The Speeches of
FANNIE LOU HAMER

The Speeches of
FANNIE LOU
HAMER
To Tell It Like It Is

Edited by Maegan Parker Brooks and Davis W. Houck

UNIVERSITY PRESS OF MISSISSIPPI
Jackson

Margaret Walker Alexander Series in African American Studies

www.upress.state.ms.us

Designed by Peter D. Halverson

The University Press of Mississippi is a member of the
Association of American University Presses.

Fannie Lou Hamer's speeches, lectures, and interviews are reprinted by
permission of Vergie Hamer Faulkner.

First printing 2011
∞
Library of Congress Cataloging-in-Publication Data

Hamer, Fannie Lou.
  [Speeches. Selections]
  The speeches of Fannie Lou Hamer : to tell it like it is / edited by Maegan Parker
Brooks and Davis W. Houck.
     p. cm. — (Margaret Walker Alexander series in African American studies)
  Includes bibliographical references and index.
  ISBN 978-1-60473-822-3 (cloth : alk. paper) — ISBN 978-1-60473-823-0 (ebook)
1. African Americans—Civil rights—History—Sources. 2. Civil rights
movements—United States—History—Sources. 3. African Americans—Civil
rights—Mississippi—History—Sources. 4. Civil rights movements—Mississip-
pi—History—Sources. 5. United States—Race relations—History--Sources. 6.
Mississippi—Race relations—History—Sources. I. Brooks, Maegan Parker. II.
Houck, Davis W. III. Title.
  E185.97.H35A5 2011
  973'.04960730092—dc22
  [B]   2010025165

British Library Cataloging-in-Publication Data available

To my parents, Greg Parker and Patti Fluke, who taught me how to find profound wisdom in the struggle of everyday life
    —M.P.B.

and

To Felecia Bivens and Natashia Hinson-Turner, who daily walk up the Freedom Road with Mrs. Hamer
    —D.W.H.

Contents

Showing Love and Telling It Like It Is

The Rhetorical Practices of Fannie Lou Hamer

"The education has got to be changed in these institutions," Fannie Lou Hamer boldly declared while addressing students at the University of Wisconsin–Madison. Invited to speak at the campus's Great Hall in January 1971, Hamer wasted no time before indicting those in power. "We got to tell the truth even in these institutions because there's one thing about it, folks—you elderly folks my age is almost hopeless," she admitted, but "you got to know now that the children know what's going on and you not going to be able to fool them any longer." If the near-decade Hamer had spent traveling the nation, testifying about her experiences and challenging America to live up to its principles had taught her nothing else, Hamer learned that Americans possessed an anemic view of their history. The informal education Hamer gleaned through her civil rights activism incited her to "think about some of our past history," like "when you never taught us, white America, that it was a black doctor that learned to save blood plasma to give a blood transfusion—you never taught that in the institution," she insisted, chastising the faculty and administrators seated before her. "And you never taught us that the first man to die in the Revolution was Crispus Attucks, another black man." Having "found out" these, and "so many other things" about the overlooked and suppressed accomplishments of African Americans, Hamer took it upon herself to encourage students at college campuses across the country "to work to make this a better place," imploring them to follow her example and "deal with politics and the history of this country that's not in the books."[1]

As Fannie Lou Hamer traveled from Harvard to Seattle University, from Berkeley to Carleton, Shaw, Florida State, and Duke—without manuscript, just telling all those who would listen "what it is and telling it like it is"—some audience members doubtlessly wondered: who *is* this woman speaking in a southern black vernacular dressed in clothing that reflects her impoverished status, and what does she have to teach *us?* In fact, that patronizing sentiment was expressed by audience members on college campuses, at political conventions, and in organizational meetings alike. In 1969, when Hamer received an honorary doctorate from Tougaloo College in Jackson, Mississippi, for instance, a cohort of middle-class black alumni objected to the accolade because she was unlettered.[2] Seasoned activists like Roy Wilkins, executive secretary of the National Association for the Advancement of Colored People (NAACP), were similarly critical of the attention Hamer garnered; in fact, Hamer remembered Wilkins calling her "ignorant" and encouraging her, and the Mississippi Freedom Democratic Party (MFDP) she represented, to leave the 1964 Democratic National Convention (DNC).[3] Even President Lyndon B. Johnson took issue with her unlettered grammar. During a meeting of notable civil rights activists gathered to consider the two at-large convention seats that Johnson grudgingly offered the MFDP at the 1964 DNC, Bayard Rustin asked if Fannie Lou Hamer would be considered for one of those two seats, to which vice presidential hopeful Hubert Humphrey replied: "The President will not allow that illiterate woman to speak from the floor of the convention."[4] Perhaps most surprisingly, members of the Student Nonviolent Coordinating Committee (SNCC), an organization that eschewed hierarchical structure and exercised considerable disrespect for respectability, questioned the value of Hamer's contribution. During a heated organizational meeting, when she spoke out against the proposed expulsion of whites from SNCC, several black staffers remarked that her comments held little weight because she was "not at their level of development."[5]

Thankfully, there were others—people like Charles McLaurin, who consistently assured Hamer: "You're somebody, you're important," like Ella Baker, who helped cultivate Hamer's political philosophy, and like Bob Moses, who encouraged Hamer to express this philosophy at mass meetings, national conventions, and speaking engagements across the nation.[6] Fortunately, there were also those movement participants like Moses Moon (formerly Alan Ribback) and Sue (Lorenzi) Sojourner, who so appreciated the power of Hamer's story and the inspirational quality of her voice that they recorded speeches she delivered before southern audiences. Beyond this, northern activist families like the Sweets and the Goldsteins of Madison, Wisconsin, also captured and preserved Hamer's addresses before a variety of audiences there. This collection was made possible by the generosity of these activists, friends, and prescient others who, like SNCC's Prathia Hall, recognized "how desperately America needs the blood transfusion that comes from the Delta of

Mississippi." Contrary to the sentiments expressed by Wilkins, Johnson, and some latecomers to SNCC, activists like McLaurin, Baker, and Moses realized that "the people are our teachers," and like Hall they believed, "People who have struggled to support themselves and large families, people who have survived in Georgia and Alabama and Mississippi, have learned some things we need to know."[7]

Strong reactions to Hamer's words, coupled with convictions, like Hall's, about their pedagogical import, add to the constellation of questions encircling Hamer's oratorical career. Being mindful that Hamer so moved audiences—both positively and negatively—leads one to wonder not just who is Fannie Lou Hamer and what does she have to teach us, but also how did she learn to speak in a manner that elicited such polar responses and how did she come to speak before the array of audiences she encountered? Answers to these questions require both culling the biographical aspects of her noteworthy life and considering the rhetorical elements of her upbringing.[8] An exploration of lessons Hamer learned in the home, on the plantation, and as a lifelong member of the black Baptist Church, for example, begins to explain how someone with little formal education and even less access to institutionalized power was able to channel growing but inchoate feelings of dissatisfaction into compelling rhetorical action. What's more, long before Hamer received civic training from leaders within the movement, she was already developing her own formidable rhetorical skills, which she later employed in her voter registration, community organizing, and fundraising efforts.

The seeds of what grew to be Fannie Lou Hamer's remarkable rhetorical abilities—her confidence, her keen understanding of race relations, her biting sense of humor, her southern black Baptist preaching style, and her mastery of biblical allusion—were sown at home and nourished within southern black churches. When Fannie Lou Hamer was born Fannie Lou Townsend in 1917, the twentieth child of sharecropper parents who lived and worked in the Mississippi Delta, the Townsends were undoubtedly grateful for another healthy child and the fifty dollars landowners typically paid sharecropping families to swell their workforce.[9] The Townsend family moved to Ruleville from Montgomery County when their youngest child was two years old; once there, they carved out a meager existence in a dilapidated shack on E. W. Brandon's plantation. The sharecropping system, which replaced slavery as a means of controlling the black population and securing cheap labor, was maintained in such a way that the workers remained indebted to the landowners and, even in a good year when a large and industrious family like the Townsends could pick fifty or sixty bales of cotton, they still would not turn a profit.[10]

Even as a child, Fannie Lou recognized sharecropping as fundamentally exploitative and asked her mother why their family was not white. "The reason I said it," she explained, was "we would work all summer and we would work until it get so cold that you would have to tie rags around your feet and sacks . . . to keep your feet warm while we would get out and scrap cotton." After all this work, she insisted, "We wouldn't have anything; we wouldn't have anything to eat; sometime we wouldn't have anything but water and bread." The white landowners, on the other hand, "would have very good food" and yet "they wasn't doing anything," she observed. To her child's mind, the solution seemed simple: "to make it you had to be white, and I wanted to be white." Her mother quickly challenged this desire, telling Fannie Lou that "there was nothing in the world wrong with being black."[11] "Be grateful that you are black," Lou Ella Townsend instructed her daughter. "If God had wanted you to be white, you would have been white, so you accept yourself for what you are and respect yourself as a black child." Reasoning further, Lou Ella advised, "When you get grown . . . you respect yourself as a black woman; and other people will respect you too."[12]

This message was reinforced by particular verses of songs and hymns Mrs. Townsend would sing to her children. Hamer remembered her mother working in the fields or cleaning their small shack while singing, "I would not be a white man / White as a drip in the snow / They ain't got God in their heart / To hell they sure must go," which she would follow with the related stanza "I would not be a sinner / I'll tell you the reason why / I'm afraid my Lord may call me / And I wouldn't be ready to die."[13] Beyond restoring a sense of race pride in her daughter, Lou Ella's allusion to divine justice left Fannie Lou with an understanding that the sharecropping system did not leave white people unscathed. Years later, Fannie Lou Hamer would draw upon this reasoning to suggest that the races were inextricably bound—both ensnared by segregation and in need of one another to liberate themselves from its effects.

Fannie Lou's father, and his strong ties to the black Baptist Church, further reinforced the lessons of self-respect and race pride Lou Ella Townsend taught her daughter. In addition to sharecropping, James Lee Townsend also served as a minister. As the child of a black Baptist preacher, Hamer was not unlike scores of notable male civil rights orators who grew up learning lessons from the Bible in their home and hearing their fathers preaching the Word from the pulpit. This familial connection to the church later revealed itself in her public addresses, as Hamer would often couple her mother's transformative lesson— that God intended for her to be black and that she should not covet the station of her white oppressor—with scripture such as Psalm 37, which reads: "Do not fret because of evildoers, nor be envious of the workers of iniquity. For they shall soon be cut down like the grass, and wither as the green herb." Moreover, Hamer developed an unparalleled ability to, as Drew native and fellow MFDP activist Dr. L. C. Dorsey describes it, "cast the struggle that blacks had against the role of the church in the human struggle."[14] This competency was likely cultivated within her religious community, as some black Baptist preachers during this era emphasized the "practical rather than the theoretical aspect of Christian theology." As a collective, moreover, black Baptists are known for "relating a relevant theology to slavery in the South and white racism throughout the nation."[15] During the course of Hamer's own speaking career, she was similarly praised for making biblical allusions "clear so that all could understand."[16]

The strength of Hamer's message, though, lay not only in its lucidity. As numerous audience members attest, the depth and intensity of Hamer's faith, conveyed through the delivery of her speech, was also quite contagious. For instance, Owen Brooks, who worked for the United Church of Christ in the Delta region during the civil rights movement, remembers that "she didn't just sing about 'we shall overcome.' She believed. She believed it with all of her might." Brooks elaborates, "She was able to make it clear for all who listened what she stood for, what she in fact believed in, and that her faith was strong."[17] Both in terms of content—"a heritage of biblical teaching applied to this world"— and style, which audience members recognized as coming from "the preachers down at the churches," Hamer's religious background echoed through her discourse.[18] In this manner, explains Dorsey, the church functioned as her "training ground."[19] Mississippi native and cofounder of the Hamer Institute, Dr. Leslie McLemore, agrees; he places Hamer's expertise within the context of southern African American culture. "Her experience was like so many experiences of African Americans in the South who were church-going people," McLemore says. He clarifies: "You learn how to preside over meetings. You learn how to conduct meetings. You learn how to give a speech. You learn all of this in the church . . . so she had all of that training."[20] Although the training Hamer received and the biblical types she utilized were part of southern black Baptist heritage common to many African Americans, Hamer nevertheless emerged as a distinctive voice within her rural black southern community. Part of that uniqueness can be attributed to Hamer's gender. Given the patriarchal structure of the southern black Baptist church, for instance, the leadership role and preacher persona Hamer adopted were indeed unusual.[21]

Another factor contributing to the emergence of Fannie Lou Hamer's distinctive voice was the confidence that the Townsends bred within their children by providing protection and enjoyment for them. Hamer characterized her mother as a "fantastic woman," whom she often remembered "getting on her knees and praying that God would let all of her children live."[22] Faced with the threat of white violence and the menacing pangs of hunger, this prayer was a desperate and constant plea. Lou Ella Townsend matched her prayers with action. Day in and day out, she would carry a bucket covered with a rag into the field with her; one day, when young Fannie Lou got up the courage to peek in that bucket, she found a 9 mm Luger hidden underneath the rag. Young Fannie Lou learned that her mother armed herself to protect her children from the physical threats plantation owners might wield against them while they worked—"no white man was going to beat her kids," Hamer recalled her mother exclaiming.[23]

Mrs. Townsend and her husband also shielded their children from despair by finding joy in the least likely of places. To make the long work day go by faster for her children, for instance, Lou Ella would initiate races to see who could pick cotton the fastest—all the while singing a lighthearted song: "Jump down turn around pick a bale of cotton / Jump down turn around pick a bale a day / Ohhh, Lord pick a bale of cotton / Ohhh, Lord pick a bale a day."[24] Songs and games like these helped the children pass the twelve to fourteen hours the family typically worked on Brandon's plantation. At night, after these seemingly interminable days, the children would huddle around their father, roast peanuts, and enjoy his repertoire of jokes.[25] From her parents, thus, young Fannie Lou was learning how words—sung or delivered in jest— could be used to comfort and protect.

While Hamer characterized these fond memories amidst trying times as the only things that "kept her going," the small moments of pleasure her mother and father provided for the Townsend children also kept the resentment they felt toward white people from turning into hatred. Hamer later remarked that in spite all of her experiences with racism in Mississippi, she really did not "hate any man." As she saw things, hate was like a cancer that "eats away at a human being until they become nothing but a shell."[26] In small yet significant ways, therefore, Hamer's parents protected their children both from imminent physical danger and from the looming psychological risk of being consumed by hatred.

The children's work on the plantation kept them from attending school for more than a few months out of the year, and they went for only a few years in total—Hamer made it to the sixth grade before she began working full time in the fields. Fleeting as her educational experience was, it nevertheless had a lasting impact; she excelled in reading and in spelling and she learned that her excellence was quite pleasing to her teacher, Thornton Layne, as well as to her parents. The pleasure her success gave these people that she so respected encouraged her to work harder. Before long she was winning spelling bees and performing poetry for her parents and their adult friends. The pride that her performances gave her parents, who liked to show her off by setting her up on their kitchen table to sing, recite, and spell, also encouraged young Fannie Lou.[27] Displaying her lessons to warm receptive audiences early in life undoubtedly imbued Hamer with the confidence and experience needed to address large crowds later. By promoting Fannie Lou's performance as a child, the Townsends helped cultivate a love of public speaking within their daughter.

After she left school at the age of twelve, Hamer's adult life began to proceed in much the same way her mother's had—she labored in the fields of the Mississippi Delta, married a fellow sharecropper, and longed for a life where survival was not a constant struggle. All the while, Hamer was honing skills of intra- and interracial communication, as well as strategies to subvert unjust power configurations, that would serve her well in years to come. In 1944, Fannie Lou Townsend married Perry "Pap" Hamer, who lived on W. D. Marlow's neighboring plantation. At the age of twenty-seven, Fannie Lou Townsend became Fannie Lou Hamer and moved to the Marlow plantation, where she and her husband lived and worked for the next eighteen years of their lives. The couple was well respected among their fellow sharecroppers and instrumental to the landowner, as Pap drove tractors and Fannie Lou recorded the workers' harvest. Her formal title was "timekeeper" on Marlow's plantation, and she was chosen for this leadership position, in part, because of the reading and writing skills she had gained during her several years of schooling.

As a plantation timekeeper she served as a liaison between the Marlows and the other sharecroppers; therefore, Mrs. Hamer must have also had "trust on both sides," reasons McLemore. He explains that her position as a timekeeper reflected the confidence that the Marlows had in her; otherwise they would not have given her the job. Concomitantly, this position enabled her to help other sharecroppers, who respected her "because they knew when Marlow was not around she would use a different kind of 'p,' [a device used] to weigh cotton, to give them a full measure for the cotton they had picked." Hamer excelled in this role, McLemore posits, because of "her great ability . . . to talk to both the white boss man and to talk to her friends and neighbors on the plantation."[28]

Hamer's own reflections about her work as a timekeeper on the plantation support McLemore's contentions. To one interviewer Hamer explained how she transformed her responsible position into an outlet for her rebellious desire: "I would take my 'p' to the field and use mine until I would see him coming, you know, because his was loaded and I know it was beating people like that."[29] Through her resistive act of providing sharecroppers with a fair measure for their harvest, Hamer worked to balance the scales that had been tipped against blacks in Mississippi for hundreds of years. Hamer's rebellious though furtive behavior, furthermore, extended into all aspects of her labor. She told a Wisconsin audience that although she became formally involved in politics in 1962, she had been acting out against exploitation for many years. "I always had to work at white folks' houses," Hamer explained. "They would tell me that I couldn't eat with them or that I couldn't bathe in their tub, so what I would do was eat before they would eat and bathe when they was gone." This defiant act elicited wild applause from her listeners—clearly she had perfected the delivery of a punch line from years of listening to her father's fireside jokes. Hamer continued: "I used to have a real ball knowing they didn't want me in their tub . . . just relaxing in that bubble bath." Similarly, "When they was saying that I couldn't eat with them, it would tickle me because I would say to myself, 'Baby, I eat first!'"[30] Through these everyday acts of resistance, she explained, "I was rebelling in the only way I knew how to rebel."[31] While Hamer's subversive behavior helped balance the unequal plantation scales and restore her sense of human dignity, she declared: "I just steady hoped for a chance that I could really lash out, and say what I had to say about what was going on in Mississippi."[32] In other words, Hamer longed for the day when she could confront the culture of white supremacy to and for a much broader audience.

That chance finally came in August 1962, when Hamer's path intersected with the burgeoning black freedom movement.[33] During the summer of 1962, members of the Council of Federated Organizations (COFO), a coalition of several civil rights groups including the Southern Christian Leadership Conference (SCLC), the Congress of Racial Equality (CORE), and SNCC, traveled throughout Mississippi holding meetings in churches to inform local people of ways to secure their voting rights. The Delta was a particularly strategic area to hold voter education and registration advocacy meetings, given that blacks outnumbered whites in several counties. One such meeting was held at Williams Chapel Missionary Baptist Church in Ruleville. Hamer learned about this meeting during the August 26 Sunday service, when Reverend J. D. Story notified his parishioners that the first-ever mass meeting to be held in Ruleville would take place at their church the following evening. Though Hamer was initially skeptical, her much-trusted friend, Mary Tucker, convinced her to attend. Once there, Hamer listened attentively as James Bevel preached a sermon entitled "Discerning the Signs of Time," and James Forman followed by offering an impassioned lecture about the rights and entitlements blacks, as American citizens, possess. To someone who had been looking for an opportunity to more boldly rebel against the sharecropping system, Bevel's and Forman's messages of hope "seemed like the most remarkable thing that could happen in the state of Mississippi."[34] At that evening's "altar call," in fact, Hamer was among the eighteen people who indicated their willingness to try and register at the county courthouse in Indianola that Friday.

Once Hamer attempted to register on Friday, August 31, 1962, her life changed dramatically. She simultaneously lost her job and was expelled from the plantation where she had lived and worked for nearly two decades. Though it was intended to punish Hamer for her civic assertion, being fired from the plantation effectively freed her to work full-time for the movement. It did not take long for civil rights organizers to recognize Hamer's natural talents as a performer, the confidence and understanding her parents had instilled in her, and the skills of leadership and interracial communication she had been cultivating in churches and on the plantations where she worked. At the age of forty-four, when Hamer became SNCC's oldest fieldworker, though, she also became the prime target for local white supremacist terror. She bravely endured threats on her life while traveling around the Delta encouraging other blacks to register and vote.

Hamer was not only brave in her registration advocacy; she was also creative and resourceful, using songs and motivational speeches to encourage and comfort black Deltans. Her rhetorical talents quickly earned her invitations to travel outside the Delta to citizenship workshops and movement meetings across the South. On her return trip from one such workshop in June of 1963, Hamer and several other activists were arrested and taken to a jailhouse in Winona, Mississippi. While being held captive on spurious "disorderly conduct" and "resisting arrest" charges, Hamer endured a beating so severe that she continued to suffer its effects for the remainder of her life. The brutal beating, like being fired from Marlow's plantation a year earlier, was a calculated attempt to punish and deter her civil rights activism; it had just the opposite effect. As soon as she was well enough to do so, Hamer began testifying about the abuse and the blatant desecration of American principles her beating represented. Most notably, Hamer first caught America's attention, and sent President Lyndon B. Johnson into a state of outright panic, with her live nationally televised testimony about the Winona beating, delivered before the Credentials Committee at the Democratic National Convention in 1964.

Although it is the moment in her activist career and the speech for which she is best known, our collection illustrates that the 1964 DNC speech was just the beginning of a struggle on behalf of the poor and disenfranchised that Hamer waged for more than a decade. After the MFDP's challenge failed to unseat the all-white delegation, for instance, Hamer was among the group of SNCC members whom famed performer and ardent civil rights supporter Harry Belafonte sponsored to travel to Guinea and meet with President Sékou Touré. Upon her return from West Africa, she spoke with Malcolm X at a rally in Harlem to drum up support for the MFDP's 1965 congressional challenge. As a lead witness for this challenge, she also testified about voter discrimination before a closed hearing of the House Elections Subcommittee and was among the first three black women ever seated in that congressional chamber. In the summer of 1966, she walked alongside Martin Luther King, Jr., when the Meredith March crossed her home county. Following a statewide election in 1967, furthermore, Hamer was instrumental in ensuring that Robert Clark, the first black legislator to win an election in Mississippi since Reconstruction, be seated without delay. Then, she received a standing ovation when she took her own seat as a delegate to the Democratic National Convention held in Chicago in 1968. In 1969, Hamer began a food cooperative in Sunflower County, which she helped to support through national fundraising efforts and the honoraria she received from speaking engagements. She was back in Chicago in 1970 being honored with a Citizen's Achievement Award and addressing the crowd gathered at Loop College as the featured speaker in their "Decade of Civil Rights History." She campaigned for the Mississippi Senate in 1971, while still managing to leave her mark on the founding of the National Women's Political Caucus with a forceful and forthright speech. Though the number of speaking engagements Hamer was able to meet after she fell ill in 1971 decreased considerably, the scores of requests pouring into her Ruleville home did not. Hamer not only received countless requests to speak; she also garnered numerous honors toward the end of her career—including the Mary Church Terrell and the Paul Robeson awards and honorary doctorates from Tougaloo College and Shaw and Howard universities. The city of Ruleville even instituted an annual "Fannie Lou Hamer Day." Despite these and many other accolades, Hamer was often gravely ill, penniless, and exhausted as she labored for the causes of civil and human rights until shortly before her death in 1977.[35]

Even as she worked tirelessly to promote specific causes like voter registration, representative government, and poverty politics, Hamer's speeches engaged broader issues and offered long-lasting lessons. Speaking before audiences outside of her home state, for example, Hamer's addresses incorporated searing details of her life growing up and becoming politically active in one of the most segregated states in the union. In testifying about the exploitative labor practices that kept her family hungry and powerless, or the retaliation she suffered upon becoming civically engaged, Hamer was also revealing the limits of America's democratic system. She often contended that "nobody's free until everybody's free." Unpacking this aphorism for an audience in Harlem, Hamer questioned: "Now how can a man be in Washington, elected by the people, when 95 percent of the people cannot vote in Mississippi?"[36] Those unrepresentative representatives sent from her state, Hamer elaborated, were not only making decisions that affected Mississippians; their votes on policies had an effect upon all Americans. She challenged an audience in Madison, proclaiming even more explicitly that "until I am free, you are not free either. And if you think you are free, you drive down to Mississippi with your Wisconsin license plate and you will see what I am talking about." Hamer's lived experiences—both before and after her political awakening—imbued her with wells of lessons upon which she drew to educate her various audiences about "the history that's not in the books."

Hamer's words, the story of her life and activist struggles they tell, not only challenge conventional views about America's history and its principles, but they also provide a reorientation regarding what we remember about the twentieth century black freedom movement that so dramatically altered our nation's social and political fabric. At the most basic level, this collection of Hamer's speeches belies the all-too-common bifurcation of rhetoric *from* action in both historical and historiographical accounts of the movement. Movement participants like Ella Baker, Septima Clark, and Reverend Edwin King all bemoaned the "preacher-talk" and "grandstanding" they heard from prominent black preachers and provocative Black Panthers, reasoning that grand rhetorical performances often diverted attention away from the less glamorous work of grassroots organizing and the cultivation of local leadership.[37] Historians have echoed these critiques. Disparaging Stokely Carmichael's transformation from a SNCC fieldworker to a nationally recognized Black Power spokesperson, for example, Charles M. Payne contends that he initiated a "pattern of substituting rhetoric at the top for program at the bottom."[38] Speaking more broadly about SNCC's mid-decade transformation, Clayborne Carson writes: "Rather than encouraging local leaders to develop their own ideas . . . SNCC was becoming merely one of many organizations seeking to speak on behalf of black communities."[39] The division drawn by historical figures and historians alike between speaking on behalf of black people and empowering people to find their own voice often intersects with the historiographical distinction between the media-magnet national leaders who aimed to spark mass mobilization and the humble local movement participants who "micro-mobilized" by organizing at the grass roots.[40]

In more recent years, historical scholarship has moved away from an exclusive preoccupation with "larger than life" figures such as Martin Luther King, Jr., and Malcolm X and has championed grassroots activists and activism.[41] If movement rhetoric is conceived of as little more than aurally pleasing promises and performances that diverted attention away from meaningful progress or as self-promoting statements that disempowered the masses, then it is easy to abandon this object of inquiry in pursuit of more meaningful activism. But the manner in which Hamer used discourse to awaken Americans to the problems that surrounded them and to empower her audiences to see themselves as part of the solution suggests that rhetoric was neither an appendage to nor a diversion from her activism. Whether spoken to United States congressional representatives or to Mississippi sharecroppers, Hamer's rhetoric embodied and supported; it taught, incited, and inspired, proving that her speech was itself a powerful form of action. Additionally, the mere act of speaking in volatile places such as the county courthouses and even church pulpits underwrote Hamer's rhetorical activism. The rhetoric of civil rights activists like Hamer thus calls into question the bright line drawn between movement rhetoric and action, inviting a reconsideration of the role speech played in propelling the civil rights struggle.

Just as Hamer's embodied words promise to revise historical accounts of movement rhetoric's relationship to social change, this collection of her speeches also extends the larger scholarly shift away from an exclusive focus on monumental televisual aspects of the black freedom movement and toward a renewed appreciation of grassroots activism.[42] This shift has contributed to a richer understanding of the movement by demonstrating that women were not only organizing and fulfilling vital supporting roles, but that women—black, older, and economically disadvantaged women like Fannie Lou Hamer—were also on the front lines of important, yet less popularly considered, movement challenges.[43] Including women such as Hamer in the narrative of civil rights history complicates aspects of the popular story, as Hamer advocated unity and decried the futility of fragmentation; she was simultaneously a civil rights supporter and an advocate of Black Power philosophy. But she was nothing if not discerning. She poked holes in the ideology of separatism, even as she critiqued aspects of the push for integration, and she warned feminists about the danger of building coalitions that would elide important differences. Focusing on the discourse of an activist who seamlessly incorporated ostensibly incongruent movement ideologies, therefore, creates a different sketch of this pivotal period in our history—one that provides an alternative depiction both of how change occurred and of who helped bring this change about.

The contention that Hamer's discourse provides an alternative perspective regarding such a vital movement in our nation's history is a multilayered claim. One piece of evidence supporting this complex contention can be found in the substance of her addresses—the life experiences, opinions, and political views her speeches convey. Yet another form of support for this central claim lies in what she embodied—the fact that she was an older impoverished and unlettered woman made her a nontraditional advocate during this period of the larger black freedom movement. And yet another piece of evidence supporting the claim that Hamer's discourse provides an alternative perspective can be found in the very lexical, grammatical, and syntactical quality of her discourse. By this we mean to suggest that Hamer's southern black vernacular was not just a marker of difference or evidence of the oppression about which she spoke, but her large- and small-scale patterns of speech in effect provide an alternative model of oratory during this era.

The careful reader of this collection will no doubt observe, for instance, Hamer's consistent use of double negation and overpluralization, as well as use of the verbs "been" and "done" to indicate habitual or recently completed action. These grammatical and lexical markers combine with a distinct syntactical pattern, in which there is no marked beginning or end to sentences that are commonly linked to one another in a hypotactic fashion, using an abundance of connectives like "and" and "but." As a collective, these features support the trademark structural and stylistic elements of Hamer's discourse—including image making, testifying, dissembling, mimicry, and circumlocution. When taken together the lexical, grammatical, syntactical, and stylistic aspects of Hamer's speech reflect what we have termed her southern black vernacular. Although there is no shortage of labels with which to categorize the distinctive sounds, structures, patterns, and rhetorical strategies manifest in the speech of African Americans—labels like African American Vernacular English, Black Dialect, and Ebonics are among the most commonly used—we find the label "southern black vernacular" to be the most descriptive of Hamer's speech. Preceding "black vernacular" with the qualifier "southern," for instance, is descriptive of her clearly discernable regional accent, and it also encapsulates phrases she commonly used like "raising Cain," which are employed by southerners of all races. Specifying the region that influences Hamer's speech functions as both a descriptive gesture and also as a means to particularize it—not all of the patterns of speech spoken by blacks share the regional markers found in Hamer's discourse. Additionally, the designation "black" acknowledges aspects of Hamer's racialized experience that influenced her speech.[44] When describing Hamer's discourse, moreover, we find the term "vernacular" more precise than either "dialect" or "language" because the etymology of "vernacular"—taken from the Latin *vernaculus* and *verna*—evokes a sense of being both "native to a region" and "subservient to something else." In this respect, "vernacular" echoes the particularity indicated by the regional distinction, as it simultaneously represents the relationship of power and domination that Hamer challenged through her words.[45]

The decision about how to represent Hamer's oral discourse on the written page was even more difficult than our choice of how to adequately label and describe it. In an attempt to capture its distinction, some past accounts of Hamer's speeches have represented her discourse phonetically. In his memoir *Stranger at the Gates*, for instance, Tracy Sugarman frequently represents Hamer's speech phonetically—transcribing phrases she used like "going to" as "gonna" and words like "tomorrow" as "tomorra."[46] Similarly, in the introduction to their edited collection, *Rhetoric, Religion, and the Civil Rights Movement, 1954–1965*, Davis W. Houck and David E. Dixon mention that when "translating sounds into written words, we have also tried to maintain the vernacular that any given speaker employed." Reasoning that "so much of the rhetorical power of their message comes from their purposeful adoption . . . of a given vernacular," Houck and Dixon try to emulate it by dropping the "g" from gerunds like running and representing phrases such as "had been" as "hadda," for instance.[47] As a general convention, however, the pronunciation of words in a given vernacular is not transcribed, and we were uncomfortable with making the words of a poor black woman the exception to this rule. So, for this collection, we have decided to transcribe the full form of the words Hamer spoke.[48] Since we also agree with those who contend that there is immense rhetorical power and purpose in the vernacular, we have done our best to translate the grammatical, syntactical, and stylistic components of Hamer's spoken word to the written page.

From this translation, at least two interrelated structural markers of Hamer's southern black vernacular emerge and warrant comment. Readers are sure to notice, for example, her circumlocutory style combined with her gift for oral editing. These aspects of her discourse, much like her unlettered grammar, garnered both praise and derision. Circumlocution, also known as indirect speech and commonly thought to be evasive in purpose, can also function enthymematically as a means of inviting the audience into an address by urging them to make connections between seemingly divergent topics. Hamer's speeches often function in just this way. While traversing a wide range of ideas without formally stating the connections between her thoughts though, Hamer incited some audience members to brand her discourse as less invitational and more "thematically inconsistent."[49]

There were, however, those who heard her speak more often and came to understand that Hamer's use of circumlocution not only invited her audience members to craft meaning by supplying connections between ostensibly disparate ideas, but that Hamer's indirect speech also reflected her keen ability to adapt to particular audiences. As noted above, Hamer's background imbued her with a deep appreciation for the power of the spoken word. It was not just that her parents, teachers, and fellow church members reveled in her performances; the fact that literacy was uncommon among blacks in her Delta community also reinforced the primacy of oral expression. As a result, Hamer rarely wrote her speeches out beforehand. In fact, she embarrassedly acknowledged trying this once to disastrous effect, which compelled fellow activist Victoria Gray Adams to respond: "My God! You don't need to. You tell what you understand, what you're feeling and why you think it's important now and don't you worry about notes or writing it out beforehand. I have to do some of that but you don't."[50] In place of the ability to prepare and recite neatly organized manuscripts, Hamer had a much more rare and perceptive gift that enabled her to combine a core set of topics, life experiences, biblical lessons, and shared expressions into addresses that became seared into the memories of her respective audiences. Reverend Edwin King aptly explained this ability of Hamer's by comparing it to another of her remarkable gifts. "She was an extraordinarily good cook of down-home foods." He suggested that she "liked to mix, to make whatever she was feeding people at midnight after they would come home from jail or somewhere else, to fix the perfect spices or recipe for her guest." He explained further that "after she became the orator," she began "picking and choosing the spicy parts she'd put in her speeches." King contended that this aspect of Hamer's speechmaking was so characteristic of her as a person; she was always "doing the best she had with whatever she had. The food, or words, or voice or song—choosing among it what was needed to persuade or to comfort or to please."[51]

Though it was less common than her extemporaneously composed and passionately delivered addresses, Hamer did occasionally speak from a script and in a narrowly directed manner. She acknowledged her manuscript, for example, at several places during the incisive testimony she delivered before the

House Elections Subcommittee in 1965. Similarly, a manuscript bearing her signature and replete with words underlined for emphasis remains of what appears to be a stump speech she gave in Ruleville during her 1971 campaign for the Mississippi Senate.[52] Including scripted speeches such as these in our collection provides the reader with a sense of Hamer's range as a public speaker—she could be loud and fiery; yet she could also be quiet and forceful.

One of our goals for this collection is to do justice to the vast array of Hamer's public discourse. In selecting speeches for inclusion, we sought to represent the full fifteen years of her career as a public activist—from 1962 to 1977—and we came close here with speeches ranging from 1963 to 1976. We also wanted to make manifest the diversity of geographical locations at which she spoke; we were able to recover speeches Hamer delivered in eight different states in addition to the District of Columbia. Beyond demonstrating the range of Hamer's speeches across space and time, we wanted this collection to reflect the variety of rhetorical occasions to which Hamer responded. Here we have a record of speeches and testimonies Hamer delivered at political conventions, during a Vietnam War moratorium rally, at the founding of the National Women's Political Caucus, and in a Mississippi courtroom. We have even coupled these speeches and testimonies with the last full-length oral history interview Hamer granted, a recent oral history interview we conducted with her daughter, and a bibliography of additional primary and secondary sources by and about Hamer.

Our overarching goal in compiling this collection was to allow Hamer to tell her own story through an extensive array of texts that have heretofore never been experienced by those outside her immediate audiences. After years of sleuthing through archives, libraries, government documents, and private collections across the country, we gathered close to thirty recordings from which we selected the twenty speeches and testimonies featured in this collection. This is the first book to exclusively showcase Hamer's powerful talents as an orator, and we suspect that the collection can be added to—that there are more of her texts that we were unable to locate, but that we hope will soon be unearthed. Thanks to the careful historical work of Hamer's biographers, for instance, we are aware that she spoke in the Northwest and in several mid-Atlantic states, and yet we were unable to locate the texts to demonstrate this travel. Just as we are mindful that the collection is not exhaustive in terms of geographical representation, we also know that the date and location designations we have assigned to several of the speeches within the collection could be more precise. For the address Hamer gave at a mass meeting in Indianola, for example, which was archived as having been delivered in "Summer 1964," we contacted original audience members who heard Hamer deliver the speech so as to arrive at a closer estimation of the date. In other speeches, such as the one Hamer gave before the National Council of Negro Women, the recording had never been catalogued, much less designated with a date and location, so both assignments are our best guesses based upon contextual information and references Hamer made within the speech itself.[53] We agreed that tolerating an intermittent lack of precision was a small price to pay for the ability to compile one of the first collections wherein many rhetorical practices of a prominent female civil rights activist are exclusively featured.

We trust it will not be the last of its kind. We not only anticipate that a collection such as this will encourage the finding of additional long lost recordings of Hamer's speeches, but we also would like it to serve as an invitation for scholars to shine the spotlight on the rhetorical careers of other less widely known activists. In Fannie Lou Hamer's case, most Americans only know about her eight-minute testimony before the Credentials Committee at the 1964 Democratic National Convention—if they have ever heard of her at all. This collection makes plain that, profound as the DNC speech was and is, there is much more to her oratorical oeuvre than that one testimony. A collection such as this also raises the question: how many other gifted speakers never had that moment of national audibility to launch them into the limelight? How many other recordings of speeches are stashed away in the attics and basements of octogenarian civil rights supporters across the country? We are confident that there are many and that those voices—like the voice of Fannie Lou Hamer—have much to teach us.

For now, we invite you to enjoy the lessons Hamer's words provide. Beyond the instruction, we suspect that you will also feel the love. As her daughter Vergie Hamer Faulkner put it in the oral history interview that concludes our collection: Fannie Lou Hamer "showed love. She showed love in everything she did. She showed love in her cooking, raising her children, being a wife to her husband. She showed love most of all when she get up there and she'd speak."[54]

MAEGAN PARKER BROOKS
DAVIS W. HOUCK

Notes

1. Fannie Lou Hamer, "Until I Am Free, You Are Not Free Either," speech delivered in Madison, Wisconsin, January 1971 (included within).

2. Kay Mills includes this anecdote in her biography of Hamer, *This Little Light of Mine: The Life of Fannie Lou Hamer* (New York: Plume, 1993), 248–249. Former Tougaloo College chaplain Reverend Edwin King also mentioned it in our interview with him. Interview with Reverend Edwin King by Maegan Parker Brooks, June 15, 2007, Jackson, Mississippi.

3. Hamer shared this painful memory in an interview; see interview with Fannie Lou Hamer by Anne and Howard Romaine, 1966, Wisconsin Historical Society, Madison, Wisconsin.

4. Chana Kai Lee, *For Freedom's Sake: The Life of Fannie Lou Hamer* (Urbana: University of Illinois Press, 1999), 95, footnote 50. Lee quotes from an interview Anne Romaine conducted with Reverend Edwin King, who was at the meeting where the offensive remark was made.

5. The dismissal of Mrs. Hamer by black separatists within SNCC is discussed widely. Most references cite James Forman's autobiography *The Making of Black Revolutionaries* as the source for this anecdote. Describing a SNCC meeting held at "Peg Leg Bates's" in 1966, Forman contextualizes the comment in the following manner: "Some people with college educations showed their disdain toward people who were slow readers or could not read at all. A few black staffers were making such comments as 'Mrs. Hamer is no longer relevant' or 'Mrs. Hamer isn't at our level of development.' This conflict was related to the debate over whites, for the same middle-class blacks who spoke this way of working-class people like Mrs. Hamer also refused to look at the 'white question' in anything more than a racial context." James Forman, *The Making of Black Revolutionaries* (Seattle: Open Hand, 1985), 475.

6. Hamer remembers McLaurin's support in an oral history with Dr. Neil McMillen, April 14, 1972, and January 25, 1973, in Ruleville, Mississippi. Oral History Program, University of Southern Mississippi, Hattiesburg, Mississippi (included within).

7. Quotation for epigraph taken from Guy Carawan and Candie Carawan, eds., *Freedom Is a Constant Struggle: Songs of the Freedom Movement* (New York: Oak Publications, 1968), 109.

8. This collection is indebted to the biographical works of Hamer that have come before it. Not only did author Kay Mills share full-text versions of speeches with us; the careful historical reconstruction of Hamer's activist career, carried out by an array of biographers, pointed us in the directions that helped us locate even more speeches. In chronological order, previous studies of Fannie Lou Hamer include: June Jordan, *Fannie Lou Hamer* (New York: Thomas Y. Crowell, 1972); Susan Kling, *Fannie Lou Hamer: A Biography* (Women for Racial and Economic Equality, 1979); David Rubel, *Fannie Lou Hamer: From Sharecropping to Politics* (Englewood Cliffs, NJ: Silver Burdett, 1990); Kay Mills, *This Little Light of Mine: The Life of Fannie Lou Hamer* (New York: Penguin, 1993); Kay Griffin-Jeuchter, "Fannie Lou Hamer: From Sharecropper to Freedom Fighter," (master's thesis, Sarah Lawrence College, 1990); Chana Kai Lee, *For Freedom's Sake: The Life of Fannie Lou Hamer* (Urbana, IL: University of Illinois Press, 1999).

9. There is a bit of uncertainty regarding the actual county of Hamer's birth. In oral histories and most speeches, she reports that she was born in Montgomery County; however, in her 1963 trial testimony, she claims she was born in Tomnolen, Mississippi, which is in the neighboring Webster County.

10. For a fascinating history of cotton as well as the details of the sharecropping system, see Stephen Yafa, *Cotton: The Biography of a Revolutionary Fiber* (New York: Penguin, 2005), especially 176–180.

11. Fannie Lou Hamer, "Fannie Lou Hamer Speaks Out" *Essence*, October 1971, 54.

12. Interview with Fannie Lou Hamer by Robert Wright, August 6, 1968, Oral History Collection, Civil Rights Documentation Project, Moorland-Spingarn Research Center, Howard University, Washington, D.C.

13. Ibid. Fannie Lou Hamer, "Songs My Mother Taught Me," audio-recording accompanying papers, Amistad Research Center, Tulane University, New Orleans. Tape produced by Bernice Johnson Reagon, financed by the We Shall Overcome Fund and the National Endowment for the Humanities, 1980. Songs taped by Worth Long.

14. Interview with Dr. L. C. Dorsey by Maegan Parker Brooks, June 11, 2007, Jackson, Mississippi.

15. Leroy Fitts, *A History of Black Baptists* (Nashville, TN: Broadman, 1985), 222.

16. Interview with Owen Brooks by Maegan Parker Brooks, June 14, 2007, Jackson, Mississippi.

17. Ibid.

18. Interview with Reverend Edwin King by Maegan Parker Brooks.

19. Interview with Dr. L. C. Dorsey by Maegan Parker Brooks.

20. Interview with Dr. Leslie McLemore by Maegan Parker Brooks, June 13, 2007, Jackson, Mississippi.

21. The gender roles Hamer adopted, which were unconventional during this time and in this region of the country, were enabled in no small part by her supportive husband. As Hamer's daughter notes in the oral history interview included within this collection, Perry Hamer supported his wife "in every way." This support included adopting unconventional gender roles himself, like caring for the couple's children while Hamer traveled around the country speaking and working for the movement. For more about Perry Hamer, see Maegan Parker Brooks's oral history interview with Vergie Hamer Faulkner (included within).

22. Hamer, "Fannie Lou Hamer Speaks Out," 54.

23. Ibid.

24. Hamer, "Songs My Mother Taught Me."

25. Jordan, *Fannie Lou Hamer,* 12.

26. Hamer, "Fannie Lou Hamer Speaks Out," 54.

27. Jordan, *Fannie Lou Hamer*, 15.

28. Interview with Dr. Leslie McLemore by Maegan Parker Brooks.

29. Interview with Fannie Lou Hamer by Robert Wright.

30. Hamer, "Until I Am Free, You Are Not Free Either" (included within).

31. Hamer uses this same characterization of her behavior in both the Robert Wright interview and in her "Until I Am Free, You Are Not Free Either" speech.

32. Interview with Fannie Lou Hamer by Robert Wright.

33. At least two different accounts exist regarding the beginning of Fannie Lou Hamer's civil rights activism: one account, promulgated principally by Charles Evers and passed along by several scholars, suggests that Hamer was an early participant in the Regional Council of Negro Leadership (RCNL), a progressive civil rights organization founded in Cleveland, Mississippi, by the legendary physician Dr.

T. R. M. Howard in 1951. A second and more plausible account is that Hamer's activism dates to August 1962 when she attended a meeting at Williams Chapel Church and heard SNCC's James Bevel and James Forman encourage local Ruleville blacks to attempt to register to vote. The plausibility of this second account is accentuated by the fact that Hamer never mentions the RCNL in her autobiography nor does she attribute her activist awakening to an RCNL meeting in any oral history or speech.

34. Interview with Fannie Lou Hamer by Project South, 1965. Project South Papers, Stanford University, Department of Special Collections, Palo Alto, California.

35. Just a year before she died, for example, Fannie Lou and Perry Hamer received a $2,250.45 bill from a collection agency demanding payment of $50 a month. As noted in a March 10, 1976, letter from the "Miscellaneous" box of documents accompanying her papers. Amistad Research Center, Tulane University, New Orleans, Louisiana.

36. "I'm Sick and Tired of Being Sick and Tired," speech delivered with Malcolm X at the Williams Institutional CME Church, Harlem, New York, December 20, 1964 (included within).

37. Charles Payne cites the critiques issued by Ella Baker and Septima Clark; see *I've Got the Light of Freedom: The Organizing Tradition and the Mississippi Freedom Struggle* (Berkeley, CA: University of California Press, 1995), 378–389. Reverend Edwin King shared the following sentiments regarding "preacher-talk" in an interview: "The preachers," who, for years, "were the only politicians in the black community could make anything sound fantastic and wonderful." Preacher-talk, as he defined it, is "just the most exciting thing to say at the moment," a way to arouse one's audience with no intention of follow-through. "We would refer to people like Charles Evers as having preacher-talk in some of his most outrageous statements that even he couldn't really mean." Reverend King suggested that some of Martin Luther King, Jr.'s more grandiose proclamations also fell into this category of rhetoric that excites, but does not deliver. Interview with Reverend Edwin King by Maegan Parker Brooks.

38. Payne, *I've Got the Light of Freedom*, 378.

39. Clayborne Carson, *In Struggle: SNCC and the Black Awakening of the 1960s* (Cambridge: Harvard University Press, 1981), 234.

40. Belinda Robnett suggests that women often served in the capacity of "micro-mobilizers" and what she also terms "bridge leaders" for the movement. For an in-depth explanation of these concepts, see "Women in the Student Non-violent Coordinating Committee: Ideology, Organizational Structure, and Leadership," in *Gender and the Civil Rights Movement*, ed. Peter Ling and Sharon Monteith (New York: Garland, 1999), 131–168.

41. In "The Social Construction of History," the bibliographic essay appended to Charles M. Payne's *I've Got the Light of Freedom*, he posits poignantly that "we can be sure that social analysis which does not somehow make it clear that ordinary, flawed, everyday sorts of human beings frequently manage to make extraordinary contributions to social change, social analysis which does not make it easier for people to see in themselves and in those around them the potential for controlling their own lives takes us in the wrong direction." See Payne, *I've Got the Light of Freedom*, 440; this book played a pivotal role in shifting historiographical attention from the grandiose to the grass roots.

42. The following works responded to Payne's reorientation and focused, particularly, on women's contributions—see, for example: Belinda Robnett, *How Long? How Long? African Women in the Struggle for Civil Rights* (New York: Oxford University Press, 1997); Robnett, "Women in the Student Non-violent Coordinating Committee," 131–168; Barbara Ransby, *Ella Baker and the Black Freedom Movement: A Radical Democratic Vision* (Chapel Hill: University of North Carolina Press, 2003); Lynne Olson, *Freedom's Daughters: The Unsung Heroines of the Civil Rights Movement from 1830 to 1970* (New York: Scribner, 2003); Christina Greene, *Our Separate Ways: Women and the Black Freedom Movement in Durham, North Carolina* (Chapel Hill: University of North Carolina Press, 2005); and Davis W. Houck and David E. Dixon, eds., *Women and the Civil Rights Movement, 1954–1965* (Jackson, MS: University Press of Mississippi, 2009).

43. Rhetorical scholarship that recovers the organizing tradition, women's voices, and alternative forms of persuasion used by these advocates includes: Karlyn Kohrs Campbell, ed., *Women Public Speakers in the United States, 1925–1993: A Bio-Critical Sourcebook* (Westport, CT: Greenwood, 1994). Richard J. Jensen and John C. Hammerback, "Working in 'Quiet Places': The Community Organizing Rhetoric of Robert Parris Moses," *Howard Journal of Communications* 11 (2000): 1–18; Janice D. Hamlet, "Fannie Lou Hamer: The Unquenchable Spirit of the Civil Rights Movement," *Journal of Black Studies* 26 (1996): 560–576; K. L. Sanger, "Functions of Freedom Singing in the Civil Rights Movement: The Activists' Implicit Rhetorical Theory," *Howard Journal of Communications* 8 (1997): 179–195; W. Stuart Towns, ed., *We Want Our Freedom: Rhetoric of the Civil Rights Movement* (Westport, CT: Praeger, 2002); Davis Houck and David E. Dixon, eds., *Rhetoric, Religion, and the Civil Rights Movement: 1954–1965* (Waco, TX: Baylor University Press, 2006); Marilyn Bordwell DeLaure, "Planting Seeds of Change: Ella Baker's Radical Rhetoric," *Women's Studies in Communication* 31 (2008): 1–28; and Houck and Dixon, *Women and the Civil Rights Movement, 1954–1965*.

44. Here, we are drawing upon the groundbreaking work of linguist Geneva Smitherman, who was among the first to provide a book-length consideration of "Black Dialect," which she defined as "an Africanized form of English reflecting Black America's linguistic-cultural African heritage and the conditions of servitude, oppression and life in America. Black Language is Euro-speech with an Afro-American meaning, nuance, tone, and gesture." *Talkin and Testifyin: The Language of Black America* (Detroit: Wayne State University Press, 1977), 2–3. Over the years, Smitherman has moved away from using the term "dialect" to describe the language of black Americans—both because of the derogatory connotations "dialect" carries in public discourse and because she believes the language of African Americans has "deep-structure linguistic differences, in addition to 'deep' differences in rhetorical style and strategies of discourse"; see *Talkin that Talk: Language, Culture, and Education in African America* (New York: Routledge, 2000), 16. In her more contemporary work, therefore, Smitherman uses the labels "Black or African American Language" instead of "dialect" to describe the distinctive speech patterns featured in the discourse of some Americans of African descent—but her definition of the new labels remains remarkably consistent with her earlier definition of "Black Dialect"; see *Word from the Mother: Language and African Americans* (New York: Routledge, 2006), 3.

45. For great rhetorical scholarship on the vernacular, see James Jasinski, "Vernacular," in *Sourcebook on Rhetoric: Key Concepts in Contemporary Rhetorical Studies* (Thousand Oaks, CA: Sage, 2001), 599–602; Gerard A. Hauser, *Vernacular Voices: The Rhetoric of Publics and Public Spheres* (Columbia: University of South Carolina Press, 1999); Kent A. Ono and John M. Sloop, "The Critique of Vernacular Discourse," *Communication Monographs* 62 (1995): 19–46; Robert Glenn Howard, "A Theory of Vernacular Rhetoric: The Case of the 'Sinner's Prayer' Online," *Folklore* 116, no. 2 (2005): 175–191; Robert Glenn Howard, "Toward a Theory of the World Wide Web Vernacular: The Case for Pet Cloning," *Journal of Folklore Research* 42, no. 3 (2005): 323–360; Robert Glenn Howard, "The Vernacular Web of Participatory Media," *Critical Studies in Media Communication* 25, no. 5 (2008): 490–513.

46. See Tracy Sugarman, *Stranger at the Gates: A Summer in Mississippi* (New York: Hill and Wang, 1966), 117–119. See also Sugarman's slightly revised *We Had Sneakers, They Had Guns: The Kids Who Fought for Civil Rights in Mississippi* (Syracuse, NY: Syracuse University Press, 2009).

47. See Davis W. Houck and David E. Dixon, Introduction and "Fannie Lou Hamer" in *Rhetoric, Religion, and the Civil Rights Movement, 1954–1965*, 14 and 784–794, respectively.

48. Of course, we are not the first scholars to address this vexatious issue. See, for example, Karlyn Kohrs Campbell, "Agency—Promiscuous and Protean," *Communication and Critical/Cultural Studies* 2 (2005): 1–19.

49. Thomas S. Flory, "Abstracter's Introduction" to "Presentation and Responses to Questions by FANNIE LOU HAMER" January 29, 1976, at the University of Wisconsin–Madison, Measure for Measure files, Tape 782 A.

50. As remembered by Reverend Edwin King, interview with King by Maegan Parker Brooks.

51. Interview with Reverend Edwin King by Maegan Parker Brooks.

52. It appears to be the case that three of Hamer's scripted speeches were actually penned by her campaign manager, Charles McLaurin. We learned of this ghostwriting relationship when checking with Mr. McLaurin to verify the authenticity of a speech that the reviewer for this project called our attention to. Upon review, McLaurin informed us that he wrote that speech, titled "The New Consumer in Health," which is located in the Lillian P. Benbow collection housed at the Mississippi Department of Archives and History, and that he had also written two others for Mrs. Hamer. In fact, two of the speeches we have included here, "Is It Too Late?" and "If the Name of the Game Is Survive, Survive," are the texts McLaurin claims to have written. We decided to include those two speeches, even in light of the question over authorship, because we have evidence that Hamer actually delivered these speeches to audiences. We did not include the "New Consumer in Health" speech, however, because McLaurin informed us that this speech was just sent away to be included in a collection of what "black politicians are saying." He told us that, upon her request, he "wrote [it] and mailed it in for Mrs. Hamer." E-mail correspondence between Davis W. Houck and Charles McLaurin, January 13, 2010.

53. Kenneth Chandler, archivist at the Mary McLeod Bethune Council House, which is home to the National Archives for Black Women's History, went above and beyond the call of duty in not only locating old Hamer recordings but in repairing and digitizing them.

54. Phone interview with Vergie Hamer Faulkner by Maegan Parker Brooks, July 11 and July 14, 2009 (included within).

The Speeches of
FANNIE LOU HAMER

"I Don't Mind My Light Shining,"

Speech Delivered at a Freedom Vote Rally in Greenwood, Mississippi, Fall 1963

Of the many strategic innovations introduced in Mississippi by the Student Non-violent Coordinating Committee and the Council of Federated Organizations, perhaps none was more consequential than the Freedom Vote of fall 1963. The joint creation of Allard Lowenstein and Bob Moses, the Freedom Vote was a "mock election" designed to dramatize, especially to the federal government, that disenfranchised black Mississippians would cast a ballot if given the opportunity. In addition, in order to vote for meaningful racial progress in the state, black Clarksdale pharmacist Aaron Henry and white Tougaloo College chaplain Reverend Edwin King were recruited to run as an integrated ticket for governor and lieutenant governor, respectively.

As the campaign gathered momentum and publicity by late October, Freedom Vote rallies were held across the state. At one such rally, held in the SNCC-headquartered town of Greenwood in the Delta, Fannie Lou Hamer delivered a brief but impassioned address to her fellow black Deltans. In this, the earliest known recording of Hamer's speechmaking, she borrows extensively from the Old and New Testaments not only to legitimize her role of rhetorical leadership—Jesus had answered her prayer and opened a way for her to speak—but to have Scripture also function as something of a cudgel: if Mississippi blacks did not take action and vote at this defining hour, they would go "straight to hell" with their oppressors.

This opening salvo in Hamer's rhetorical ministry foreshadows many of the themes she would address during the next thirteen years: the intimidation and violence she had faced immediately upon attempting to register to vote on August 31, 1962; her brutal beating on June 9, 1963, in a Winona, Mississippi, jail; the extent to which the black church was often an insular house of hypocrisy rather than a house of meaningful political action; the relationship among poverty, race, and social justice; and always the impassioned righteousness that sprang from the unswerving knowledge that she was doing God's will.

3

The Mississippi Freedom Vote was a stunning success: nearly eighty thousand ballots were cast between November 2 and 4; the arrival of white Yale University undergraduates to assist in the campaign generated local, state, and national publicity; the Henry-King political ticket foreshadowed the creation six months later of the Mississippi Freedom Democratic Party; and the influx of northern college students proved so successful that Freedom Summer of 1964 was modeled after such domestic missionary work.

*   *   *

From the fourth chapter of St. Luke beginning at the eighteenth verse: "The Spirit of the Lord is upon me because he has anointed me to preach the gospel to the poor. He has sent me to heal the brokenhearted, to preach deliverance to the captive, and recover the sight to the blind, to set at liberty to them who are bruised, to preach the acceptable year of the Lord."

Now the time have come that was Christ's purpose on earth. And we only been getting by, by paying our way to Hell. But the time is out. When Simon [of] Cyrene was helping Christ to bear his cross up the hill, he said, "Must Jesus bear this cross alone? And all the world go free?" He said, "No, there's a cross for everyone and there's a cross for me. This consecrated cross I'll bear, till death shall set me free. And then go home a crown to wear, for there's a crown for me."

And it's no easy way out. We just got to wake up and face it, folks. And if I can face the issue, you can too. You see, the thing, what's so pitiful now about it, the men been wanting to be the boss all of these years, and the ones that ain't up under the house is under the bed.

But you see, it's poison; it's poison for us not to speak what we know is right. As Christ said from the seventeenth chapter of Acts and the twenty-sixth verse, says: "Has made of one blood all nations, for to dwell on the face of the earth." Then it's no different, we just have different colors.

And, brother, you can believe this or not: I been sick of this system as long as I can remember. I heard some people speak of depression in the '30s. In the '20s, it was 'pression with me! De-pression. I been as hungry—it's a funny thing since I started working for Christ—it's kind of like in the twenty-third of Psalms when he says, "Thou prepareth a table before me in the presence of my enemies. Thou anointed my head with oil and my cup runneth over."

And I have walked through the shadows of death because it was on the tenth of September in '62 when they shot sixteen times in a house and it wasn't a foot over the bed where my head was. But that night I wasn't there—don't you see what God can do? Quit running around trying to dodge death be-cause this book said, "He that seeketh to save his life, he's going to lose it anyhow!"

So as long as you know you going for something, you put up a life. That it can be like Paul, say, "I fought a good fight." And I've "kept the faith." You know, it had been a long time—people, I have worked, I have worked as hard as anybody. I have been picking cotton and would be so hungry—and one of the poison things about it—wondering what I was going to cook that night. But you see all of them things was wrong, you see? And I have asked God, I said, "Now Lord"—and you have too—ain't no need to lie and say that you ain't. Said, "Open a way for us." Said, "Please make a way for us, Jesus." Said, "Where I can stand up and speak for my race and speak for these hungry chil-dren." And he opened a way and all of them mostly backing out.

You see, he made it so plain for us. He sent a man in Mississippi with the same name that Moses had to go to Egypt. And tell him to go down in Mis-sissippi and tell Ross Barnett to let my people go. And you know I feel good, I feel good. I never know today what's going to happen to me tonight, but I do know as I walk alone, I walk with my hand in God's hand.

And, you see, you know the ballot is good. If it wasn't good how come he trying to keep you from it and he still using it? Don't be foolish, folks: they going in there by the droves and droves and they had guards to keep us out of there the other day. And dogs. Now if that's good enough for them, I want some of it too.

You see, as I said, it was on the tenth of September when they shot in the house for me sixteen times, but I didn't stop. Now some of the time since then I got hungry, but I got consolation because I had got hungry before I got in it. Wasn't going to be no more hungry now than I was then. Then, on the ninth of June, this year, I was beat in a jailhouse until I was hard as metal. And I told the policeman, I said, "It's going to be miserable when you have to face God." I said, "Because one day you going to pay up for the things you have done." I said, because, as the Scripture says, "Has made of one blood all nations." He said, "It's a damn lie," said, "Abraham Lincoln said that." So that's pitiful—I'm telling you the truth, but it's pitiful, you see—that people can have so much hate that will make them beat a person and don't know they doing wrong.

But open your New Testament when you get home and read from the twenty-sixth chapter of Proverbs and the twenty-seventh verse: "Who so dig-geth a pit shall fall down in it." Pits have been dug for us for ages. But they didn't know, when they was digging pits for us, they had some pits dug for themselves. And the Bible had said, "Before one jot of my word would fail,

Heaven and earth would pass away. Be not deceived for God is not mocked. For whatsoever a man soweth, that shall he also reap."

All we got to do—that's why I love the song "This Little Light of Mine"— from the fifth chapter of Matthew, He said, "A city that's set on a hill cannot be hid." And I don't mind my light shining; I don't hide that I'm fighting for freedom because Christ died to set us free. And he stayed here until he got thirty-three years old, letting us know how we would have to walk.

And we can come to this church and we can shout till we look foolish, be- cause that's what we're doing. And we can come out here and live a lie and like the lie and we going just as straight to hell, if we don't do something. Because we got a charge to keep too. Until we can sing this song of Dr. Watts: "Should earth against my soul engage and fiery darts be hurled, but when I can smile at Satan's rage and face the frowning world." Thank you.

Federal Trial Testimony, Oxford, Mississippi, December 2, 1963

As her Continental Trailways bus arrived at Staley's Café in Winona, Mississippi, on the morning of June 9, 1963, Fannie Lou Hamer could not have known her life was about to change dramatically. Nor did she likely know the extent to which local law enforcement officials had so brutally and swiftly suppressed any civil rights activity there long before her arrival.

Hamer, along with her traveling companions Annell Ponder, James West, June Johnson, Rosemary Freeman, and Euvester Simpson were traveling back to the Delta after a week-long voter education workshop in Charleston, South Carolina, led by the legendary teacher-activist Septima Clark. Unbeknownst to the road-weary travelers, Winona and Montgomery County officials were not eager to heed the 1961 Interstate Commerce Commission ruling, which effectively integrated interstate travel. In fact, in State Sovereignty Commission documents, local officials were feted for realizing "that each person has a responsibility in helping to resist those who would destroy our way of life by attempting to carrying [sic] out governmental department orders or decrees." Such resistance entailed re-segregating the lunch counter and the restrooms at Staley's in the fall of 1961.

Into this thicket of white intransigence Hamer and her friends walked. While several members of the party were badly beaten in the local jailhouse following their arrest, none was more savage than the beating ordered by the state highway patrolman and chief of police to be administered by two black prisoners— Sol Poe and Roosevelt Knox—on Fannie Lou Hamer. She would carry the beating with her until her death fourteen years later. It was a beating provoked, in her frequent retelling, by her civil rights activism back home in Ruleville. Largely because of the brutal beatings, and the seemingly irrefutable physical evidence therein, the Justice Department took an interest in the case—something the federal government was still slow to do in 1963.

The government brought suit against Earle Wayne Patridge, Thomas J. Herod, Jr., William Surrell, John L. Basinger, and Charles Thomas Perkins in U.S. District Court in the Northern District of Mississippi, Western Division. Its star witness was Fannie Lou Hamer, who testified at length in Oxford on December 2, 1963. Despite her steadfast and moving account of what happened on June 9, 10, and 11, and the damning evidence provided by her travel companions, the twelve-member all-white and all-male jury deliberated for a mere seventy-five minutes; on December 6, they found each defendant not guilty of violating the activists' civil rights.

Whenever Fannie Lou Hamer spoke publicly after being bonded out of the Montgomery County Jail, the gruesome details of Winona were almost never spared; the "incident," regardless of how many times she recounted it North and South, never failed to move both the speaker and her disbelieving audiences. Her accounts of the Winona beating also dramatically conveyed the larger sickness of white supremacy, as she carefully characterized her experience as symptomatic of a systemic illness rather than simply a small-town act of unpunished sadism.

* * *

Would you state your full name.

FLH. Mrs. Fannie Lou Hamer.

Q. Where do you live?

FLH. 626 East Lafayette Street, Ruleville, Mississippi.

Q. What does your family consist of, Mrs. Hamer?

FLH. Four.

Q. Who are the members of your family?

FLH. My husband and two daughters.

Q. Where were you born?

FLH. I was born in Webster County, Tomnolen, Mississippi.

Q. Where have you lived?

FLH. I've been in Sunflower County, not out of Sunflower County a year for forty-four years.

Q. Lived all your life in Mississippi.

FLH. That's right.

Q. Now, are you associated at the present time with any organization that has among its purposes the encouragement of Negroes to vote in Mississippi?

FLH. Yes.

Q. What's that organization?

FLH. I'm a field secretary for the Student Nonviolent Coordinating Committee.

Q. How long have you been connected with that organization?

FLH. I began working in December of '62.

Q. What type of work have you been doing?

FLH. Trying to get people to register to vote.

Q. Have you been doing any type of work in connection with that committee other than relating to voting?

FLH. Well, I worked . . . I teaches citizenship class for SCLC—Southern Christian Leadership Conference.

Q. And what do you teach in those classes?

FLH. The duties of citizenship under a constitutional form of government.

Q. Mrs. Hamer, do you know Annell Ponder?

FLH. Yes.

Q. How long have you known her?

FLH. Since March.

Q. During the period of time you have known her where has she been staying?

FLH. Greenwood.

Q. Did you go with a group on a trip to Charleston, South Carolina, in June of this year?

FLH. Yes.

Q. Was Annell Ponder with that group?

FLH. Yes.

Q. Did you recall on what day you returned from Charleston?

FLH. We left Charleston the eighth of June and we arrived at Winona, Mississippi, the ninth.

Q. How did you travel?

FLH. Continental Trailways.

Q. What time did the bus get to Winona?

FLH. I would say . . . I didn't know definitely, but I would say between eleven and twelve o'clock.

Q. Did some of your party get off of the bus?

FLH. Yes.

Q. . . . at Winona?

FLH. Yes.

Q. Did you get off with the first ones who got off?

FLH. No.

Q. Would you just tell the jury what happened after the bus got to Winona? Just tell them in your own words. Now don't tell them what anyone else may have told you, but just tell what you saw and what you heard, but not any conversation you had with the other people who were with you, except when one of the defendants may have been present. Do you understand?

FLH. It was two got off at first. They said on the bus they was going to use the washroom. Then it was four others say they was going into the bus terminal to eat.

Q. All right. Just go ahead and tell the members of the jury, if you would, what happened, what you observed.

FLH. I was looking through the window, and it wasn't too long before the four that went in the restaurant at the bus terminal to get food . . . It wasn't long before they came out, and I got off of the bus to see what it . . . you know, what caused them to come out so quickly. Miss Ponder said they had been . . .

Q. Objected to.

Q. Don't tell what Miss Ponder said.

FLH. Okay.

Q. Just tell us what you did . . . and what the other people did.

FLH. I got back on the bus, and after I got back on the bus it wasn't too long before I seen them getting in a light-colored car. I had Miss Ponder's iron, and I left my bag and my luggage on the bus, because I planned to get right back, but I got off, and somebody screamed from the car that they was in, said, "Get that one there." And it was this man with the glasses on told me that I was under arrest.

Q. Now, may the record show that the witness is indicating . . . Would you state whether it's the first one in the row here or the last one?

FLH. It's the second one . . .

Q. From which end?

FLH. With the glasses on.

Q. From which end?

FLH. From this end down here.

Q. May the record show the witness is indicating the defendant, Patridge. All right, Mrs. Hamer. Go ahead.

FLH. As I started to get in the car, he kicked me. This man was in the front with him.

Q. Now which man are you indicating?

FLH. This man with the red tie on.

Q. May the record show the witness is indicating the defendant, Perkins. All right, Mrs. Hamer. Would you go ahead?

FLH. They drove me on to this county jail.

Q. Was anyone else in that car other than the defendant, Patridge, the defendant, Perkins, and yourself?

FLH. That's all. It was the three of us.

Q. Were there two cars . . . is this . . . were there two cars?

FLH. The other car had gone on with the others.

Q. All right.

FLH. That's right.

Q. Go ahead and tell the jury what happened when you got to the jail.

FLH. When . . . as we were going on to this jail, Mr. Wayne . . . Mr. Earle Wayne Patridge would ask me questions, and as I would try to answer he would . . .

Q. Go ahead. Tell the jury what was said in the car as you were going to the jail.

FLH. He asked what was we trying to do. I say, "I wasn't doing anything," I say, "because I had just got off of the bus." I say, "What had I done?" He would tell me to hush and, you know, would talk . . . he would talk . . . he would never raise his voice, but he would talk, you know, awful.

Q. Well, just tell us what was said, Mrs. Hamer.

FLH. I say, "I haven't done anything." I say, "I didn't go in the bus terminal and I didn't do anything but just got off of the bus." I say, "Why was I arrested?" And then he would say cuss words to me and he would tell me to hush. So, I just hush.

Q. Where did the car take you?

FLH. They taken me to this jail.

Q. That's the Montgomery County Jail in Winona?

FLH. Yes.

Q. Just tell the jury what happened when you got to the jail.

FLH. When we got inside the jail, this man at the end...

Q. Now . . .

FLH. He had on a dark pair of blue trousers . . .

Q. Now are you indicating . . .

FLH. After we got out . . .

Q. The defendant . . .

FLH. And went inside the jail . . .

Q. Mrs. Hamer, are you indicating the defendant, Surrell, who is sitting at the nearest to me?

FLH. That's right.

Q. All right.

FLH. Well, as we got out and went into the jail, he had on navy blue pants and a lighter blue shirt, he walked over, the rest was already inside, because this first car had got there before we did. So as we, as I walked inside the jail, he walked over to James West and jumped on his feet.

Q. Mrs. Hamer, I'd like to direct your attention to Government Exhibit Number One, which is a diagram of the floor plan on the jail. Do you recognize that as roughly showing the layout in the jail?

FLH. I do.

Q. Well, would you point out to the jury where you were taken in the jail and where this incident happened that you have just described?

FLH. I was taken through this place right here. It was a big, some kind of drum in this place, and I was taken to this place right here.

Q. Well, were you taken first into what's labeled there as the "booking room"?

FLH. Yes. At first . . .

Q. Well, would you . . .

FLH. I was in here . . .

Q. Just tell the jury what happened in the booking room, if anything?

FLH. They carried me to this cell right here, myself and Euvester Simpson, and locked us up in this cell.

Q. All right. Did you see where the others were taken, if anywhere?

FLH. No.

Q. You can take your chair again, if you will. Mrs. Hamer, how long, about how long, was it from the time you were arrested at the terminal until you were put in that cell, would you say?

FLH. I would say about forty minutes, from the time, you know, to get down to the jail and then put in the cell.

Q. Would you tell the jury what happened, if anything, after you were put in that cell?

FLH. After I was put in the cell, the state highway patrolman, because he had a sign across his shirt, was kind of . . . looked like silk, and it had wrote on this sign "John Basinger," and then it was an insignia on the arm that said he was a state highway patrolman . . .

Q. Do you see that man . . .

FLH. Yes; I do.

Q. . . . in the courtroom today?

FLH. Yes; I do.

Q. Where is he?

FLH. He's the third one, and he has on glasses.

Q. May the record show the witness is indicating the defendant, Basinger? I'm sorry, Mrs. Hamer. Go ahead. Tell the jury . . .

FLH. But anyway, he came in the cell, and Mr. Earle Wayne Patridge was with him, and the man said, he told me the day he was carrying me to jail his name was Jenkins. So, that's what I thought his name was, but I know his; and he asked me, Mr. Basinger.

Q. Now, what man told you his name was Jenkins?

FLH. That man with the black tie on, the first one.

Q. Are you indicating the defendant, Surrell . . .

FLH. Yes.

Q. . . . who is sitting closest to me?

FLH. Yes.

Q. All right.

FLH. But he carried me in this cell and he asked me where I was from, and I told him, and he said he would check. He talked awhile, and then he went out, and . . .

Q. Well, tell us what he said.

FLH. He just asked me where I was from, and I told him, Ruleville, Mississippi, and he said, "I'm going to check." Say, "What was you all trying to do? Demonstrate or something?" I said, "No sir. I was not off of the bus." I said, "There wasn't anybody." I said, "They was just trying to get food, the others was, and I wasn't off the bus," and I say, "I haven't . . ." and he cut me off; never allowed to get finished; never allowed hardly at no time to finish what I was trying to say.

Q. Did he come back to the cell?

FLH. Yes.

Q. Was anyone with him when he came back to the cell?

FLH. He was by hisself when he came back.

Q. Tell the jury what happened when he came back to the cell.

FLH. He came back and told me to come out.

Q. Did you go out?

FLH. That's right.

Q. What happened after you went out with him?

FLH. He walked, he carried me to another cell. Now, this cell, I don't know where it was, but it was a bunk in there. It was two Negroes in this other cell.

Q. Men or women?

FLH. Men.

Q. Had you ever seen them before?

FLH. No.

Q. Go ahead and tell us what happened.

FLH. Mr. Basinger gave the first one, he was dark, with a round face, looked like about twenty-five, he gave him a blackjack. It was a piece of, black leather thing, and it was wide, and it was heavy, and he told the first one, says, "I want you to make that bitch wish she was dead." And the Negro told me to stretch out on the cot, on my face, and that's what I did, and he beat me. He beat me something terrible. He beat me a long time.

Q. What part of your body did he beat?

FLH. From here back. This side, I had polio when I was five or six years old, and I was holding my hands behind to try to keep as much of the weight off of this side as I could, and I just, just taken a beating, and I never at no time resisted, because it wasn't any need, because at the time I was being beat it was five men there, which was the man that say his name was Mr. Jenkins, Mr. Basinger, and the man with the red tie on. They was in the room, and the first one beat me, and then Mr. Basinger told the second one to take the blackjack, and I asked the second one, I say, "How can you do it?" And . . .

Q. Now, when you say "the second one," who do you mean?

FLH. The second Negro.

Q. All right.

FLH. I asked him, I say, "How can you do it?" And he say, "You better get your arms out of the way." And he had already begun. During this time it was just, it was hurting so bad, just you know, the same thing. My dress was coming up. I had on a gathered skirt. I pushed my dress down, and the man that say his name was Mr. Jenkins . . .

Q. You mean the defendant, Surrell?

FLH. That's right. He pulled my dress up and ordered the first Negro that had whipped me to set on my feet while the second one beat me, and during the time the second one was beating, I was screaming so loud, this one got up, with the red tie on, and began beating me in my head, from the back of my head, and I just hugged my arms then around, tried to muffle out the sounds until it was over.

Q. How long did it go on?

FLH. I don't know, but when, when they was finished my hands was navy blue and I was hard. I was hard like metal. And he told me then to get up, Mr. Basinger did, and go back to my cell, and I was, it was like I was drunk or something; but I couldn't, I couldn't lay down, you know, on the back, and it would just make me scream, and I just had to try to get up.

Q. Mrs. Hamer, tell me this: would you describe the cot that you were stretched out on?

FLH. It was just a bunk bed, with a tick, a little mattress on it, and it look like an army blanket was on it.

Q. What color army . . .

FLH. It was green, you know. A dark green blanket was on it.

Q. Mrs. Hamer, was that your last contact with those officers that evening, Sunday evening? I mean that day?

FLH. It was.

Q. When did you see them again?

FLH. Monday night.

Q. Were you in the same cell on Monday night?

FLH. Yes.

Q. Tell the jury what happened Monday night.

FLH. Monday night Mr. Fowler, he said his name was Fowler, that was the jailer, he came and told me to get up out of my cell, and when I had gone into the room they asked us, they asked me about making, they made pictures.

Q. You say "they" asked you. Who was there?

FLH. Mr. Earle Wayne Patridge; Mr. Basinger. We first, at first I did, I had to write a statement, and I wrote what Mr. Basinger told me to write.

Q. What did he tell you to write?

FLH. He told me to write that since I had been in jail I had been treated good; I had been fed, and had nobody mistreated me, and said I was writing it of my own free will. He told me to write it.

Q. Did you write it?

FLH. Yes.

Q. Why did you write it?

FLH. He had his gun, and I know what I had gone through that Sunday, and I didn't have no other choice. But I asked him one time, I say, "Do you mean I had been treated good and can't sit down?"

Q. Did you write it as well as you could?

FLH. No.

Q. What did you do?

FLH. I wrote it, I wrote it terrible. I wrote it just real bad.

Q. Was that occasion when you wrote the statement in the daytime or nighttime, Mrs. Hamer?

FLH. It was at night.

Q. And was your photograph taken in the daytime or nighttime?

FLH. At night.

Q. The same night?

FLH. The same night.

Q. I'm not sure I caught whether you said who took your photograph.

FLH. Mr. Basinger.

Q. Who else was there at that time?

FLH. Mr. Basinger; Mr. Earle Wayne Patridge. I, I remember those two.

Q. Were you taken to trial?

FLH. Yes.

Q. When were you taken to trial?

FLH. On Tuesday.

Q. Mrs. Hamer, I'll direct your attention to Government Exhibit Number Three, and you'll note that there's a building indicated in the upper right of the diagram, the Montgomery County Jail.

FLH. Yes.

Q. Then down the street there's the Montgomery County Court House, and across the street from it is the city hall. Where was your trial conducted?

FLH. It wasn't at a courthouse, and this placed looked more like it right here. It looked like it right here. It looked like it here; but, anyway, it was being repaired.

Q. The city hall was?

FLH. Yes, if that was the city hall.

Q. All right.

FLH. It was torn up.

Q. Were the other members of your group taken to trial on the same time you were?

FLH. Yes.

Q. All right. Would you describe to the jury how you were taken to the trial and who took you and what happened?

FLH. We began walking, but I was sore and I couldn't walk too very well.

Q. Do you remember who was with you when you were walking?

FLH. Mr. Earle Wayne Patridge was with us, and as I began walking, and couldn't walk too good, he asked Mr. Jenkins to carry us in the black car.

Q. Now, when you refer to Mr. Jenkins, are you indicating, at the end here, the defendant, Surrell?

FLH. Yes. That's what he told me his name was.

Q. Did you ride in a car with him . . .

FLH. Yes.

Q. ... to the place where you were tried?

FLH. Yes.

Q. Would you tell the jury what happened at the trial?

FLH. When we got to the trial, we was standing in, in one of the little rooms, you know, just all of us I would say was called "prisoners." We was in the little room, and when one walked to the door, now, that is one thing, I'm not sure who walked to the door and ordered me to come in, as one by one, and when they called me in Mr. Earle Wayne Patridge and some of the ones I had seen that Sunday was on the jury seat, and it was a man, I saw him yesterday, but today I don't see him; but he told me that I was charged with disorderly conduct and resisting arrest. I says, "Not either one so," I said, "because I didn't do anything but get off of the bus, and I don't think that was against the law."

Q. Mrs. Hamer, were you found guilty at the trial?

FLH. I pleaded not guilty.

Q. I know, but what did the court decide at the trial?

FLH. I was guilty.

Q. How did you ... Did you return from the place of trial to the county jail?

FLH. In the same black car that Mr. Jenkins was driving.

Q. And each time you say Mr. Jenkins you're referring to the defendant, Surrell?

FLH. Yes.

Q. Correct?

FLH. That's what he, he told me that was his name.

Q. Did others ride in the car back to the jail with you?

FLH. Back to jail. All of us rode together.

Q. Was there any conversation in the car as you went back to jail?

FLH. He told me about, asked me did I know any of the waitresses, and I told him some of those people was my relation that lived at Kilmichael, Mississippi, and he said he was friends with them because they had, he had let them use his tractor; and one time, during the time we were going on to jail, I said I would like to see these people when they face God, with the kind of thing they have done to us, and he said, "Don't say it to me, because you haven't seen me. I wasn't on duty yesterday." But, you see, I remembered too many things about it.

Q. Now, you've mentioned at one time he said his name was Jenkins. When did that occur?

FLH. I asked him when we were going on what was his name.

Q. Was that on the trip back to the jail or the trip from the jail, the first trip, from the jail to . . .

FLH. Back to the jail.

Q. What was said?

FLH. I asked him what was his name, and he paused a few seconds and said, "Mr. Jenkins."

Q. When were you released?

FLH. On the twelfth.

Q. What day of the week was that?

FLH. Wednesday.

Q. On the day you were released from the county jail did you see any of the defendants there at the jail?

FLH. I saw Mr. Earle Wayne Patridge.

Q. Did you see any other defendants?

FLH. Yes. I saw the chief.

Q. Did you see any of the other defendants there at the jail?

FLH. I'm not sure, but I know I saw those two.

Q. Did you receive any injuries from the beating that you have described to the jury?

FLH. Yes.

Q. What injuries did you receive?

FLH. I was, I was real hard, just real hard, from my back down to the calf of my leg, and as soon as we had gotten out of jail I went to see Dr. Garner in Greenwood.

Q. When did you completely recover from the injuries you received?

FLH. I haven't recovered.

Q. What effects do you still have?

FLH. Dr. Searcy say . . . I have a hurting, and it's hard places, you can feel. It's hard places in my hip, and at times I just be sore.

Q. Mrs. Hamer, did representatives of the Federal Bureau of Investigation photograph you in Washington, D. C.?

FLH. Yes.

Q. When was that?

FLH. It was on, let me see, the Wednesday I got out of jail. On a Saturday.

Q. The Saturday . . .

FLH. Yes.

Q. . . . after . . .

FLH. Wednesday.

Q. . . . you were out of jail?

FLH. That's right.

Q. Have you ever been arrested on any other occasion?

FLH. No.

Cross Examination

Q. Fannie Lou Hamer, is it?

FLH. That's right. Mrs. Fannie Lou Hamer.

Q. Now, as I understand, you and the other group who were with you started your trip on this occasion in . . . where in South Carolina?

FLH. Charleston, South Carolina.

Q. Charleston, South Carolina. And you had gone over there to attend a school for the purpose of preparing yourselves to continue the work of the, what? Student Nonviolent . . .

FLH. Voter education.

Q. Oh, the voter education?

FLH. Yes.

Q. In Mississippi? Is that right?

FLH. That's right.

Q. When you left South Carolina, where were you headed?

FLH. Back to Greenwood.

Q. Back to Greenwood?

FLH. And from there on to Ruleville.

Q. Ruleville?

FLH. That is right.

Q. Now, was Greenwood at that time sort of the headquarters for this movement in that section of Mississippi?

FLH. Yes.

Q. And did you come straight through on the same bus or did you have to change buses?

FLH. We had to, we had to change bus. We wasn't on a chartered bus.

Q. Did the bus stop at Columbus?

FLH. Yes, it did.

Q. And then you came on through from Columbus, and your next stop was Winona?

FLH. That's right.

Q. When you stopped in Winona, a group got off of the bus to go into the lunchroom; is that right?

FLH. That's right. Four people.

Q. Had there been any discussion between you and the other members of this group that were arrested about whether or not they would go into the white lunchroom?

FLH. No.

Q. No discussion about that?

FLH. No.

Q. But you then saw them come out of the lunchroom rather quickly or quicker than you thought that they should be coming out; is that right?

FLH. Yes.

Q. And I believe you said you got off of the bus to find out why they were coming out so quick?

FLH. Yes.

Q. Were you particularly interested why they were coming out so quick?

FLH. I just wanted to know.

Q. The truth of the business is you knew when they got off they were going in to integrate that lunchroom and you were getting out to find out what happened, weren't you? Now, that's the truth of it, isn't it?

FLH. No, because we knew from the ICC ruling in 1961 that that had already passed. They had a right to eat in the bus terminal.

Q. I'm not talking about what they had a right to do; I'm not talking about the ICC ruling, but you knew when they got off . . .

FLH. I did not know, because I hadn't ever been in the terminal in Winona.

Q. You did not know that that was their purpose?

FLH. No.

Q. Then why were you so interested in why they had come out so soon?

FLH. I just wanted to know.

Q. Why didn't you stay on the bus until they came back to the bus to find out?

FLH. I just didn't do it.

Q. In other words, you saw them come out pretty soon and you got out to see what happened, did you? That's the truth of it, isn't it?

FLH. I got off of the bus to see what had happened, why they came out so early.

Q. I see.

FLH. I say that at the beginning.

Q. Were they headed back toward the bus when they came out?

FLH. Did they head back toward the bus?

Q. When they came out the first time . . .

FLH. They walked on across, on the side where the bus was, and stopped.

Q. And stopped?

FLH. Yes.

Q. And you got off?

FLH. They wasn't on the street. They was on the place where the bus was, and I got off and walked to them.

Q. To find out what happened?

FLH. That's right.

Q. I see. Now, then, after talking with them a minute, you got back on the bus; is that right?

FLH. That's right.

Q. Then did they start back in toward the café?

FLH. No.

Q. They did not?

FLH. They did not.

Q. Were you looking at them?

FLH. That's right.

Q. What did they do?

FLH. It wasn't, it wasn't too long before they was getting in a white car.

Q. I see.

FLH. And I . . .

Q. You looked . . .

FLH. And when they started getting in this white car, that's when I got Annell's iron that I had and got off of the bus with the iron.

Q. Now, you saw the four of them . . .

FLH. It was more than four. It was five at the time was standing on the outside.

Q. You saw June Johnson and James West and Annell Ponder and Euvester Simpson and Rosemary Freeman getting into a car, didn't you?

FLH. Yes.

Q. In other words, you saw them when they were being arrested and were being put into a car? That's what you knew had happened, didn't you?

FLH. Yes.

Q. Now, did you see the officers who were at that car?

FLH. I did not. I couldn't tell, you know.

Q. They got in the car?

FLH. Yes.

Q. Did you or someone call out or come out of the bus and call out to Annell Ponder and ask, "What you want us to do?"

FLH. I called Annell. I called her.

Q. And asked her, "What do you want us to do?"

FLH. I said, "Annell," and I was holding up the iron. And she said, "Go ahead, Mrs. Hamer. Get back to the bus." Somebody from the car she was in at that time said, "Get that one, too."

Q. Some officer from the car called with instructions to arrest you, didn't he?

FLH. That's right; somebody did.

Q. And then that car drove off with them in it, didn't it?

FLH. Yes.

Q. And the officer who had come up about that time, who arrested you, was Mr. Patridge, the sheriff, wasn't it?

FLH. Yes.

Q. He had not participated in arresting the others? In other words, he was not with the others at that time, was he?

FLH. I didn't see him.

Q. Two other officers drove off with them; is that right?

FLH. I don't know. I didn't see how many officers it was drove off with them. I heard one person say, "Get that one." I don't know how many was in the other car. I know how many was in the car I was in.

Q. Now, how far were you then from that car when the officer called out to "get that one"?

FLH. From what car?

Q. From the car that they were getting in?

FLH. I wasn't too far, because at no time, I wasn't far from the bus and the cars wasn't far from the bus.

Q. What I mean is this: June Johnson and those others were being loaded into a car.

FLH. And when this person called out and said, "Get that one there," this car left, and then Mr. Earle Wayne Patridge...

Q. Now . . .

FLH. . . . arrested me.

Q. That's right.

FLH. That's the way it was.

Q. That's right. What I'm getting at is this: this officer from that other car called out and said, "Get that one." How far were you standing from the car where he called out from? About how far?

FLH. I don't know.

Q. Point out something.

FLH. About, I would say about as far from here to the window over there, because I was closer to the bus than I was to the car.

Q. That's right. In other words, you were about as far as from where you are to that window, which is some fifty or sixty feet, isn't it?

FLH. From here to the first part of the window.

Q. Yes.

FLH. About what I would say.

Q. That's about fifty or sixty feet, isn't it?

FLH. Something like that.

Q. Or maybe a little further? And where was Mr. Patridge, the sheriff, when you first saw him?

FLH. He drove around this car. When this man said, "Get that one there," he drove around and jumped out of the car and said, "You're under arrest."

Q. In other words, Mr. Patridge had just driven up, hadn't he. . .

FLH. I guess he had . . .

Q. . . . in his car . . .

FLH. . . . because that's when . . .

Q. . . . and one of these officers called out to him to "get that one," and he got out of his car and put you under arrest, didn't he?

FLH. Yes. He told me I was under arrest, and he opened the back door, and as I started to get in the car, that's when he kicked me.

Q. He kicked you?

FLH. Yes.

Q. Did you get in the back seat?

FLH. That's right.

Q. And Mr. Patridge kicked you?

FLH. That's right. The man with the glasses on.

Q. Now, was anybody in the car with him?

FLH. Yes. The one with the red tie on.

Q. That's Mr. Perkins. He was in the car with Mr. Patridge?

FLH. That's right.

Q. And who was driving?

FLH. Mr. Patridge.

Q. Was driving the car?

FLH. That's right.

Q. You were put in the car and carried to the county jail?

FLH. Yes.

Q. Following the other prisoners.

FLH. Yes.

Q. Now, you were not brought to that jail or arrested by Mr. Surrell, this gentleman here, were you?

FLH. No; I wasn't arrested by Mr. Jenkins.

Q. Well, his name is Mr. Surrell and, if you don't mind, I'll refer to him as Surrell, and if you would, that is his name. I understand you tell the court he told you his name was Jenkins.

FLH. He did.

Q. You didn't see him at the bus station, did you?

FLH. I didn't. I did not see him at the bus station . . .

Q. And he . . .

FLH. . . . because . . .

Q. . . . did not put you under arrest?

FLH. No.

Q. He did not take you to jail?

FLH. No.

Q. Mr. Patridge, the sheriff, did not go to the jail in the other car that the other prisoners were in, did he?

FLH. No. Mr. Patridge carried me.

Q. I see. Now, when you got to the jail, now when you were carried to the jail, you drove in this driveway and stopped and went through this hall, down this hall, and into the booking room here, didn't you.

FLH. Yes.

Q. Who went in with you?

FLH. Mr. Earle Wayne Patridge and the man with the red tie on.

Q. That's Mr. Perkins?

FLH. That's right.

Q. The two went in with you?

FLH. Yes.

Q. And you entered this door into the booking room?

FLH. Yes.

Q. Now in this booking room there was a table or high-top desk right along this wall, wasn't it, where they keep the docket and enter names on?

FLH. I didn't notice all of that, but I know it was a big something, like . . .

Q. Well, it was a table against this wall . . .

FLH. Yes.

Q. . . . wasn't it?

FLH. Yes.

Q. There was a big still in there, wasn't it?

FLH. It was something. It was a big round something.

Q. And wasn't it sitting along here, sitting along here?

FLH. It was in there, if I'm not . . .

Q. Was there a little refrigerator in there?

FLH. Yes, it was something.

Q. Was that along here, between these two entrances?

FLH. I'm not sure about the Frigidaire, because I wouldn't, you know, I wasn't paying no attention to the Frigidaire.

Q. That's right. Now, there is a solid door, metal door, across this entrance that goes into the colored cell block, isn't there?

FLH. A solid door?

Q. That's right.

FLH. Yes.

Q. And it was closed?

FLH. Yes.

Q. Then there's a solid door that shuts off these two cells, isn't it?

FLH. Yes.

Q. Now, when you were taken in there by Mr. Patridge and Mr. Perkins, who was in that room when they got you in there?

FLH. All of the rest was standing around . . .

Q. In . . .

FLH. . . . in this room.

Q. Did they take your names at that time?

FLH. No.

Q. You were talked to at that time?

FLH. I wasn't talked to too much. I just remember very clearly as we walked in this room, when we got to this jailhouse, when we walked in this room . . . Anyway, Mr. Surrell walked over and jumped on James West's feet.

Q. All right. Was Mr. Surrell already in there when you got there?

FLH. He was, when I seen him, he was in there.

Q. When Mr. Patridge and Mr. Perkins brought you in there, Mr. Surrell, that gentleman sitting on the end, was in the room . . .

FLH. He was in the room . . .

Q. . . . when you were there?

FLH. . . . when I got there.

Q. And you saw him go over and step on James West's feet?

FLH. Yes.

Q. Now, Mr. Patridge is not the man that went over and stepped on James West's feet, is he?

FLH. No; he is not the man.

Q. Mr. Surrell is the man?

FLH. That's right.

Q. And he was in that room when you got there?

FLH. Yes, he was.

Q. All right. How long were you kept in that room before you were taken to the cell?

FLH. I don't know exactly, but . . .

Q. Well, give me your best judgment.

FLH. It wasn't long. You know, I didn't have no watch, keeping of the time . . .

Q. Well . . .

FLH. . . . but we wasn't kept there long.

Q. Would you say . . . What I'm trying to get at: was it about five minutes or ten minutes or what?

FLH. I'm not sure, because the whole thing, from the jailhouse on until I was put in this cell over there was about, I would say about forty minutes. So, I can't determine the time between, the time, how long I was in and how long I was . . .

Q. Well, just a short time after you got in here you were put in here, weren't you?

FLH. I was put over there.

Q. In here?

FLH. Yes.

Q. Now, was there any other act of violence in this room at the time, other than Mr. Surrell jumping on James West's feet?

FLH. Not while I was in there.

Q. I see. Who was taken in here and put in these cells?

FLH. In the cell there?

Q. Both of them.

FLH. I was put in the cell that I showed you.

Q. Right here?

FLH. That's right.

Q. Who was in there with you?

FLH. Euvester Simpson.

Q. Euvester Simpson?

FLH. Yes.

Q. Who was put in here?

FLH. Rosemary Freeman and June Johnson.

Q. June Johnson and Rosemary Freeman?

FLH. Yes, but they wasn't brought when we were put in there. They wasn't in the cell at the time.

Q. Were you all carried in first?

FLH. Yes, I was put in my cell before they was.

Q. Were you put in . . . were you the first one put in?

FLH. Yes.

Q. Then how soon after you was Euvester?

FLH. Euvester and I were put in about the same time.

Q. The same time?

FLH. Yes.

Q. Then how long after you got in there were these two brought in here?

FLH. I didn't notice the time.

Q. Well, give me your best judgment. Almost immediately?

FLH. No, it wasn't immediately.

Q. About how long?

FLH. I don't know, because I heard them screaming. I heard screaming. I just heard the screaming, and then, after then, they brought them, and I couldn't see too well to see around because, as you see this . . .You don't mind me showing you, do you?

Q. No.

FLH. You see, from right here, I could just come to the door. I couldn't see around here too good, but I could just hear these in here crying.

Q. Now, you heard some screaming?

FLH. Yes.

Q. Where did you hear the screaming coming from?

FLH. It seemed to be coming from this booking room.

Q. From this booking room.

FLH. It wasn't in the cell. I'm sure it wasn't in the cell.

Q. Now, at the time of the screaming you heard you and . . . is it Euvester Simpson?

FLH. Euvester Simpson.

Q. . . . Euvester Simpson were in here, weren't you?

FLH. Yes.

Q. Had somebody else been brought and put in here?

FLH. The time, after the time of the screaming?

Q. At the time of the screaming.

FLH. Well, they brought Rosemary Freeman first.

Q. Did you hear screaming before she was brought in?

FLH. I heard screaming after she was brought in, too.

Q. All right. Then who was brought in next, after Rosemary Freeman?

FLH. June Johnson.

Q. June Johnson was brought in next?

FLH. Yes.

Q. Then who was brought in next?

FLH. I heard screaming. I heard awful sounds, and I heard somebody praying, and said, "O God, forgive them, because they don't know what they
was doing." And then I could hear somebody saying, "Can't you say, 'Yes,
sir,' nigger? Can't you say, 'Yes, sir,' nigger?" And this person said, "Yes."
I'm just telling you the sounds I heard. Say, "Yes, I can say, 'Yes, sir.'" Say,
"Say, 'Yes, sir,' nigger." Say, "I don't know you well enough." And I could
hear screaming again . . .

Q. Now . . .

FLH. . . . and I don't know how long that lasted, but after while Miss Ponder
passed by, you see, and I could see, because I could see through there,
and she was, they was leading her some place, but her eye was swelled;
her hair was standing up on her head, and she was going, you know, up
against . . .

Q. Where were they bringing her?

FLH. I don't know.

Q. You were in here?

FLH. Yes.

Q. And you were looking through the door here?

FLH. Yes.

Q. And where was she? In this area here?

FLH. I just don't know what part she was in when I saw them pass...

Q. Well, you couldn't see . . .

FLH. . . . through the little aisle.

Q. You couldn't see through here because that door was closed, wasn't it?

FLH. That door . . .

Q. This . . .

FLH. . . . that I was in . . .

Q. No. This door right here, leading into the cell block.

FLH. The door that I, the iron door, that big, heavy door, wasn't closed. I
could see out in this little hall. I could see very clear.

Q. I see.

FLH. I saw Miss Ponder.

Q. Now, you were in this cell here?

FLH. Yes.

Q. And the only place to see out of this cell was through a barred door here,
wasn't it?

FLH. Yes.

Q. Well, where were you looking through? This way?

FLH. I was looking across, and I could see her. She passed against, she passed against the wall here. She was up against the wall, with her hands up, just going against the wall like that, when I seen her.

Q. Now, look at this diagram. This diagram here has been introduced as showing the layout of that jail, not exactly to scale, but substantially the layout, and this is the cell you were in, isn't it?

FLH. Yes.

Q. Now, that's a solid . . . is that a solid wall there?

FLH. You see, I don't know too much about diagrams . . .

Q. Well, let's . . .

FLH. . . . but I, you know . . .

Q. It shows it is here.

FLH. Yes.

Q. And the only way you can see out of that cell is through a barred door right there, isn't it?

FLH. It had bars in it . . .

Q. That's right.

FLH. . . . but it wasn't closed.

Q. That's right. Look at this.

FLH. Yes.

Q. And what you saw you saw from that cell, didn't you?

FLH. Yes, from that door.

Q. And the only way you could look out of the cell was through that barred door, wasn't it?

FLH. Yes.

Q. All right. Then you were looking through here, and where did you see Annell Ponder? Where was she standing when you saw her?

FLH. She wasn't standing. She was moving.

Q. Where was she walking?

FLH. She was going against, I could really show you if you would have this, if it would be possible that I could be at this jail to show you, and you would see what I was talking about.

Q. All right.

FLH. But I saw Annell Ponder against the wall, with her clothes torn, and she was leaning back like this.

Q. Was she in the booking room?

FLH. I'm not sure.

Q. Was she in this corridor, this area here?

FLH. I'm not sure. It could have been that place, but I know I seen her.

Q. You couldn't see from your cell into the booking room, could you?

FLH. I saw Annell Ponder.

Q. All right. Look here and tell me whereabouts she was standing.

FLH. She wasn't standing.

Q. All right. Where was she moving? Point out where she was when you saw her.

FLH. I don't know whether she was in the little space there or not, but I did see Annell Ponder.

Q. Now, as a matter of fact, from in this cell, you can't see in that booking room at all, can you?

FLH. In the booking room?

Q. That's right.

FLH. Oh.

Q. From this cell.

FLH. I don't know how the diagram is. I could see very clear. I could see. I could see. You know, I could see this whisky distillery. I looked when they was making a picture out in that room. I did see. I could see.

Q. While you were in this cell?

FLH. That's right.

Q. You could see in the booking room?

FLH. I could peep out.

Q. Peep out through here?

FLH. Yeah, with the door open. Now, with the door closed I couldn't do it.

Q. All right. You could peep out here?

FLH. Yes.

Q. And you could look through this solid wall?

FLH. No. It wasn't a solid wall.

Q. Well, were you looking around this way?

FLH. I don't know how that is drawn, that is, you know, look like I might couldn't see; but I'm sure. I know I saw it.

Q. This is the government's drawing . . .

FLH. Yes.

Q. . . . drawn from the floor plan.

FLH. Yeah.

Q. And, as a matter of fact, you're going to tell this jury that while you were in this cell, right here, you could see in this booking room?

FLH. Yes.

Q. There was a still against this wall, wasn't there? Wasn't it? You remember that still that was in there?

FLH. I told you I saw the thing. I didn't know what it was.

Q. Could you see it from your cell?

FLH. Yes. It was very obvious. Across this cell place it was . . .

Q. All right.

FLH. . . . this big, old drum thing.

Q. Could you see the table or the desk thing they write on from your cell?

FLH. No. I wasn't, you know, I didn't even see it.

Q. All right. But you saw Annell Ponder while she was in this booking room?

FLH. Yes.

Q. Now, when they took her out of the booking room, where did they put her?

FLH. They put her across from me. It might have not been this place. It might not have been . . .

Q. Was it here?

FLH. Yes. It looked like a place like that.

Q. All right. And could you see from your cell . . .

FLH. I could.

Q. . . . this place?

FLH. I never did see Annell, but I could see this big, huge door she was shut up in.

Q. And could you see from your cell to this door here?

FLH. Yes.

Q. And, while you were in that cell, you could see Annell Ponder while she was in the booking room?

FLH. I saw her pass. I didn't say she was standing. I saw her pass the cell that I was in. She was on the outside of the cell, but she passed. And one other thing I would like to say: this is the man right there that sentenced me. I had looked for him. I thought he was on the other seats, but I couldn't see him.

Q. Where is he?

FLH. Right there.

Q. Which one?

FLH. This one right here with the blue suit on.

Q. That is the man . . .

FLH. Yes.

Q. . . . that sentenced you?

FLH. That's right.

Q. That's the judge that sentenced you?

FLH. That's the man told me I was charged with disorderly conduct and resisting arrest.

Q. Is that the man that pronounced sentence on you?

FLH. That's him.

Q. Is that the judge that tried you? That's the man [Rupert Ringold] who sat as judge that put the sentence on you?

FLH. Just like the man, it was; just like him.

Q. Now, I believe you say that you were taken back in a cell somewhere and two colored prisoners whipped you; is that right?

FLH. That's right.

Q. Can you show where you . . .

FLH. I don't know. I know where that cell was. I was carried to a cell, and that's what I know.

Q. Were you taken out of your . . .

FLH. Yes; I was taken out of my cell.

Q. And brought out back into the booking room?

FLH. I was carried to a cell.

Q. And you were carried to a cell?

FLH. Yes.

Q. And while you were in that cell two colored prisoners whipped you?

FLH. Yes.

Q. Now, who was in there when that happened?

FLH. The man there with the red tie on . . .

Q. That's Mr. Perkins.

FLH. . . . Mr. Earle Wayne Patridge, but he didn't stay, but Mr. . . . what you say his name is?

Q. Mr. Surrell.

FLH. Mr. Surrell, Mr. John Basinger and the man with the red shirt on is the one that was in the room.

Q. While you were being whipped?

FLH. Yes.

Q. Now, you say Mr. Patridge came in there, but he left?

FLH. Yes. He just walked in, but he walked, he didn't stay in that room. He was not in there.

Q. He was not in at the time . . .

FLH. No, he was not.

Q. . . . you were actually being whipped?

FLH. He was not.

Q. He didn't see you?

FLH. No, he didn't.

Q. Now, I believe you said you got out of jail Wednesday; is that right?

FLH. I did.

Q. And when you left the jail you went to Greenwood?

FLH. Yes.

Q. And you were examined there by Dr. who?

FLH. Garner.

Q. Beg pardon.

FLH. Garner.

Q. G-a-r-n-e-r?

FLH. That's right.

Q. Is that a woman doctor?

FLH. That's a woman doctor.

Q. Colored woman doctor?

FLH. Yes.

Q. Dr. Garner?

FLH. That's right.

Q. Then from Greenwood where did you go?

FLH. I went to Birmingham, Alabama, and I flew from Birmingham, Alabama, to Atlanta, Georgia.

Q. You and Annell Ponder go together?

FLH. Yes.

Q. You went to Birmingham and then to Atlanta?

FLH. Yes.

Q. And that's where Annell lives, I believe?

FLH. Yes. That's her home, where she was born, and . . .

Q. And you got to Atlanta when? That night?

FLH. In Atlanta. She doesn't live in Atlanta. She lives in Mississippi, but we went to Atlanta; but we weren't going to Annell's home.

Q. Where does Annell live?

FLH. Her home, where she originally from, Atlanta, Georgia; but she lives in Mississippi now.

Q. Where does she live?

FLH. Greenwood.

Q. You tell the jury that Annell Ponder is now a resident of Mississippi?

FLH. Yes.

Q. And lives in Greenwood?

FLH. Yes.

Q. I see. Where did you go when you got to Atlanta?

FLH. We went to, the first night, when we got to Atlanta, we went to Mrs. Ponder's home. It's Annell Ponder's mother.

Q. I see.

FLH. And spent the night.

Q. Now, that was Wednesday night?

FLH. Yes, it was. It was almost day, Thursday.

Q. Then Friday did you go, you flew to Washington?

FLH. Yes.

Q. Get your plane out of Atlanta?

FLH. Yes.

Q. Do you mind telling us who paid your fare to go to Washington?

FLH. The fare was paid.

Q. By who?

FLH. By SCLC.

Q. By SCLC. That's the Southern Christian, what's the rest of it? What's the official name?

FLH. Southern Christian Leadership Conference.

Q. The Southern Christian Leadership Conference. And that's headed by Dr. Martin Luther King, isn't it?

FLH. Yes.

Q. Did you and Annell discuss this matter with Dr. King or any other representatives of the SCLC before you went to Washington?

FLH. Yes. We talked with Dr. King. We talked with . . .

Q. In other words, you reported to Dr. King in Atlanta about what happened; is that right?

FLH. We talked, maybe talked with the press conference in Atlanta.

Q. You gave them, you had a press conference; is that right?

FLH. Yes.

Q. Then you talked with Dr. King; is that right?

FLH. Yes.

Q. Then did he make an appointment for you with Mr. Barrett of the Justice Department in Washington?

FLH. No. I was begging somebody. I don't know. He might have, but I told them I wanted to go to Washington to show in person what had happened to us, because . . .

Q. And, so, the Southern Christian Leadership Conference paid your way for you and Annell Ponder to fly to Washington, and you went straight to the Justice Department when you got there, didn't you?

FLH. No, I didn't go straight to the Justice Department. I went to a hotel.

Q. Well, then you did go to the Justice Department?

FLH. Yes.

Q. And conferred with Mr. St. John Barrett, the gentleman who is sitting there, didn't you?

FLH. Yes.

Q. If the court please, we have no further questions of this witness.

Redirect

Q. Mrs. Hamer, counsel has asked you about the trial in the city hall of Winona, and you have testified that Mr. Ringold, one of the attorneys for the defendants here, was at the trial. Were there other men at the trial?

FLH. I remember very clearly it was one, I don't know, a big, huge straw hat rolled up around; but I don't know . . .

Q. About how many men were there?

FLH. I . . .

Q. About how many, would you say?

FLH. I don't know, because I didn't count them.

Q. Well, do you know the official positions of each of the men who were there at the trial?

FLH. No; I didn't.

Q. Now, counsel has also asked you about coming up to Washington and who you saw at the Department of Justice. Did you see Mr. Robert Owen, an attorney in the department up there . . .

FLH. Yes.

Q. . . . for a few minutes?

FLH. A few minutes.

Q. And then he referred you to me?

FLH. Yes.

Q. Is that right?

FLH. Yes.

Q. Had you had any prior contact with me at all?

FLH. No.

Q. Did you have any reason to think that I was expecting you?

FLH. I wasn't sure.

Q. I have no further questions.

Testimony Before a Select Panel on Mississippi and Civil Rights, Washington, D.C., June 8, 1964

Fannie Lou Hamer's testimony was an integral part of a hearing that the Council of Federated Organizations (COFO) orchestrated to expose the volatile climate into which the Mississippi-bound Freedom Summer volunteers would soon enter. The hearing took place at the National Theatre on June 8, 1964. It featured twenty-four speakers who testified before a board of distinguished panelists, including former president of Sarah Lawrence College Harold Taylor, the president of the American Sociological Society, Gresham Sykes, Harvard research psychiatrist Robert Coles, novelist Joseph Heller, journalist Murray Kempton, and Justice Justine Wise Polier. U.S. Representative William Fitts Ryan, who was among the hearing participants, moved to have the proceedings read into the Congressional Record on June 16—a motion that received unanimous consent. In addition to the exposure Ryan's motion engendered, the panelists also compiled information gathered from the hearing into a report entitled "Summary of Major Points in Testimony by Citizens of Mississippi." This report formed the basis of their recommendation that federal authorities provide protection for COFO's Freedom Summer voter registration and education project.

The proceedings capture Hamer's first attempt to share her riveting personal account of terror and injustice in Mississippi with a national audience. In offering testimony about her own experiences, Hamer also represents larger social problems like police brutality, segregationist retaliation, and the invasion of privacy that kept African Americans in the Delta from challenging the blatant imbalance of power. Of the several privacy invasions Hamer recounts throughout the testimony, her discussion of forced sterilization during the question and answer period is perhaps the most notable—this was an issue that personally affected her, but about which she rarely spoke. Even here, Hamer does not specifically mention that after she sought medical attention for a uterine tumor in 1961,

the doctor performed a hysterectomy without her consent. She does, however,
provide an arsenal of injustices that brightly underscore the need for federal
intervention into Mississippi politics.

* * *

MR. FREEDMAN: Mrs. Hamer, what is it that brings you before the panel
today?

MRS. HAMER: To tell about some of the brutality in the state of Mississippi. I
will begin from the first beginning—August thirty-first in 1962. I traveled
twenty-six miles to the county courthouse to try to register to become a
first-class citizen. I was fired the thirty-first of August in 1962, from a plantation where I had worked as a timekeeper and a sharecropper for eighteen
years. My husband had worked there for thirty years.

I was met by my children when I returned from the courthouse, and my
girl and my husband's cousin told me that this man my husband worked
for was raising a lot of Cain. I went on in the house and it wasn't too long
before my husband came and said this plantation owner said I would have
to leave if I didn't go down and withdraw.

About that time, the man walked up, Mr. Marlow, and said, "Is Fannie
Lou back yet?"

My husband said, "She is." I walked out of the house at this time.

He said, "Fannie Lou, you have been to the courthouse to try and register," and he said, "We are not ready for this in Mississippi."

I said, "I didn't register for you. I tried to register for myself."

He said, "We are not going to have this in Mississippi, and you will have
to withdraw. I am looking for your answer, yea or nay." I just looked. He
said, "I will give you until tomorrow morning and if you don't withdraw,
you will have to leave. If you do go withdraw, it's only how I feel. You might
still have to leave." So I left that same night.

On the tenth of September, they fired into the home of Mr. and Mrs.
Robert Tucker sixteen times for me. That same night, two girls were shot at
Mr. Herman Sisson's. Also they shot Mr. Joe McDonald's house. I was fired
that same day and haven't had a job since.

In 1963, I attended a voter registration workshop and was returning
back to Mississippi. At Winona, Mississippi—I was arrested there—some
of the folk had got off the bus. Miss Annell Ponder, June West Johnson,
Euvester Simpson, Rosemary Freeman, and James West got off the bus to

go into the restaurant to get food. Two of the people decided to use the restroom. I saw them come right straight out of the restaurant. I got off the bus to see what had happened.

Miss Ponder said, "They won't let us eat." She said, "There was a chief of police and a highway patrolman inside, and they ordered us out."

I said, "Well, this is Mississippi." I got back on the bus, and about the time I just got sat down good, I looked out the window and they were getting Miss Ponder and the others into the highway patrolman's car.

I stepped off the bus to see what was happening, and one screamed, "Get that one there." I was picked up by the police, Earl Wayne Patridge, told me I was under arrest. He opened the door, and as I started to get in, he kicked me. They carried me to town to this county jail.

We were carried to the booking room. Soon as we walked inside, I was in the car with Earle Wayne Patridge, and one plainclothesman—I don't know if he was a policeman or not. He didn't have on police clothes, had a crew haircut. They would ask me questions going on to jail, and as I would go on to answer, they would curse me and tell me to hush.

I was carried on to the booking room and carried from the booking room to a cell. After I was locked up in a cell with Miss Euvester Simpson, I began to hear the sounds of licks and I could hear people screaming. I don't know how long it lasted before I saw Miss Ponder, the Southside supervisor for the SCLC, pass the cell with both her hands up. Her eyes looked like blood and her mouth was swollen. She passed my cell. Her clothes was torn. She backed and they carried her again out of my sight.

After then, the state highway patrolman—because it was on the insignia on his arm and another silver plate across his pocket—walked into my cell with two other white men. He asked me where I was from and I told him. He said, "I am going to check." They left my cell and it wasn't too long before they returned, and he said "You damn right, you from Ruleville," and he called me a bad name. He said they would make me wish I was dead.

I was carried out of the cell into another cell where there were two Negro prisoners. The state highway patrolman gave the first Negro a long blackjack that was heavy. It was loaded with something, and they had me lay down on the bunk facedown, and I was beat. I was beat by the first Negro until he was exhausted. After I was beat by the first Negro, the state highway patrolman ordered the other Negro to take the blackjack. The second Negro, he began to beat. The state highway patrolman ordered the first Negro that had beat me to sit on my feet. One of the white men that was in the room—my dress would work up because it had a large skirt, but I was trying to keep it down and trying to shield the licks from the left side because I had polio when I was a child. During the time that I was trying to work my dress down and keep the licks off my left side, one of the white men walked over and pulled my dress up. At this time I had to hug around the mattress to keep the sound from coming out.

MR. FREEDMAN: Mrs. Hamer, you referred to the woman from the SCLC. Is that a religious organization, as I understand it?

MRS. HAMER: Yes, Southern Christian Leadership Conference.

MR. FREEDMAN: Is there anything that you would like to add to your statement before you are questioned?

MRS. HAMER: We have a curfew in our town, Ruleville. Also, the night police there is a brother to J. W. Milam, that lynched Emmett Till in Sunflower County—the boy that was fourteen years old and put in Tallahatchie River. We have a curfew only for Negroes. It was a little before Christmas, my husband got up at five o'clock to go to the washroom. As he walked out, we heard a knock at the door, and he opened the door. He said, "Come in." Two policemen walked in, Mr. Milam and Mr. Dave Fleming, and asked him what was he doing up at this time of night.

Not only have I been harassed by the police, I had a call from the telephone operator after I qualified to run as congresswoman. She told me, "Fannie Lou, honey, you are having a lot of different callers on your telephone. I want to know, do you have any outsiders in your house? You called somebody today in Texas. Who was you calling, and where are you going? You had a mighty big bill."

I said, "The bill was paid."

"Well, I wouldn't let no outsiders come into my house."

I said, "What do you mean outsiders?"

"Well, we are going to check on this, and we just don't want no people from outside your house coming in and making outside calls."

I would like to add right now, the people I was with in Boston had to call the doctor to get some relief for my back that I still suffer with.

CHAIRMAN TAYLOR: Mrs. Hamer, may I ask, what was the charge on which you were arrested on the bus incident?

MRS. HAMER: Well, during the time I asked the jailer, "Would you leave the door open so I could catch air."

During the time the door was open, I heard discussion: "Now what is we going to charge them with?" Somebody said something. He said, "Well, you are going to have to get up something better than that. Man, that is the end of the wire."

So, I actually didn't know what we were charged with until they got ready to have our trial, and we were charged with resisting arrest and disorderly conduct.

DR. SYKES: We are all concerned about what might possibly happen in Mississippi this summer. Can you tell us about some things that have happened, what is going on now? But what do you think might happen with people going to Mississippi this summer?

MRS. HAMER: Well, I can say there will be a hot summer in Mississippi and I don't mean the weather, because people are really getting prepared. They have been riding with the guns. But Ruleville is a very small town; there are about two thousand people in there. I see now they have a tank and they are keeping the dog riding on the back of the truck so if the truck stops, the dog won't have anything to do but jump off. And the mayor, he would ride around and tell folk don't let the outside people come into their homes, because after they stay awhile, they would just beat them up. But they say, "Don't say nothing to old Fannie Lou Hamer about it." I am not even going on that street.

My husband was fired the day after I qualified to run as a congresswoman in the Second Congressional District. Last week he had gotten a second job. The mayor went out on this job on which he was working, so he will probably be fired by the time I get back home.

DR. COLES: First of all, this curfew, is this legally done, or is this done—how is this known that there is a curfew?

MRS. HAMER: As long as there is a white man says that a Negro violated, it is legal with them.

DR. COLES: There is no public statement?

MRS. HAMER: No, you just get arrested, a Negro, if you are out after twelve o'clock.

DR. COLES: Is it a local ordinance? That is what we want to know. Is there a local law that says that if you are on the streets after twelve o'clock you are violating the law?

MRS. HAMER: It must be, because I know you do get arrested.

DR. COLES: Has anyone challenged this?

MRS. HAMER: No.

DR. COLES: The other thing that I would like to find out is, who do you pay your telephone bills to? Is this the Southern Bell Telephone Company?

MRS. HAMER: That is right.

DR. COLES: Now, this is the town telephone operator, is it?

MRS. HAMER: The long distance operator—they operate out of Cleveland, Mississippi, because I asked her for her name. She told me her name, and she said that it was just too much. And also, they take the telephone wire loose from the telephone post and got it right in front of the house and clipped on the main line.

DR. COLES: All I can say is I lived in a town in Georgia, and no telephone operator ever talked to me like this.

MRS. HAMER: Well, it was the first time for me, but it did happen. One of the other things that happened in Sunflower County, the North Sunflower County Hospital, I would say about six out of the ten Negro women that go to the hospital are sterilized with the tubes tied. They are getting up a law that said if a woman has an illegitimate baby and then a second one, they could draw time for six months or a five-hundred-dollar fine. What they didn't tell is that they are already doing these things, not only to single women, but to married women.

CHAIRMAN TAYLOR: Thank you very much.

Testimony Before the Credentials Committee at the Democratic National Convention, Atlantic City, New Jersey, August 22, 1964

When the Mississippi Freedom Democratic Party (MFDP) was founded in April 1964, the event barely registered across the state, let alone in Washington, D. C. And yet in four short months, the MFDP changed the history of the Democratic Party.

The MFDP's plan was as audacious as it was savvy: black Mississippians would attempt to participate in the state's selection of Democratic Party delegates to the national convention—knowing that they would be denied that opportunity by the white power structure. With their exclusion complete—and well documented—they would then enact their own parallel delegate selection process, from the precinct level up to the state convention held on August 5, in Jackson. With thirty-four delegates selected, and with thirty-four alternates, the MFDP delegation arrived in Atlantic City on August 21.

The next part of the plan would prove to be most dramatic: the MFDP needed to convince 11 members of the 108-member Credentials Committee to issue a minority report that would go to the convention floor supporting the party's request to be seated instead of the elected white delegation. Once on the floor, if eight states requested a roll call vote, then each state's delegation would be forced to go on the record and reveal its loyalties. Going into the convention, MFDP legal counsel Joseph Rauh thought they had the votes. He was probably even more sanguine about the outcome by Saturday evening, August 22.

As part of its strategy, the MFDP had selected several of its best speakers to make the case on live television before the Democratic Party's Credentials Committee. Even the nation's most eloquent voice for civil rights, Dr. Martin Luther King, Jr., was overshadowed on this day by Ruleville's first lady. President Johnson hastily called a press conference to take the cameras off of the mesmerizing sharecropper as she addressed the committee. But his interruption actually backfired: the television networks caught on to his diversionary tactic and aired Hamer's speech later that evening during their primetime newscasts.

In this short address delivered before millions, Hamer briefly narrates the three events that were an intimate part of her rhetorical repertoire: her first attempt to register to vote; her employer's angry reaction and the violence engendered by stepping out of her "place"; and her brutal beating in a Winona, Mississippi, jail. Delivered with righteous indignation and in an unlettered vernacular, Hamer's testimony stunned an incredulous country.

Despite her riveting testimony and the best efforts of the MFDP, they could not offset the power politics unleashed by Lyndon Johnson. Ultimately, the MFDP delegation rejected the administration's best offer: two at-large seats for Aaron Henry and Edwin King. Hamer summarized the group's decision thus: "We didn't come all this way for no two seats."

*   *   *

Mr. Chairman, and to the Credentials Committee, my name is Mrs. Fannie Lou Hamer, and I live at 626 East Lafayette Street, Ruleville, Mississippi, Sunflower County, the home of Senator James O. Eastland and Senator Stennis.

It was the thirty-first of August in 1962, that eighteen of us traveled twenty-six miles to the county courthouse in Indianola to try to register to become first-class citizens. We was met in Indianola by policemen, highway patrolmen, and they only allowed two of us in to take the literacy test at the time. After we had taken this test and started back to Ruleville, we was held up by the city police and the state highway patrolmen and carried back to Indianola where the bus driver was charged that day with driving a bus the wrong color.

After we paid the fine among us, we continued on to Ruleville, and Reverend Jeff Sunny carried me four miles in the rural area where I had worked as a timekeeper and sharecropper for eighteen years. I was met there by my children, who told me that the plantation owner was angry because I had gone down, tried to register. After they told me, my husband came, and said the plantation owner was raising Cain because I had tried to register. And before he quit talking the plantation owner came and said, "Fannie Lou, do you know—did Pap tell you what I said?"

And I said, "Yes, sir."

He said, "Well, I mean that." Said, "If you don't go down and withdraw your registration, you will have to leave." Said, "Then if you go down and withdraw, then you still might have to go because we are not ready for that in Mississippi."

And I addressed him and told him and said, "I didn't try to register for you. I tried to register for myself." I had to leave that same night.

On the tenth of September 1962, sixteen bullets was fired into the home of Mr. and Mrs. Robert Tucker for me. That same night two girls was shot in Ruleville, Mississippi. Also, Mr. Joe McDonald's house was shot in.

And June the ninth, 1963, I had attended a voter registration workshop— was returning back to Mississippi. Ten of us was traveling by the Continental Trailways bus. When we got to Winona, Mississippi, which is in Montgomery County, four of the people got off to use the washroom, and two of the people—to use the restaurant—two of the people wanted to use the washroom. The four people that had gone in to use the restaurant was ordered out. During this time I was on the bus. But when I looked through the window and saw they had rushed out, I got off of the bus to see what had happened. And one of the ladies said, "It was a state highway patrolman and a chief of police ordered us out."

I got back on the bus and one of the persons had used the washroom got back on the bus, too. As soon as I was seated on the bus, I saw when they began to get the five people in a highway patrolman's car. I stepped off of the bus to see what was happening and somebody screamed from the car that the five workers was in and said, "Get that one there." And when I went to get in the car, when the man told me I was under arrest, he kicked me.

I was carried to the county jail and put in the booking room. They left some of the people in the booking room and began to place us in cells. I was placed in a cell with a young woman called Miss Euvester Simpson. After I was placed in the cell, I began to hear sounds of licks and screams. I could hear the sounds of licks and horrible screams. And I could hear somebody say, "Can you say, 'yes, sir,' nigger? Can you say 'yes, sir'?" And they would say other horrible names.

She would say, "Yes, I can say 'yes, sir.'"

"So, well, say it."

She said, "I don't know you well enough." They beat her, I don't know how long. And after a while she began to pray, and asked God to have mercy on those people.

And it wasn't too long before three white men came to my cell. One of these men was a state highway patrolman and he asked me where I was from. And I told him Ruleville and he said, "We are going to check this." And they left my cell and it wasn't too long before they came back. He said, "You's from

Ruleville all right," and he used a curse word. And he said, "We are going to make you wish you was dead."

I was carried out of that cell into another cell where they had two Negro prisoners. The state highway patrolmen ordered the first Negro to take the blackjack. The first Negro prisoner ordered me, by orders from the state highway patrolman, for me to lay down on a bunk bed on my face.

And I laid on my face and the first Negro began to beat. And I was beat by the first Negro until he was exhausted. I was holding my hands behind me at that time on my left side, because I suffered from polio when I was six years old. After the first Negro had beat until he was exhausted, the state highway patrolman ordered the second Negro to take the blackjack. The second Negro began to beat and I began to work my feet, and the state highway patrolman ordered the first Negro had beat me to sit on my feet—to keep me from working my feet. I began to scream and one white man got up and began to beat me in my head and tell me to hush. One white man—my dress had worked up high—he walked over and pulled my dress, I pulled my dress down and he pulled my dress back up.

I was in jail when Medgar Evers was murdered.

All of this is on account of we want to register, to become first-class citizens. And if the Freedom Democratic Party is not seated now, I question America. Is this America, the land of the free and the home of the brave, where we have to sleep with our telephones off of the hooks because our lives be threatened daily, because we want to live as decent human beings, in America? Thank you.

"We're On Our Way,"

Speech Delivered at a Mass Meeting in Indianola, Mississippi, September 1964

So many black Deltans wanted to see the woman from their community whose testimony was broadcast before the nation that soon after Mrs. Hamer returned from Atlantic City, she was finally able to speak at a mass meeting in Indianola, Mississippi. Although speaking in a small church twenty-six miles outside of Ruleville might not seem like a telling measure of Hamer's growing popularity, the fact that her campaign manager, Charles McLaurin, had been trying for the past two years—without success—to secure a speaking venue in Indianola demonstrates that Hamer's national notoriety had begun to exert an influence on local politics.

The setting for this forty-five-minute speech was a mass meeting held in early September 1964. Mass meetings, like the one Hamer attended at Williams Baptist Church on the eve of her political awakening, were a vital part of the black freedom movement's grassroots contingent; in many ways, they cultivated the ground out of which the larger movement for social change grew. Featuring freedom songs, religious sermons, and secular speeches, the format of these meetings emulated that of a church service, and the content extended biblical lessons familiar to the meeting's attendees. Despite the growing threat of church bombings and fires, the setting was still relatively comfortable for most southern blacks to whom the space represented community and permitted privacy from those whites who sought to control most other aspects of their existence.

Put simply, Hamer's rhetorical purpose at this particular mass meeting was to encourage black Mississippians to register and vote. As her own experiences with voter registration attested, however, if you were black in Mississippi, there was nothing simple about voting. Convincing her audience to undertake such a risky endeavor, therefore, required Hamer to adopt two interrelated personae in her Indianola address—that of a preacher and of a fellow community member. Throughout the speech, Hamer balanced these two relationships with her audience in a manner that simultaneously instructed them on how to act and empowered them to see their own potential for activism. She used her bond with the audience, grounded in their similar life experiences, as a bridge to meet them where they were and move them forward along the path to civic engagement. She acknowledged their fears and inhibitions, but did not become mired in commiseration; instead, Hamer challenged her audience to overcome their fears and realize their political potential.

* * *

Thank you very much. Good evening, ladies and gentlemen. I am very glad to be here for the first time in Indianola, Mississippi, to speak in a mass meeting. And you just don't have a idea what a pleasure this is to me. Because we been working across—for the past two years—and Mr. Charles McLaurin worked very hard trying to get a place here during the time that I was campaigning and he failed to get a place. But it's good to see people waking up to the fact—something that you should've been awaken years ago.

First, I would like to tell you about myself. As McLaurin say, my name is Mrs. Fannie Lou Hamer and I live at 626 East Lafayette Street in Ruleville, Mississippi. It was in 1962, the thirty-first of August that eighteen of us traveled twenty-six miles to this place, to the county courthouse, to try to register to become first-class citizens. When we got here to Indianola, to the courthouse, that was the day I saw more policemens with guns than I'd ever seen in my life at one time. They was standing around and I never will forget that day. One of the men called the police department in Cleveland, Mississippi, and told him to bring some type of big book back over there. But, anyway, we stayed in the registrar's office—I'm not sure how long because it wasn't but two allowed in the room at the same time. After we got out from the registrar's office, I was one of the first persons to complete, as far as I knew how to complete, on my registration form. And I went and got back on the bus.

During the time that we was on the bus, the policemens kept watching the car—the bus—and I noticed a highway patrolman watching the bus. After everybody had completed their forms, and after we started back to Ruleville, Mississippi, we were stopped by the highway patrolman and the policeman, and was ordered back to come to Indianola, Mississippi. When we got back to Indianola, the bus driver was charged with driving a bus the wrong color! This is the gospel truth, but this bus had been used for years for cotton chopping, cotton picking, and to carry people to Florida, to work to make enough to live on in the wintertime to get back here to the cotton fields the next spring and summer. But that day the bus had the wrong color.

After we got to Ruleville, about five o'clock, Reverend Jeff Sunny drove me out into the rural area where I had been working as a timekeeper and a share-cropper for eighteen years. When I got there I was already fired. My children met me and told me, said, "Momma," said, "this man is hot!" Said, "He said you will have to go back and withdraw, or you will have to leave."

During the time he was talking, it wasn't too long before my husband came and he said the same thing. I walked in the house, set down on the side of my little daughter's bed and then this white man walked over and said, "Pap, did you tell Fannie Lou what I said?"

He said, "Yes, sir," and I walked out.

And he said, "Fannie Lou, did Pap tell you what I said?"

I said, "He did."

He said, "Well, Fannie Lou," said, "you will have to go down and withdraw or you will have to leave."

And I addressed and told him, as we have always had to say, "Mister," I say, "I didn't register for you," I say, "I was trying to register for myself."

He said, "We're not ready for that in Mississippi." He wasn't ready, but I been ready a *long* time. I had to leave that same night.

On the tenth of September in 1962, sixteen bullets was fired into the home of Mr. and Mrs. Robert Tucker for me. That same night, two girls was shot at Mr. Herman Sisson's in Ruleville. They also shot in Mr. Joe McDonald's house that same night. Now, the question I raise: is this America, the land of the free and the home of the brave? Where people are being murdered, lynched, and killed, because we want to register and vote?

When my family and I decided to move back in Sunflower County in De-cember, the car that we had been paying on for the last three years, it was taken. We didn't have many things and part of them had been stolen. But just to show you that God want people to stand up—so, we began at this address, 626 East Lafayette Street.

Last February, my husband was arrested because I said, "I don't believe that I've used nine thousand gallons of water." And don't have a bathtub or run-ning water in the house. Can't you see justice in disguise? Can't you see justice in disguise? One morning about five o'clock, my husband got up to use the washroom. There was a knock on our door; he said, "Come in."

That was two policemens. "What are you doing up at this time of night?" Five o'clock in the morning. Can you see how justice is working in Mississippi?

You see the point is about this, and you can't deny it, not either one of you here in this room—not Negroes—we have prayed for a change in the state of Mississippi for years. And God made it so plain He sent Moses down in Egypt-land to tell Pharaoh to let my people go. And He made it so plain here in Mississippi the man that heads the project is named Moses, Bob Moses. And He sent Bob Moses down in Mississippi, to tell all of these hate groups to let his people go.

You see, in this struggle, some people say that, "Well, she doesn't talk too good." The type of education that we get here, years to come you won't talk too good. The type of education that we get in the state of Mississippi will make our minds so narrow it won't coordinate with our big bodies.

This is one of the next things that I don't like: every church door in the state of Mississippi should be open for these meetings; but preachers have preached for years what he didn't believe himself. And if he's willing to trust God, if he's willing to trust God, he won't mind opening the church door. Because the first words of Jesus's public ministry was: "The spirit of the Lord is upon me because he has anointed me to preach the gospel to the poor. He has sent me to proclaim and bring relief to the captive." And you know we are living in a captivated society today. And we know the things we doing is right. The thirty-seventh of Psalms said, "Fret not thouselves because of evildoers, neither be thy envious against the workers of iniquity for they shall be cut down like the green grass and wither away as the green herb. Delight thouselves in the Lord and verily thou shalt be filled." And we are determined to be filled in Mississippi today.

Some of the white people will tell us, "Well, I just don't believe in integration." But he been integrating at night a long time! If he hadn't been, it wouldn't be as many light-skinned Negroes as it is in here. The seventeenth chapter of Acts and the twenty-sixth verse said: "Has made of one blood all nations." So whether you black as a skillet or white as a sheet, we are made from the same blood and we are on our way!

We know, we know we have a long fight because the leaders like the preachers and the teachers, they are failing to stand up today. But we know some of the reasons for that. This brainwashed education that the teachers have got, he know that if he had to get a job as a janitor in this missile base that they are be building he'd probably turn something over and blow up the place because he wouldn't know what it was.

Righteousness exalts a nation, but sin is a reproach to any people. Sin is beginning to reproach America today and we want what is rightfully ours. And it's no need of running and no need of saying, "Honey, I'm not going to get in the mess," because if you were born in America with a black face, you were born in the mess.

Do you think, do you think anybody that would stand out in the dark to shoot me and to shoot other people, would you call that a brave person? It's a shame before God that people will let hate not only destroy us, but it will destroy them. Because a house divided against itself cannot stand and today America is divided against itself because they don't want us to have even the ballot here in Mississippi. If we had been treated right all these years, they wouldn't be afraid for us to get the ballot.

People will go different places and say, "The Negroes, until the outside agitators came in, was satisfied." But I've been dissatisfied ever since I was six years old. I remember my mother has worked for one measly dollar and a quarter a day. And you couldn't say that was satisfaction. But to be truthful to you tonight, I first wished I was white. Some of you've wished the same thing. The reason I wished that was they was the only people that wasn't doing nothing, but still had money and clothes. We was working year in and year out and wouldn't get to go to school but four months out of the year because two of the months we didn't have nothing.

Now you can't tell me you trust God and come out to a church every Sunday with a bunch of stupid hats on seeing what the other one have on and paying the preacher's way to hell and yours too. Preachers is really shocking to find them out. You know they like to rear back in the corners and over the rostrum and said, "What God has done for Meshach, Shadrach, and Abednego." But what he didn't know, God has done the same thing for Fannie Lou Hamer, Annell Ponder, and Lawrence Guyot.

And I can tell you now how this happened. After I had been working for eight or ten months, I attended a voter educational workshop in Charleston, South Carolina. On the ninth of June in 1963, we was returning from the workshop. We arrived in Winona, Mississippi, about eleven o'clock. Four of the people got off of the bus to use the restaurant; two of the people got off of the bus to use the washroom. At this time, I was still on the bus. And I saw the four people rush out and I got off of the bus. And I said, "What's wrong?"

And Miss Ponder, Southwide supervisor for the Southern Christian Leadership Conference said, "It was the chief of police and a state highway patrolman ordered us to come out."

And I said, "This is Mississippi for you."

She said, "Well, I think I'll get the tag number and we can file it in our report." And I got back in the bus. One of the girls that had used the washroom got back on the bus and that left five on our outside. When I looked through the window, they was getting those people in the car. And I stepped off of the bus again. And somebody screamed from that car and said, "Get that one there," and a man said, "You are under arrest." When he opened the door, and as I started to get in, he kicked me and I was carried to the county jail.

When I got to the county jail, with the two white fellows that drove me to jail, they was calling me all kinds of names. And they was asking me questions and as I would try to answer they would cut me off. And as we got to the county jail there, when we walked into the booking room, one of the policemans walked over to one of the young men and jumped up with all of his weight on one of the Negro's feet. And then they began to place us in cells. I was placed in a cell with Miss Euvester Simpson from Itta Bena, Mississippi. And during that time they left some in the booking room. And I began to hear screams. And I began to hear howls. And I began to hear somebody say, "Can't you say 'yes, sir,' nigger?"

And I could hear Miss Ponder's voice said, "Yes, I can say 'yes, sir.'"

"So, well, say it." She said, "I don't know you well enough."

And I would hear when she would hit the floor again. And during the time they was beating Miss Ponder, I heard her when she began to pray. And she asked God to have mercy on those people because they didn't know what they was doing. I don't know how long this lasted. But after a while, Miss Ponder passed my cell. She didn't recognize me when she passed my cell. One of her eyes looked like blood, and her mouth was swollen, and she was holding up by propping against the back of the brick cell.

And then three men came to my cell: a state highway patrolman, and a police, and a plain-dressed man. The state highway patrolman said, "Where you from?"

I said, "Ruleville, Mississippi."

He said, "I'm going to check that out." And it wasn't too long before he was back. And he used a curse word and he said, "You are from Ruleville, all right." He said, "We is going to make you wish you was dead."

I was led out of that cell and to another cell where they had two Negro prisoners. Three white men in that room and two Negroes. The state highway patrolman ordered the first Negro to take the blackjack; it was a long leather blackjack and it was loaded with something heavy. And they ordered me to lay down on my face on a bunk bed. And the first Negro beat me. He had to beat me until the state highway patrolman give him orders to quit. Because he had already told him, said, "If you don't beat her," said, "you know what I'll do to you." And he beat me I don't know how long. And after a while, he was exhausted and I was too. And it was a horrible experience.

And the state highway patrolman told the second Negro to take the black-jack. And I asked at this time, I said, "How can you treat a human being like this?"

The second prisoner said: "Move your hand, lady. I don't want to hit you in your hand." But I was holding my hand behind on the left side to shield some of the licks, because I suffered from polio when I was six years old and this kind of beating, I know I couldn't take it. So I held my hands behind me, and after the second Negro began to beat me, the state highway patrolman ordered the first Negro that had beat me to set on my feet to keep me from working my feet. And I was screaming, and I couldn't help but scream, and one of the white men began to beat me in my head and told me to "stop screaming." And the only way that I could stop screaming was to take my hand and hug it around the tip to muffle out the sound. My dress worked up from this hard blackjack and I pulled my dress down, taking my hands behind and pulled my dress down. And one of the city policemens walked over and pulled my dress as high as he could.

Five mens in this room while I was one Negro woman, being beaten, and at no time did I attempt to do anything but scream and call on God. I don't know how long this lasted, but after a while I must have passed out. And when I did raise my head up, the state highway patrolman said, "Get up from there, fatso." But I couldn't get up. I don't know how long, but I kept trying, and you know God is always able. And after a while I did get up, and I went back to my cell.

That Tuesday when they had our trial, the same policemen that had participated in the beatings was on the jury seat, people. And I was charged with disorderly conduct and resisting arrest. And I want to say tonight, we can no longer ignore the fact, America is not the land of the free and the home of the brave. When just because people want to register and vote and be treated like human beings, Chaney, Schwerner, and Goodman is dead today. A house divided against itself cannot stand; America is divided against itself and without their considering us human beings, one day America will crumble. Because God is not pleased. God is not pleased at all the murdering, and all of the brutality, and all the killings for no reason at all. God is not pleased at the Negro children in the state of Mississippi suffering from malnutrition. God is not pleased because we have to go raggedy each day. God is not pleased because we have to go to the field and work from ten to eleven hours for three lousy dollars.

And then how can they say, "In ten years' time, we will have forced every Negro out of the state of Mississippi?" But I want these people to take a good look at themselves, and after they've sent the Chinese back to China, the Jews back to Jerusalem, and give the Indians their land back, and they take the *Mayflower* from which they came, the Negro will still be in Mississippi.

We don't have anything to be ashamed of here in Mississippi. And actually we don't carry guns because we don't have anything to hide. When you see people packing guns and is afraid for people to talk to you, he is afraid that something is going to be brought out into the open and on him. But I want the people to know in Mississippi today, the cover has been pulled back off of you. And you don't have any place to hide. And we're on our way now; we're on our way and we won't turn around.

We don't have anything to fear. I don't know today, I don't know tonight whether I'll actually get back to Ruleville, but all that they can destroy is the Fannie Lou that you meet tonight, but it's the Fannie Lou that God hold will keep on living, day after day.

"Righteousness exalts a nation, but sin is a reproach to any people." The beatitude of the Bible, the fifth chapter of Matthew said: "Blessed are they that moan, for they shall be comforted." We have moaned a long time in Mississippi. And he said, "The meek shall inherit the earth." And there's no race in America that's no meeker than the Negro. We're the only race in America that has had babies sold from our breast, which was slavery time. And had mothers sold from their babes. And we're the only race in America that had one man had to march through a mob crew just to go to school, which was James H. Meredith. We don't have anything to be ashamed of. All we have to do is trust God and launch out into the deep. You can pray until you faint, but if you don't get up and try to do something, God is not going to put it in your lap.

It's very plain today, some of the things that you have read in the Bible. When this man looked out and saw the number and said, "These are they from every nation." Can't you see these things coming to pass today? When you see all of these students coming here to help America to be a real democracy and make democracy a reality in the state of Mississippi. Can't you see the fulfilling of God's word?

He said, "A city that's set on a hill cannot be hid. Let your light so shine that men would see your good works and glorify the father, which is in Heaven." He said, "Blessed are ye when men shall revile you and shall persecute you and shall set almighty evil against you falsely for my sake. Rejoice and be exceedingly glad, for great is your reward in Heaven. For so they persecuted the prophets which were before you." That's why I tell you tonight that you have a responsibility and if you plan to walk in Christ's footstep and keep his commandments you are willing to launch out into the deep and go to the courthouse—not come here tonight to see what I look like, but to do something about the system here.

We are not fighting against these people because we hate them, but we are fighting these people because we love them and we're the only thing can save them now. We are fighting to save these people from their hate and from all the things that would be so bad against them. We want them to see the right way. Every night of my life that I lay down before I go to sleep, I pray for these people that despitefully use me. And Christ said, "The meek shall inherit the earth." And He said before one-tenth—one jot—of his word would fail, heaven and earth would pass away. But His word would stand forever. And I believe tonight, that one day in Mississippi—if I have to die for this—we shall overcome.

We shall overcome means something to me tonight. We shall overcome mean as much to me tonight as "Amazing Grace how sweet the sound that saved a wretch like me." Because if grace have saved a wretch like me, then we shall overcome. Because He said, "Seek and ye shall find, knock and the door would be opened, ask and it shall be given." It was a long time, but now we see. We can see, we can discern the new day. And one day the little Negro children—the little Negro boys and the little Negro girls—won't be afraid to walk down the street because of so much hate that would make a police jump on the kid. And one day, by standing up going to the courthouse to try to register and vote, we can get people that's concerned about us—because anytime you see a Negro policeman now, you can rest assured he's a Tom. Because if he wasn't a Tom, if he wasn't a Tom, he would be elected by the people, not just a handful of folk. And he'll get out on the street and beat your brains out and afraid to go around the corner and arrest a white man.

We want people, we want people over us that's concerned about the people because we are human beings. Regardless of how they have abused us for all these years, we always cared what was going on. We have prayed and we have hoped for God to bring about a change. And now the time have come for people to stand up. And there's something real, real peculiar but still it's great: there used to be a time when you would hit a Negro—a white man would hit a Negro—the others would go and hide. But there's a new day now, when you hit a Negro, you likely to see a thousand there. Because God care. God care and we care. And we can no longer ignore the fact that we can't sit down and wait for things to change because as long as they can keep their feet on our neck, they will always do it. But it's time for us to stand up and be women and men.

Because actually, I'm tired of being called "Aunty." I wondered in life what actually time would they allow for me to be a woman? Because until I was thirty-six I was a girl: "Girl this." And now I'm forty-six and it's "Aunty." But I want you to know tonight: I don't have one white niece or nephew. And if you don't want to call me Mrs. Hamer, just call me plain "Fannie" because I'm not your aunt.

You know, people had said for years and years, "The Negroes can't do anything." That's the report that they was sending out about the people of Mississippi: "The Negroes are ignorant." But just who's acting stupid now?

I heard a preacher say one night, I heard a preacher say one night that people could look at the cloud and say it was going to rain and it would rain. And still now they can't discern the signs of time. We can see the signs, people, the signs of time. And the time now is to stand up. Stand up for your constitutional right. And one day, if we keep on standing up, we won't have to take this literacy test—to copy a section of the constitution of Mississippi that we had never seen, and interpret it too. When if he had the same test, he couldn't. One day we won't have all of this to do. We'll keep right on walking, and we'll keep right on talking, and we'll keep right on marching. And when your minister say, "Well, it's all right to stand up, but don't march—
[tape break]
—I don't like bringing politics into the church." And when he says this it make me sick because he's telling a big lie because every dollar bill got a politician on it and the preacher love it. And if this man, and if this man don't choose to be a shepherd, he can be a sheep and follow the shepherd.

You know, actually, I used to have so much respect for teachers and preachers, I would be nervous when I'd be around them, but since I found out that that's the scariest two things we got in Mississippi—how, how, how can you actually trust a man and have respect for him, he'll tell you to trust God, but he doesn't trust Him himself? We want leaders in our community. And what people will say, say, "Well, if we can get rid of Fannie Lou," said, "we can get rid of the trouble." But what they don't know, freedom is like an eating cancer, if you kill me, it will break out all over the place.

We want ours and we want ours now. I question sometime, actually, has any of these people that hate so—which is the white—read anything about the Constitution? Eighteen hundred and seventy, the Fifteenth Amendment was added on to the Constitution of the United States that gave every man a chance to vote for what he think to be the right way. And now this is '64 and they still trying to keep us away from the ballot. But we are determined today, we are determined that one day we'll have the power of the ballot. And the sooner you go to the courthouse, the sooner we'll have it. It's one thing, it's one thing I don't want you to say tonight after I finish—and it won't be long—I don't want to hear you say, "Honey, I'm behind you." Well, move, I don't want you back there. Because you could be two hundred miles behind. I want you to say, "I'm with you." And we'll go up this freedom road together.

Before I leave you, I would like to quote from an old hymn my mother used to sing: "Should earth against my soul engage, and fiery darts be hurled, when I can smile at Satan's rage and face this frowning world." Thank you.

"I'm Sick and Tired of Being Sick and Tired,"

Speech Delivered with Malcolm X at the Williams Institutional CME Church, Harlem, New York, December 20, 1964

In the fall of 1964, when famed performer and avid civil rights supporter Harry Belafonte sponsored a trip to West Africa for a group of Student Nonviolent Co-ordinating Committee (SNCC) members, he hoped the journey would internationalize their perspectives as well as provide some much needed respite for the weary activists. The delegation's time in Africa not only accomplished this, but also helped strengthen ties between SNCC and the well-known African American activist Malcolm X. Two of the SNCC travelers, John Lewis and Donald Harris, decided to extend their stay and travel through other parts of Africa. Their decision proved serendipitous when they unexpectedly encountered Malcolm X at an airport in Nairobi, Kenya.

Concomitant ideological transformations—SNCC's movement from an explicitly nonviolent collective to an organization whose leaders began to champion self-defense combined with Malcolm's break from the Nation of Islam and his creation of the Organization of Afro-American Unity (OAAU)—laid the foundation for an alliance between the activists. This convergence of interests was accompanied by mutual support for SNCC programs and OAAU causes. In December 1964, for instance, Hamer and Malcolm shared the platform at Williams Institutional CME (Christian Methodist Episcopal) Church in Harlem, which housed a political rally in support of the MFDP's upcoming congressional challenge. Malcolm returned the favor, visiting Greenwood, Mississippi, in late 1964, and speaking in Selma, Alabama, on February 7, 1965. During the Harlem rally, the SNCC Freedom Singers performed and Fannie Lou Hamer spoke before Malcolm X delivered his oration, in which he worked extemporaneously to interpret and combine several core aspects of Hamer's address into his own.

Their speeches were addressed to a small, predominantly African American audience—less than a third of the attendees were white—and the content of

Hamer's speech, in particular, was far more secular than previous addresses she had delivered in church settings. Notably, Hamer's Harlem rally speech proceeded in what was becoming an effective pattern of address, adapting her personal narrative to the particular exigencies of the moment. Recounting her own experiences with oppression served Hamer's larger political objectives of garnering support for the MFDP's impending congressional challenge and of directing national attention to the endemic racism in American society. Thus, she moved beyond racism in Mississippi, challenging her black Harlem audience to recognize their own oppression. In a deft rhetorical move, she simultaneously drew attention to the limits of their power and empowered them to help with both her struggle in Mississippi and her congressional challenge. The larger problem, according to Hamer, is not just that constitutional rights are withheld from some American people; it is also that African Americans with relatively more rights and with more influence are not using their power to help African Americans with less.

In many ways, this appeal to blacks in New York, and to their white supporters, is similar to the appeals Hamer issued to African American sharecroppers in Mississippi. In both rhetorical situations, Hamer used speech to move her audience beyond acknowledging that a problem is occurring and toward the discovery that they could be part of the solution. In both the North and the South, Hamer was at once critical and congratulatory in her attempt to shame and empower her respective audiences.

*   *   *

My name is Fannie Lou Hamer and I exist at 626 East Lafayette Street in Ruleville, Mississippi. The reason I say "exist" [is] because we're excluded from everything in Mississippi but the tombs and the graves. That's why it is called that instead of the "land of the *free* and the home of the *brave*," it's called in Mississippi "the land of the *tree* and the home of the *grave*."

It was the thirty-first of August of 1962, that eighteen of us traveled twenty-six miles to the county courthouse in Indianola, Mississippi, to try to register to become first-class citizens. It was the thiry-first of August in 1962, that I was fired for trying to become a first-class citizen. When we got to Indianola on the thirty-first of August in 1962, we was met there by the state highway patrolmen, the city policemen and anybody—as some of you know that have worked in Mississippi, any white man that is able to wear a khaki pair of pants without them falling off him and holding two guns can make a good law officer—so we was met by them there. After taking this literacy test, some of you have seen it, we have twenty-one questions and some is not questions. It began with: "Write the date of this application. What is your full name? By whom are you employed?"—so we can be fired by the time we get back home—"Are you a citizen of the United States and an inhabitant of Mississippi? Have you ever been convicted of any of the following crimes?"—when, if the people would be convicted of the following crimes, the registrar wouldn't be there. But after we go through this process of filling out this literacy form, we are asked to copy a section of the constitution of Mississippi and after we've copied this section of the constitution of Mississippi we are asked to give a reasonable interpretation to tell what it meant, what we just copied that we just seen for the first time.

After finishing this form, we started on this trip back to Ruleville, Mississippi, and we was stopped by the same city policeman that I had seen in Indianola and a state highway patrolman. We was ordered to get off the bus. After we got off the bus, we was ordered to get back on the bus and told to go back to Indianola. When we got back to Indianola the bus driver was charged with driving a bus the wrong color. That's very true. This same bus had been used year after year to haul people to the cotton fields to pick cotton and to chop cotton. But, this day, for the first time that this bus had been used for voter registration it had the wrong color. They first charged this man one hundred dollars. And from a hundred dollars they cut down to fifty. And from fifty to thirty, and after they got down to thirty dollars the eighteen of us had enough among ourselves to pay his fine.

Then we continued this journey back to Ruleville. When we got to Ruleville, Reverend Jeff Sunny drove me out to this rural area where I had been existing for the past eighteen years as a timekeeper and a sharecropper. I was met there by my daughter and my husband's cousin that told me this man was raising a lot of Cain because I had went to Indianola. My oldest girl said that she believed I would have to leave there. Then my husband came and during the time he was talking this white man walked up and asked him had I made it back. And he told him I had. And he said, "Well, did you tell her what I said?" My husband told him he did and I walked out. He said, "Fannie Lou," say, "did Pap tell you what I said?" And I told him he did. He said, "I mean that. You will have to go down and withdraw or you will have to leave."

I said, "Mr. Marlow," I said, "I wasn't trying to register for you today. I was trying to register for myself." And this was it. I had to leave that same night.

On the tenth of September in 1962, sixteen bullets were fired into the home of Mr. and Mrs. Robert Tucker, where I'd been living after I was fired from this plantation. That same night, two girls was shot in Ruleville. They also shot in Mr. Joe McDonald's home that same night. And until this day the place was swamped with FBI, until this day—it's a very small town where everybody knows everybody—it hadn't been one arrest made. That's why about four months ago when the FBI came to talk to me about my life being threatened—they wanted to know what could I tell them about it—I told them until they straightened out some of the things that we had done happened, don't come asking about the things that just happened. Do something about the problems that we'd already had. And I made it plain. I said, "If there is a God and a heaven," I said, "if I was going to see you two up there, I would tell them to send me back to Mississippi because I know He wouldn't be just to let you up there." This probably don't sound too good to everybody, but if I can't tell the truth—just tell me to sit down—because I have to tell it like it is.

The third day of June, we went to a voter educational workshop and was returning back to Mississippi. We arrived in Winona, Mississippi, between ten-thirty and eleven o'clock on the ninth of June. Some of the people got off the bus to go in the restaurant and two of the people got off the bus to use the washroom. I was still on the Continental Trailways bus and looking through the window, I saw the people rush out of the restaurant and then the two people rush out had got off to use the washroom. One of the people that had got off to use the washroom got on the bus and I got off the bus. I went straight to Miss Ponder, it was five of them had got off the bus, six in all but one had got back on the bus, so that was five. I went to talk to Miss Ponder to ask of her what had happened. And she said that it was state highway patrolmen and a city chief of police had tapped them all on the shoulder with billy clubs and ordered them out. And I said, "Well, this is Mississippi."

I went back and got on the bus. When I looked back through the window they was putting those people in the patrolmen's car. I got off of the bus, holding the eyes of Miss Ponder and she screamed to tell me to get back on the bus when somebody screamed from her car and said, "Get that one, too." And a man jumped out of his car and said, "You are under arrest." As he went to open the door, he opened the door and told me to get in. And as I started to get in, he kicked me and I was carried to the county jailhouse by this county deputy and a plainclothesman. They would call me all kinds of names. They would ask me questions and when I would attempt to answer the questions, they would curse and tell me to hush.

I was carried to the county jail and when I got inside of the jail, they had the other five already in the booking room. When I walked in the booking room, one of the city policemen just walked over, a very tall man, walked over and jumped on one of the young men's feet, James West from Itta Bena,

Mississippi. Then they began to place us in cells. They left some of the people out of the cell and I was placed in a cell with Miss Euvester Simpson from Itta Bena.

After they left the people in the booking room I began to hear the sounds of licks and I began to hear screams. I couldn't see the people, but I could hear them. And I would hear somebody when they would say, "Can't you say 'yes, sir,' nigger? Can't you say 'yes, sir'?" And they would call Annell Ponder awful names.

And she would say, "Yes, I can say 'yes, sir.'"

And they would tell her, "Well, say it."

She said, "I don't know you well enough."

And I would hear when she would hit the floor again. I don't know how long this happened until after awhile I saw Miss Ponder pass my cell. And her clothes had been ripped off from the shoulder down to the waist. Her hair was standing up on her head. Her mouth was swollen and bleeding. And one of her eyes looked like blood. And they put her in a cell where I couldn't see her.

And then three men came to my cell. The state highway patrolman asked me where I was from. And I told him I was from Ruleville. He said, "We're going to check that." And they left the cell and after awhile they came back. And he told me, said, "You were right," said, "You's from Ruleville all right and we going to make you wish you was dead." I was led out of that cell and into another cell where they had two Negro prisoners. The state highway patrolman gave the first Negro prisoner the blackjack. It was a long heavy leather something made with something you could hold it, and it was loaded with either rocks or something metal. And they ordered me to lie down on the bed on my face. And I was beat by that first Negro until he was exhausted. I was beat until he was ordered by the state highway patrolman to stop.

After he told the first Negro to stop, he gave the blackjack to the second Negro. When the second Negro began to beat, it seemed like it was more than I could bear. I began to work my feet, and the state highway patrolman ordered the first Negro that had beat me to set on my feet where I was kicking them. My dress worked up real high and I smoothed my clothes down. And one of the city policemens walked over and pulled my dress as high as he could. I was trying to shield as many licks from my left side as I could because I had polio when I was six or eight years old. But when they had finished beating me, they were, while they was beating, I was screaming. One of the white men got up and began to beat me in my head.

A couple of Saturdays ago, I went to a doctor in Washington, D.C., a specialist, and he said one of the arteries behind this left eye had a blood clot.

After this happened in jail, we was in jail from Monday until Wednesday without seeing a doctor. They had our trial on Tuesday and we was charged with disorderly conduct and resisting arrest. I was in jail when Medgar Evers was killed.

What I'm trying to point out now is when you take a very close look at this American society, it's time to question these things. We have made an appeal for the president of the United States and the attorney general to please protect us in Mississippi. And I can't understand how it's out of their power to protect people in Mississippi. They can't do that, but when a white man is killed in the Congo, they send people there.

And you can always hear this long sob story: "You know it takes time." For three hundred years, we've given them time. And I've been tired so long, now I am sick and tired of being sick and tired, and we want a change. We want a change in this society in America because, you see, we can no longer ignore the facts and getting our children to sing, "Oh say can you see, by the dawn's early light, what so proudly we hailed." What do we have to hail here? The truth is the only thing going to free us. And you know this whole society is sick. And to prove just how sick it was when we was in Atlantic City challenging the National Convention, when I was testifying before the Credentials Committee, I was cut off because they hate to see what they been knowing all the time and that's the truth.

Yes, a lot of people will roll their eyes at me today but I'm going to tell you just like it is, you see, it's time—you see, this is what got all this like this—there's so much hypocrisy in this society and if we want America to be a free society we have to stop telling lies, that's all. Because we're not free and you know we're not free. You're not free here in Harlem.

I've gone to a lot of big cities and I've got my first city to go to where this man wasn't standing with his feet on this black man's neck. And it's time for you to wake up because, you see, a lot of people say, "Oh, they is afraid of integration." But the white man is not afraid of integration, not with his kids. He's afraid of his wife's kids because he's got them all over the place. Because some of his kids just might be my second cousin.

And the reason we're here today, we're asking for support if this Constitution is really going to be of any help in this American society, the fourth day of January is when we'll find it out. This challenge that we're challenging the five representatives from Mississippi; now how can a man be in Washington, elected by the people, when 95 percent of the people cannot vote in Mississippi? Just taking a chance on trying to register to vote, you can be fired. Not only fired, you can be killed. You know it's true because you know what happened to Schwerner, Goodman, and Chaney. And any person that's working down there to change the system can be counted just as another nigger.

But some of the things I've got to say today may be a little sickening. People have said year after year, "Those people in Mississippi can't think." But after we would work ten and eleven hours a day for three lousy dollars and couldn't sleep we couldn't do anything else but think. And we have been thinking a long time. And we are tired of what's going on. And we want to see now, what this here will turn out for the fourth of January. We want to see is democracy real? We want to see this because the challenge is based upon the violation of the Thirteenth, Fourteenth, and Fifteenth Amendments to the United States Constitution, which hadn't done anything for us yet. And the U.S. courts tied it to Section 201 and 226. Those people were illegally elected and they have been there—the man that I challenged, Jamie L. Whitten, has been in Washington thirteen years and he is not representing the people of Mississippi because not only do they discriminate against the poor Negroes, they discriminated up until the third of November against the poor whites, but they let them vote because they wanted their votes. But it will run until the first of July and we need your support—morally, politically, and financially, too. We need your help.

And, people, you don't know in Harlem the power that you got. But you just don't try to use it. People never would have thought—the folks they said was just ignorant, common people out of Mississippi that would have tried to challenge the representatives from Mississippi. But you see the point is: we have been dying in Mississippi year after year for nothing. And I don't know, I may be bumped off as soon as I go back to Mississippi but what we should realize, people have been bumped off for nothing. It is my goal for the cause of giving those Negro children a decent education in the state of Mississippi and giving them something that they have never had. Then I know my life won't be in vain. Because, not only do we need a change in the state of Mississippi, but we need a change here in Harlem. And it's time for every American citizen to wake up because now the whole world is looking at this American society.

I remember, during the time I was in West Africa—some of you may be here today because I don't know what it's all about, but I know I can tell you the truth, too—it was a lot of people there that was called the PIAA. "What are you doing over here? Who are you trying to please?"

I said, "All you criticize us when you at home and you're worried to death when we try to find out about our own people," I said, "If we had been treated as human beings in America, you wouldn't be trailing us now to find out what we is trying to do over here."

But this is something we going to have to learn to do and quit saying that we are free in America when I know we are not free. You are not free in Harlem. The people are not free in Chicago, because I've been there, too. They are not free in Philadelphia, because I've been there, too. And when you get it over with all the way around, some of the places is a Mississippi in disguise. And we want a change. And we hope you support us in this challenge that we'll begin on the fourth of January. And give us what support that you can. Thank you.

Testimony Before the Subcommittee on Elections of the Committee on House Administration, House of Representatives, Washington, D.C., September 13, 1965

As the U.S. House of Representatives began its eighty-ninth session, Fannie Lou Hamer, Annie Devine, and Victoria Gray stood at the door of the Capitol building intent upon challenging the electoral legitimacy of Mississippi's five white congressmen, Jamie Whitten, John Bell Williams, Thomas G. Abernathy, Prentiss Walker, and William Colmer. A host of Mississippi Freedom Democratic Party (MFDP)–backed candidates, including Hamer, Devine, and Gray, were defeated in the 1964 congressional primaries. Suspecting that the primary election had been fraudulently taken from them, several candidates attempted to run again as Independents in the general election. Not surprisingly, they were barred from doing so by the Mississippi election machinery. COFO orchestrated another "Freedom Vote" mock election in response; it was a four-day event— open to all, with polling places set up in churches and community centers to attract a broad base of voters. The results of the mock election differed markedly from the official primaries. Hamer, for instance, received 33,009 votes to Whitten's 59—a stark contrast to the primary when Whitten beat Hamer handily—35,218 to 621 votes. Like others before it, this mock election demonstrated that Mississippi blacks would vote if given the chance and that their votes would yield quite different results.

To further expose the widespread nature of voter discrimination, the MFDP recruited nearly one hundred lawyers to take depositions from over six hundred witnesses who were denied the opportunity to register and vote in the state of Mississippi. The lawyers also subpoenaed Mississippi election officials who had carried out these discriminatory actions. Ultimately, the MFDP compiled their findings into fifteen thousand pages of testimony, ensuring the MFDP a hearing with the Congressional Subcommittee on Elections.

Hamer's testimony, delivered before a closed-door session of the committee in a small meeting room on the third floor of the Capitol building, demonstrates her range as a rhetor and her ability to respond to varied rhetorical situations. Friends recall that in addition to Hamer's extemporaneously delivered, impassioned, and moving speeches she could also be quiet and forceful. In this address, Hamer was just that. One can observe Hamer indicating in several places that she was reading from a script, which was quite unusual for her; the relatively quiet nature of this speech and its apparent scripted quality do, however, reflect Hamer's adaptability. These textual markers also strategically function to achieve Hamer's rhetorical purposes. The scripted nature of the address permitted Hamer to utilize statistics, specific names, places, and offenses in support of her claims. Since part of the redress she sought included being seated in Jamie Whitten's place, her well-informed, factually based discourse also embodied that of a capable congresswoman.

Although a majority of representatives voted to dismiss the MFDP challenge on September 17, 1965, Hamer, Devine, and Gray managed to leave an indelible mark on this governing body. Upon accepting Speaker John McCormack's invitation to witness the vote, they became the first African American women to ever be seated on the floor of the U.S. Congress and the first African Americans from Mississippi to be seated there since 1882.

*   *   *

MRS. HAMER: Mr. Chairman and members of the subcommittee, my name is Fannie Lou Hamer, of Mississippi. I attempted to run for Congress as an interested candidate in the Second Congressional District of Mississippi. I too got the same treatment that Mrs. Gray and Mrs. Devine got, and some of the difference that I received in the Second Congressional District, whereas one man at Nesbit, Mississippi, went to get his name certified as a registrar, Mr. Williams, he was harassed and was told we wasn't doing anything but stirring up trouble.

In another case, Miss Penny Patch was working in Mississippi on voter registration and was told in Panola County that she could come back five days later, which would be too late to get me on the ballot as an Independent candidate in the Second Congressional District. She was told to come back because they had court for the next week.

Mr. Dave Jones, a secretary for the Student Nonviolent Coordinating Committee, did get some names and petitions to carry to the secretary of state to get my name on the ballot as the Independent candidate. He was arrested on his way to Jackson. He was arrested by the state highway patrol. The names was taken from him and he was charged with some type of disorderly conduct.

One of the things before I read I would like to say: it is pretty bad when the people can't feel safe in going to what are called police officials or state highway patrols to be protected in the state of Mississippi, because I am standing here today—and I must say this before I continue—I am standing here today suffering with a permanent kidney injury and a blood clot in the artery from the left eye from a beating I got inside of the jail in Winona, Mississippi, because I was participating in voter registration, and these orders was ordered by a county deputy, a state highway patrol. I want to say something else. When we go back home from this meeting here today, we stand a chance of being shot down, or either blown to bits in the state of Mississippi.

I want to read. You gentlemen should know that the Negroes make up 58 percent of the potential voters of the Second Congressional District. This means that if Negroes were allowed to vote freely, I could be sitting up here with you right now as a congresswoman.

You also know that Negroes are not permitted to, and have not been permitted for almost ninety years, to register and vote in this or any congressional district in Mississippi.

According to the latest figures compiled by the U.S. Commission on Civil Rights, less than 5 percent of the potential voters in my congressional district have been permitted to register and vote. In fact, in some of the counties in the Second Congressional District, not many Negroes are registered despite the fact that there are hundreds and thousands of Negroes over twenty-one in those counties.

Just as one example, in Humphreys County where Negroes outnumber whites two to one, not a single Negro out of 5,561 of voting age were on the rolls when these contested elections took place.

It is significant that one of the first federal examiners sent into the South after signing out the voting rights bills in 1965 was Leflore County in the Second Congressional District.

I would like to point out that almost seventy-two percent of the 10,274 white persons of voting age in that county are registered, whereas only one and six-tenth percent of the 13,567 Negroes over the age of twenty-one are on the voting rolls. Since the arrival of the federal examiner just a few weeks ago, more than 3,000 Negroes have managed to become registered voters. This reflects the eagerness of the Mississippi Negro to participate in the elective process.

This eagerness has so frightened officials of the state of Mississippi that the state attorney general has just started a lawsuit to keep the names of these newly elected—newly registered voters—off of the voting roll. I might add that the same suit will be brought wherever federal examiners are sent throughout the state.

In addition to the attorney general's lawsuit, Mississippi is using the same violence and terror that it has used for generations to keep my people from voting. For example, within the last two weeks in my own community a man who has been seen around the MFDP workers was brutally murdered in his home. That man was murdered. My husband helped dig his grave. They was ordered to bury him that night. They couldn't bury him because the undertaker couldn't make it, and less than seventy-two hours ago my brother was threatened over the telephone and he was told that they would get rid of him by two o'clock. This is the price we pay in the state of Mississippi for just wanting to have a chance, as American citizens, to exercise our constitutional right that we were insured by the Fifteenth Amendment.

By sweeping this challenge under the rug now and dismissing this challenge, I think we would be wrong for the whole country because it is time for the American people to wake up. All we want is a chance to participate in the government of Mississippi, and all of the violence, all of the bombings, all of the people that have been murdered in Mississippi because they wanted to vote in the Second Congressional District, like Reverend Lee and all of the others who have been killed, there hasn't been one person convicted and done no time. It is only when we speak what is right that we stands a chance at night of being blown to bits in our homes. Can we call this a free country, where I am afraid to go to sleep in my own home in Mississippi?

I am not saying that Mr. Whitten or the other congressmen helps in that, but I am saying that they know this is going on and as long as they have let it happen—some have been in office thirty-some years and never even bothered to run because they didn't have nobody to oppose them. But when we tried we have been treated like criminals and convicts. It is time for the American people in this country to wake up.

I might not live two hours after I get back home, but I want to be a part of helping set the Negro free in Mississippi. Thank you.

MR. WAGGONNER: Mr. Chairman, I have just two questions. Mrs. Hamer, do I correctly understand that you were a Democratic primary opponent of Mr. Whitten in last year's congressional election?

MRS. HAMER: That is right. I would like to answer this question too. I was a primary candidate. When we went up and asked this people who watched the polls just to see how many ballots I was getting, the people in the area where I exist now was told to stand fifty feet away and watch through a concrete wall.

MR. WAGGONNER: One other question, Mr. Chairman. Do I correctly, as well, understand that after having duly qualified and actually been a candidate in the Democratic primary, that you in turn sought to qualify and run as an Independent in the November 3, 1964, general election for this same congressional seat?

MRS. HAMER: I did.

MR. WAGGONNER: What does the Mississippi law have to say about having been a candidate in a primary and then becoming a candidate in a general election?

MRS. HAMER: My legal counsel will tell you that.

MR. ABBITT: Mr. Chairman, for the record, could we have that answer now?

MR. ASHMORE: I don't know how long he would wish to elaborate on it.

MR. KINOY: We will deal with it fully in our argument, Mr. Congressman.

MR. HIGGS: That completes our statements.

"The Only Thing We Can Do Is to Work Together,"

Speech Delivered at a Chapter Meeting of the National Council of Negro Women in Mississippi, 1967

With passage of the Civil Rights Act of 1964 and the Voting Rights Act of 1965, as well as the Johnson administration's War on Poverty, Fannie Lou Hamer's rhetorical trajectory shifted ever so subtly. Instead of relying almost exclusively on personal narratives highlighting the cruelties and violence of Mississippi's white supremacist culture, as the late 1960s played out Hamer marshaled new rhetorical strategies and tactics for bureaucratic and electoral ends. Having been outmaneuvered in Atlantic City in 1964 and in the halls of Congress in 1965, she was learning to master the bureaucratic back channels, political allegiances, and arcane policy details so instrumental to controlling resources and thus political power. Even so, her gift for drawing historical parallels and contextualizing all manner of political infighting squarely within the Judeo-Christian tradition enabled her to translate complex realities for her myriad audiences.

In this address, most likely delivered in Jackson, Mississippi, early in 1967, Hamer continues her attacks on the alliances among "chicken-eating" black ministers, white power brokers, and educated middle-class blacks. Always vigilant about how poor Mississippi blacks figured into any political equation, Hamer directed her anger specifically at the Sunflower County Progress Inc. (SCPI), a coalition of moderate blacks and whites seeking to attract Head Start monies from the federal government. The SCPI would compete directly with the Child Development Group of Mississippi (CDGM), with whom Hamer was aligned, and which was administered largely by poor, rural blacks.

That a moderate and interracial alliance, however well meaning, could prove disastrous, if not fatal, is underscored by Hamer's not-so-subtle analogy to three murders in particular: the 1961 killing of Herbert Lee by a white Mississippi politician; the ambush murder of Reverend George W. Lee, who was given up by a black Judas to local whites, on the streets of Belzoni in 1955; and the June

1963 assassination of Medgar Evers by Greenwood white supremacist Byron De La Beckwith. Hamer probably did not believe that the SCPI had murderous intent in seeking Head Start support, but even so she was exceedingly wary—perhaps hyperbolically so—of wealthier blacks making common political cause with well-connected whites. As always, Scripture and experience were her twin guides in engaging Mississippi's increasingly complicated post–Jim Crow political realities.

*   *   *

Thank you very much, Annie Devine. That was quite an introduction. I don't know whether I can live up to it or not, but I would just like to say that I am very happy to be here. I started early today and I had to go back home and we finally made it about four-thirty this afternoon. I'm glad to see white and Negro working together for the cause of human dignity. I won't have too much to say tonight, but I've been greatly shocked for the past few years and for the past seven or eight months at what I have watched in the state of Mississippi.

In 1962, 1963, 1964 and '65, when it was some of us traveling from place to place without money, without food, and at all times we didn't have really decent clothes. I remember at one time when we was traveling from place to place a co-worker of mine, we would have sometime just enough money to get a sour-pickled wiener, and a pop to go from place to place, we drank that and we would eat that wiener together and we would go on to one place to the other, and my blood pressure went up to 230! And I know some of you see me with this leg, where I'm suffering now from permanent kidney damage because of my experience in Montgomery County.

But what puzzle me now is the people that we couldn't get to say a word, not only church doors was closed in our face, but teachers said: "We got it. So what is we got to worry about?" You know, "We got ours." But today, all over the state, these same professional people that's supposed to be leaders is turning us right straight back into Reconstruction. We're going into the second phase of Reconstruction. This is a shame.

But, you see, I'm one person in this building—I don't know how the rest of you feel—but I strictly believe in Christianity. And you see people can say that you've got to have a PhD degree to live. But you see my Holy Bible tell me that He was taking from the wise and revealing it to babies. You see in the Delta area of Mississippi, I watched Friday night—was two weeks ago—I watched our principal, our professional men, and these chicken-eating ministers stand up and vote against the poor Negro people and the poor white in Sunflower

County. You see if you are professional and if you are a nonprofessional, if you are not giving service to your fellow man, well, you can be as fancy-dressed as you want to be, but just don't go to church because it's no good. Because we are our brother's keeper.

The fourth chapter of St. Luke and the eighteenth verse say: "The spirit of the Lord is upon me because he has anointed me to preach the gospel to the poor." Not to the rich. But when we come to the qualification, after people have gone through the suffering—I think in terms of what happened from 1961 up until 1967—and I think of the times when Mr. Herbert Lee in Amite County had gone to the cotton gin and was shot down by a state representative, Mr. E. H. Hurst. Then I think about Reverend Lee in Belzoni, Mississippi, that was shot down by a white man and was pointed out by a Negro preacher, says: "There he is." And then I think about Medgar Evers, that was on his way back home and was going to his wife and family and was shot in the back. And this man that was accused of killing Medgar Evers is now holding a big job and got a big stock in the Standard Oil Company. You see I raise question about this. And I think about little Jimmie Travis that was shot in the spine going outside of Greenwood, Mississippi. And then I think about the three friends of mine that we had been together only one week before they went to Oxford, Ohio—I hope I don't hold you up too long, but I just want to tell you some of the things. And tell you some of the things that you have failed to do in helping to make this a better place for all of us—I think of Andrew Goodman, Michael Schwerner, and James Chaney: three young men that gave their lives for a cause. And instead of us saying, "Let's help to train the people that's not qualified; let's try to do something that they can work for the first time to give them a chance to have a head start in life not only for their children, but for themselves too . . . ." But today we have professional people in the state of Mississippi—teachers and preachers—don't have the dignity—they have these degrees but they don't have the dignity and respect for their fellow man to stand up for a cause. You see, this makes me begin to raise a question about my children. Raise, the question is: "Do I want my child to go through a system and then come out to be ashamed to be yourself?" And be ashamed, if it is necessary to die for a cause?

We have in Sunflower County fourteen hundred children that we were able to get out of the ghettos, out of the country, and most of these children had never seen a commode in their lives. Some of these children had never had their faces washed in a face bowl—but you see, I care. When we got these children and brought them in the little town and began to work with these children as best as we could do—again the professional Negro got with the power structure white and they have done everything to drag us down. But I am going to stand. You see, I have a principle and not only do I have a principle, I have a charge.

And I think about the sixth chapter of Ephesians and the eleventh and the twelfth verse that say, "Put on the whole armor of God that he may be able to stand against the wiles of the devil. For we wrestle not against flesh and blood." We are not wrestling against flesh and blood today, people, but against principalities—powers of darkness. The rulers of darkness of this world, which is the power structure. Spiritual wickedness in high places—that's the ministers. We have a long fight and this fight is not mine alone. But you are not free whether you white or whether you black, until I am free. Because no man is an island to himself. And until I'm free in Mississippi, you are not free in Washington; you are not free in New York.

If you think about what happened to Adam Clayton Powell, you can see that we are not free. Now there's a lot of people criticize this man. But when we think of the way Adam Clayton Powell was on the seat and then at the time they was talking about this on the television, talking about Adam Clayton Powell, I looked at fifteen thousand pages of evidence. We had fifteen thousand pages of evidence, three volumes, to prove why those five men shouldn't be seated in Congress, and they there today. They right there. They wasn't unseated.

We are being used from coast to coast for political football. And only thing that's going to make us exist—and the only thing that's going to carry us through: first place, we've got to have God on our side. And I'm not just fighting for myself and for the black race, but I'm fighting for the white; I'm fighting for the Indians; I'm fighting for the Mexicans; I'm fighting for the Chinese; I'm fighting for anybody because as long as they are human beings, they need freedom. And the only thing we can do, women and men, whether you white or black, is to work together. Because, you see, whether you got a degree or no degree, all wisdom and knowledge come from God. And if you don't have that, I'm afraid we won't make it.

I would just like to close with a little quote from a hymn my mother used to sing:

"Should earth against my soul engage and fiery darts be hurled, when I can smile at Satan's rage, and face this frowning world." Thank you.

"What Have We to Hail?,"
Speech Delivered in Kentucky, Summer 1968

In this address to a predominantly white audience in Kentucky, Fannie Lou Hamer tells her story with particular emphasis on her first attempt at voter registration. Part of Hamer's unique agility as a speaker was her ability to amplify a given story based on the speaking occasion. Before her Kentucky auditors, Hamer provides an extended treatment of the events surrounding August 31, 1962—to highlight both the absurd arbitrariness of Jim Crow justice and the potentially lethal consequences of expressing one's citizenship rights in the Mississippi Delta. The story functions, too, as Hamer's civil rights baptism, one that she never uncoupled from her Christianity.

Before discussing her nationally prominent roles at Atlantic City in 1964 and her attempts to win a congressional seat in 1965, Hamer offers one final revealing anecdote about her hometown. Emmett Till, whose 1955 death captured international headlines, was murdered on a plantation in Sunflower County very close to Ruleville in the early morning hours of August 28. In an incident that bears eerie resemblances to the Till case, J. W. Milam's brother, police officer S. L. Milam, entered the Hamer residence in the early morning hours of January 1963, with a flashlight in one hand and a loaded gun in the other—simply to intimidate the family.

Hamer weaves her mention of Till into the latter half of this speech as well. Before promoting interracial unity, she works to defend the ideal of integration from the erroneous attacks of its detractors. To do so, Hamer reminds the audience of Emmett Till's ostensible offense: whistling at a white woman, which evoked the specter of racial "amalgamation." Accusations that black men posed a threat to white women was the spurious first premise of a century's worth of segregation, intimidation, and lynchings. Not only was it hypocritical of white men to invoke such fears when they had raped black women for generations, argued Hamer, but the "pedestal" upon which white southern women were placed by white southern men's virulent defense of their "purity" encouraged the belief that white women were "more than" black women. Rather than people being torn apart by these constructed divisions, false accusations, and unfounded fears, Hamer prescribed seeing one another as human beings—of "one blood" in the Christian covenant—as the only antidote to generations of racial injustice.

*   *   *

Thank you very kindly. I don't know whether I'll get this type of rap when I'm finished tonight or not because I'll be talking, I think, somewhat about "Is politics a hindrance to racial progress?" and then "Do black people have a future in America?" I think we have to start somewhat at its beginning of how I become involved in human rights. And we have to think and draw the line as our goal in talking about the future of black people in this country and how it relates to politics.

In 1962, in Mississippi—the Delta area—I'm from the ruralest of the rural-est, poorest of the poorest U.S.A.—the home of Senator James O. Eastland, Sunflower County, where we have thirty-eight thousand blacks, seventeen thousand whites, fourteen thousand potential voters (black), eight thousand white, 150 percent of the white are registered, and we don't have quite 50 percent of the blacks registered. And the reason I say "150 percent of the white are registered" is because they's still voting that's dead and they's still voting that's not born in Mississippi.

The thirty-first of August 1962, after the Student Nonviolent Coordinating Committee, along with the Southern Christian Leadership Conference, came into Mississippi in August of '62—I never will forget—it was Monday night after the fourth Sunday in August that I attended the first mass meeting in Ruleville that I had ever gone to in my life. Going to this mass meeting, James Bevel, from the Southern Christian Leadership Conference, preached a sermon from the twelfth chapter of St. Luke and the fifty-fourth verse, "discerning the signs of time," and he tied it to voter registration. Then Jim Forman got up and talked about how it was our constitutional right as citizens that we should have a right to register and vote in Mississippi. That night they asked who would go down the following Friday to try to register. I was one of the eighteen that went down on Friday to try to register for the first time in my life.

It was eighteen of us traveled by an old bus that a Negro fellow used for hauling cotton choppers, cotton pickers, and he would also go to Florida every year in the winter months, you know, to make enough for people to exist down there in Mississippi. We went down to the courthouse and when we got there we went into the clerk's office. He asked us what did we want, and I told him we had come to try to register. He said, "Well, all of you will have to leave out of here except two." And I was one of the two persons that stayed in to take—this is what they call the "literacy test." The literacy test consists of about twenty-one questions. It began by "What is your full name?" "Write the date of this application." "By whom are you employed?"—meaning you'd be fired by the time you got back to where you was going. "Where is your place of residence in the district?"—that was giving the Ku Klux Klan and the White Citizens' Council your address. And then it said, "If there's more than one person of the same name in this precinct, by which name do you wish to be called?"

Then the registrar would point out a section of the constitution of Mississippi. That was strange to me because up until August 1962, I didn't know Mississippi had a constitution. And he would point out a section and tell us to copy the section. And after we had copied, to give a reasonable interpretation. After we had finished, it was about four-thirty when all eighteen had finished filling out the literacy form, it was a hard thing to go through because we met people there with cowboy boots on, rifles, and dogs, and some of them looked like—I know you've seen Jed Clampett with the *Beverly Hillbillies*—but they wasn't kidding, that was the difference. But anyway, we had taken this literacy form test and started back to Ruleville. When we got on the way back, about two miles out of Indianola, we was stopped and ordered to get off of the bus. We got off of the bus and they told us to get back on the bus. We got back on the bus and they carried us back to Indianola, where the bus driver was finally charged a hundred dollars for driving a bus the wrong color. There was too much *yellow* in the bus that day. That's the truth—I'm not kidding—but, anyway, they finally charged us thirty dollars and eighteen of us had enough to pay this fine, and we went on to Ruleville after we had paid the fine and got back on the bus.

But when I got out into the rural area where I had worked eighteen years as a timekeeper and sharecropper, my oldest daughter and her little cousin met me and told me that the man that I had worked for was just blazing mad because I had gone down that day to try to register. I went on to the house and finally my husband came and he told me the same thing. Right after he finished talking, the landowner came and asked my husband had I made it back, and he told him I had, so I got up and walked out, and he said, "Did Pap tell you what I said?"

And I said, "Yes, sir"—because this has been the pattern in the South. It's just been in the last two or three years and it's a whole lot of people say "Yes, sir," "Yes, ma'am," until today—but I told him that my husband had told me.

And he said, "Well, you'll have to go back and withdraw or you'll have to leave," and I said, "I didn't go down there to register for you, I went down there to register for myself." I had to leave on that night, the thirty-first of August. On the tenth of September 1962, sixteen bullets was fired into the home of Mr. and Mrs. Robert Tucker—that's the place that I was staying in Ruleville. That night, two girls was shot. And this has been the pattern of harassment we have got in Mississippi because of our participation in voter registration and politics.

Early in 1963, we had a knock at our door. And we got up and opened the door, my husband did, and that was a police from the next town, they call him "Sundown Kid," and S. L. Milam. S. L. Milam is the brother of J. W. Milam and I know that all of you have read about that or heard about that, one of the brothers helped to lynch Emmett Till—the kid that was fourteen years old and whistled in Mississippi and they called it a "wolf whistle" and he was murdered in 1955. And this was the man's brother, a night policeman in Ruleville, Mississippi.

But I didn't stop; I started going about voter registration work in Mississippi. Then on the ninth of June 1963, is when I was arrested in Winona, Mississippi. And I was beaten in jail until I have a damaged kidney for life and a blood clot that has almost blocked the sight in my left eye. But I haven't stopped because I know we have to have a change, not only for blacks in Mississippi, but for the poor whites as well.

We tried very hard to work with the red-blooded Democratic Party in the state of Mississippi. We tried to go in from the precinct level. When I went up to visit the precinct meeting in Ruleville, Mississippi, my husband had got a job but he was fired the next day. When they wouldn't allow us to go into their regular Democratic meeting, we organized what is now called the Mississippi Freedom Democratic Party. It was organized at the Masonic Temple in Jackson, Mississippi, in 1964. And some of you remember seeing us because I was a vice chairman of the delegation that went to Atlantic City, New Jersey, to challenge the seating of the regular delegation from Mississippi in 1964. That is the time when we found out what politics was like—not only in Mississippi, but in the United States because I saw people threatening—I heard of people being threatened—because they dared to take a stand with the Mississippi Freedom Democratic Party.

I never will forget one meeting we had with the man that's now vice president of the United States. We had a meeting in Atlantic City with him because he wasn't nominated at that time. And that's where Mr. Joe Rauh told us if we didn't "cool off" of what we was doing and keep pressing to make that fight, a fight to come on the floor, that Mr. Hubert Humphrey wouldn't be nominated that night for vice president of the United States. And I asked the question of "was his position more important to him than four hundred thousand black people's lives in Mississippi?" And I wasn't allowed to meet again.

But they did have other leaders, that hadn't been in Mississippi, to tell us what we should expect and what we should accept and they wanted us to take a compromise—two votes at large. We refused to accept the compromise on the grounds of: if there's something supposed to be mine three hundred years ago, I just don't want anybody to hand me part of it today. I want every bit of what's mine. I'm not going to take it by just a taste now and a taste another hundred years, because I'll never know what it was like and I don't want it like that. Anyway, we didn't accept the compromise and we went back home to Mississippi. We was stopped in Knoxville, Tennessee, by the Klansmen and it taken five loads of patrolmen to guard us from Knoxville to Chattanooga, Tennessee, on our way back home from that National Democratic Convention. We had to go straight on back to Mississippi and go in court, because we had been summoned to not go to that convention. And they filed a suit against us and we filed a suit against them asking, "Why we shouldn't go?" So we went to the convention.

After that, we tried again unsuccessfully to get on ballots to run as candidates and I tried to run in the Second Congressional District for a congresswoman. When they refused to let my name go on the regular ballot, we made up our own ballot with the same candidates that they had—only we had my name added. And I ran against Jamie Whitten, which is the congressman there now. But something else strange had happened because they seen the power that the black people had in the Second District, and one night I went to bed and I didn't turn over and I didn't move, but I woke up in the First Congressional District. So that's where I am now.

But, anyway, it was the Second then—Second Congressional District. I received 33,009 votes against Jamie L. Whitten's 49. That made us come to Washington in 1965 with a challenge to challenge the five representatives from Mississippi. We got to Washington and on the fourth of January 1965, the three women—the three black women—from Mississippi went up before the door of the House, not to be seated, but to challenge the seating of the five until we could have people to study and challenge their seats and go into

Mississippi and take depositions to see did they really deserve to be seated in Congress? We were turned away from the door of Congress and told there we couldn't come in unless we was a congressman or congresswoman. Now while the power structure was so busy watching the three black women, they didn't see the Nazi guy go in and he was wearing a black hat and a tail and all the makeups to it, trying to make us feel bad. When one of the newsmen asked me what did I think about it, I asked him: "Which one of the congressmens was it?"

And he said, "Mrs. Hamer, you should be ashamed of yourself."

I said, "Why, you told me"—you know, I was told at the door that I couldn't go in unless you was a congressman or congresswoman, so he was definitely inside because I seen him when they dragged him out.

But what I'm trying to say is while this country is so engaged in just watching black folks, they don't see other people that's coming into the United States and could be here definitely to take over the United States because they're watching and studying other skins to keep us down. The challenge wasn't dismissed then. We asked lawyers to come to Mississippi and help us to prove that these five men shouldn't be in Congress. We had a team of 125 lawyers that came to Mississippi to take that position and we were able to get fifteen thousand pages—three volumes—of evidence to prove why the five representatives shouldn't be seated in Congress. But the thirteenth of September 1965, we got a telegram from the speaker, Mr. McCormick, said they wanted to have a hearing to discuss the *dismissal* of the challenge. We went to Washington before the Subcommittee on Elections and the way we were treated in Washington wasn't any different than the way we were treated in Mississippi because it was closed to the public. And they told us in Washington—said, "We won't say you Negroes are not right, but if we let *you* get way with it, they'll be doing that all over the South."

So the seventeenth of September 1965, we was met and escorted across to the gallery by Congressman William Fitts Ryan from New York City, Congressman Donnie Edwards from California, Congressman Byrd from California, and Congressman Hawkins, that escorted us into the gallery until they called for this challenge to come to the floor. When they called for it to come to the floor, we went down out of the gallery to be on the floor while they argued the challenge. But when we got there, they had congressmens from Detroit, Michigan, and New York City and other places to block our entrance there. It was there that I think about a lot of times how Congressman Powell, when he told me that day—said, "I think you people should stay off the floor because if you go on the floor of Congress today you'll be the first black women that have ever gone on the floor of Congress in the history of the United States."

So I said, "You get your pencil out and start writing because we going to make it today because I'm going to that floor." We went on the floor of Congress and they dismissed the challenge. Now what this means—they talking about racial progress—but this mean it is worse now than it was almost a hundred years ago. Because John R. Lynch placed this same type of challenge in Washington, D. C.—a black man from Mississippi. He succeeded almost a hundred years ago. We failed in 1965.

But what we have to think about again—the five men is still there in Congress and we got all type of evidence to prove that they shouldn't be seated there. Because, the first place, Mississippi was just readmitted back to the Union in 1870, when they had to sign an agreement that they wouldn't do anything to disenfranchise the citizens to keep them from registering to vote—and they've done everything since then to keep people from registering to vote. But still the five mens are there in Congress, but 1966 they unseated Powell in Washington, D.C. See, people got to think about what's happening to us because it wasn't actually unseating Powell—it was unseating *us* when Powell was unseated in Congress in 1966. But still, when they censored Senator Dodd, they patted him on the back and gave him the go-ahead to be a good boy—"just don't get caught anymore." See, this is not Mississippi's problem; this is America's sickness. And I had to send the president a telegram—I don't think he's liked me so well since then. They kept on coming out with the thing, "The Great Society." And I asked him to bring some of the troops home from Vietnam and in Dominican Republic at the time and protect American citizens because, I said, "If this society of yours is a 'Great Society,' God knows I'd hate to live in a bad one."

This is the kind of thing that we have gone through in Mississippi and this is the voice in our destiny. And some of the threatening letters, and some of the telegrams that I've got during the time that I was in Atlantic City, wasn't from Mississippi. I got telegrams and letters from Chicago and other places in the North of the racist white cat telling what we shouldn't have done and what should happen to us. I'll never forget one of the things that was told to me during the time that I was in Atlantic City, when I got a letter and they had a lot of our pictures there and they had a red heart with something through the heart and they had a little reading under there that told me to go back to Africa.

So every audience that I've spoken to since then—I don't know whether that man is in that audience or not—but I tell him we'll make a deal: after they've sent all the Australians back to Australia, the Koreans back to Korea, the Chinese back to China, give the Indians their land back, and get on the *Mayflower* from whence they come, we will go home. See, it's time for America to wake up and know that we're not going to tolerate—we're not begging anymore. And I'm not going to say it's not any more of us going to die, because I'm never sure when I leave home whether I'll get back home or not. But if I fall while I'm in Kentucky, I'll fall five feet and four inches forward for freedom and I'm not backing off it. And nobody will have to cover the ground that I walk on as far as freedom is concerned because *I* know as well as *you* should know that no man is an island to himself, and until I'm free in Mississippi, you're not free in no other place. And it's time that we stop accepting these brainwashed ideas that we've had that nobody can be right in this country except Mr. Charley because Mr. Charley's days is numbered now. And we going to move on up.

You don't want to hear that—I know you don't want to hear it, but as we are here, you know, in all the little petty things that you fight, you tell us we should integrate the schools. We get three in the schools and you start complaining about that. And it's like a little poem that I saw Marlon Brandon, I think this guy was named. He writes for *Freedomways* magazine. And he had a little poem there—it was a cartoon—it said, "This is a story of folks black like me—no longer slaves but not yet free, told what they can do and told what they can't, told what they should do and told what they shant, told what to do and told what to don't, damned if we do and damned if we don't." And this has been the pattern. This has been the pattern—not only in Mississippi, but this has been the pattern in America, people, and it's time for folks to see that. Because one of the first questions you ask—you kept me from getting an education and they say, "Well, don't you think that education is needed?" Yes, we need education—we're going to educate our kids, but you're going to have to deal with us while our kids is getting this education. And it's time for people to wake up as American citizens, not only black people but white people as well, because a nation that's divided is definitely on its way out.

And we have problems from coast to coast. The same people that they's giving all the guns to do the shooting is the people that's been causing the problems in the first place. And as far as a person's chance in America as a black person, what our chances are, if you survive, we will too. And if we crumble, you going to crumble too. And it's time for America to face this and for us to work together because this scapegoat that you've got—talking about your son marrying my daughter, or my daughter marrying your son—I couldn't care less. But we want to be treated as human beings. My little daughter is the product of what's called an integrated school. And the suffering the kid is going through—I wouldn't put her in there another year for nothing. But then when I take her out, they'll say we segregated ourselves. It's time for America to straighten up and straighten out some of its problems because it's long overdue.

These are the problems that Dr. King was talking about in Memphis, Tennessee. And you'll get tired and you'll be ready to boo when I say what happened to Dr. King, that wasn't only Memphis, that was America's problem to have that man killed because you don't want to face the truth. But the truth is the only thing that's going to free us. And I'm fed up and sick and tired of you saying that you can't stand for integration when you started it, when they started unloading the ships of the black people when we began to come in from Africa. *You* started it because I have cousins as white as any of you in here with blue eyes and gray hair—and a black man didn't do it.

You don't want to hear the truth—I know you're upset, but we just going to upset you more. I love you, the reason I'm upsetting you. And we going to have to face the problem that we have in America today and stop going to church acting this big lie because we know the most segregated hour in America is eleven o'clock church service, where you see white and black hypocrites go to church in all of these fine clothes and come out and if you see a kid there raggedy or see a man drunk, you turn up your nose and say, "Now what's wrong with him?" When you never have questioned, "Why is that man drunk?"—because it was something that drove him to drink.

We have a grave problem that's facing us today in this country and if we're going to make democracy a reality, we better start working now. Because I cannot stand when people stand to sing the national anthem, "O say can you see, by the dawn's early light, what so proudly we hail . . ." I ask myself the question, "What do we have to hail?" When actually "the land of the free and the home of the brave" means "the land of the tree and the home of the grave" in Mississippi. It's time for us to wake up, and if we going to make democracy a reality, we have to work to eliminate some of the problems with not only blacks but the poor whites as well. Because the poor whites have been used too; because the power structure told him, "Because your skin is a little different, you're better than they are." But you're not better than the black man because the fourth chapter of St. Luke and the eighteenth verse, where Christ was dealing with poor people, and he said, "The spirit of the Lord is upon me because he has anointed me to preach the gospel to the poor." And that didn't just mean black, that meant people. And to show you we're no different, the seventeenth chapter of Acts and the twenty-sixth verse says, "has made of one blood all nations." So whether you're white, black, or polka dot, we made from the same blood, brother, and we are on our way.

We have a grave problem in the United States today and we realize that we're not fighting *men* today, but we're fighting the devil himself. Because the sixth chapter of Ephesians and the thirteenth verse say, "Put on the whole armor of God that he may be able to stand against the wiles of the devil, for we wrestle not against flesh and blood, but against principalities, against power, against the rule of the darkness of *this* world, spiritual wickedness in high places"—that means when a white minister, a black minister, will stand behind a podium and preach a lie in church on Sunday.

And I want to say to the black students, "Stand up and be a man, a woman, wherever you are, because you're as much as anybody else." And stop trying to be white, because if you live four hundred years from tonight, if you wake up you're going to be black, baby. And we have to accept this and do the best we can *out* of it.

But when I hear people say, "I wonder what's wrong, I just wonder what's wrong that people's having all these riots?" Have you *ever* thought about *why* we're having all of the riots, and all the reasons we're having uprisings all across the United States? I've never been in a riot in my life, but I'm not as young as a lot of these young people that will be having them from here on out. America created this problem. Because *I* forgive America, even though we were brought here on the slave ships of Africa and not only was the dignity taken from men—the black men—but also the women had to bear, not only their kids, but they had to bear the kids for the white slave owners.

But we forgive America for that. But we're looking for this check now, that's long past due. And to have a great country, not only will we have to have political power, but we will have to have economic power as well. So let's each of us ask ourselves a question tonight: "Must I be carried to the sky on flowery beds of ease, while others fight to win the prize and sail through bloody seas?" Thank you.

Speech on Behalf of the Alabama Delegation at the 1968 Democratic National Convention, Chicago, Illinois, August 27, 1968

Unlike at the 1964 Democratic National Convention, the controversy plaguing the 1968 gathering stemmed less from domestic racial politics than it did from protests of the country's foreign policy—most notably, the war in Vietnam. With commotion in the streets, the three Credentials Committee hearings, initiated by civil rights activists in Georgia, Alabama, and Mississippi, received less national attention than had the Freedom Democrats' 1964 challenge. There were also fewer questions about the legitimacy of the challenging groups' claims. The activist coalition from Mississippi, for example, had carefully followed the national Democratic Party's rules for the formation of an integrated, representative party, whereas the official delegation from Mississippi had blatantly disregarded these provisions. Their delegation did not include a single black member, not even from congressional districts where over 70 percent of the population was African American; this patent disregard for the national party's pledge to never again seat a segregated delegation made the committee's verdict relatively easy—eighty-five members voted to seat the integrated coalition in place of the segregated delegation and only ten voted against this provision. When she took her hard-won seat on the convention floor, Hamer—with her official credentials badge strung across her chest—received a standing ovation.

Victory was not as swift for the integrated Alabama and Georgia delegations. Led by the politically embattled Julian Bond, the Georgia challengers managed to receive half of their state's delegate seats for the convention. Alabama's delegation, on the other hand, needed all the help they could get when their case was brought to the convention floor. On August 27, 1968, during the second evening session, Hamer delivered a short speech on their behalf.

Hamer's 1968 DNC speech is not emotional in tone, nor circumlocutory in style, and it does not feature her sardonic, yet endearing, wit. Instead, much like the scripted 1965 testimony she delivered before the House Elections Subcommittee, Hamer's DNC speech is convicting and incisive. Echoing the three simple words Hamer used to capture the national imagination four years before—"Is this America?"—she now asks: Is this the Democratic Party? More than raising a critical question, however, the strength of her political persona enables her to confront the national Democratic Party's hypocrisy head-on.

Despite her strong advocacy, the integrated Alabama delegation was not seated at the 1968 convention in Chicago. As Hamer makes manifest in her testimony before the Democratic Reform Committee—the twelfth speech in our collection—the party's refusal to seat the Alabama delegation was just one of several disappointments Hamer faced at the 1968 DNC.

✷   ✷   ✷

Mr. Chairman, Governor Hughes, I am here speaking for the national Democratic Party from Alabama. In 1964, Fannie Lou Hamer was on the outside trying to get in. We know the long pattern of discrimination, not only in Mississippi, but also in the state of Alabama. We also know that Governor Wallace is running today for president of the United States, and he is only pledged as a Democrat in the state of Alabama.

It is time for us to wake up, America. We always talk about a minority, but we don't even say minority when you carry our sons to fight in Vietnam.

I support Dr. Cashin from Alabama because it's time for us to stop pretending that we are, but act in the manner that we are, and if we are the Democratic Party of this country, we should stop tokenism—and just so many this year and four years later seat another delegation.

It is time, tonight, to seat the delegation with the national Democratic Party from Alabama and that be Dr. Cashin and his delegation that represent all the people, not just a few—representing not only the whites, but the blacks as well. Thank you.

"To Tell It Like It Is,"

Speech Delivered at the Holmes County, Mississippi, Freedom Democratic Party Municipal Elections Rally in Lexington, Mississippi, May 8, 1969

Fannie Lou Hamer always called Sunflower County home, but she was never shy about venturing into surrounding counties—especially when it involved an election with a Mississippi Freedom Democratic Party member on the ballot. In 1967, for example, Hamer worked to get Holmes County schoolteacher Robert G. Clark elected to the state house of representatives. Clark defeated twelve-year incumbent James P. Love by a mere 116 votes, thus ending seventy-four years of white-only rule in the Mississippi State Legislature. Clark also had the able organizing assistance of Sue and Henri Lorenzi, white activists who helped organize the rural and predominantly black (72 percent) county.

In the spring of 1969, Hamer returned to Holmes County for an MFDP election rally. While she was always passionate, regardless of audience, Hamer's Lexington interlocutors were in for a real rhetorical treat on May 8. Just five days before the primary election, Hamer exhorts her black audience members to remember their past persecutions, not to sell out to the white power structure, and to keep in mind that a snake, even a momentarily benign one, was still a snake—white or black. Hamer also warned her charges that even a consequential rhetorical change should give pause: just because she was now "Miss Hamer" instead of "Fannie Lou Hamer" to some, and though they were no longer "niggers" but "nigras," the state's political suitors had not necessarily changed their beliefs.

She argues convincingly that blacks should vote for black MFDP candidates, not on the grounds of a black supremacy argument—which would plague many Black Power advocates—but on her (and their) unique positioning as witnesses to generations of Jim Crow practices; from the back of the bus, they had an unobstructed view of white behavior. As a consequence they had become the "greatest actors in the world," which also meant that blacks could spot a phony—white

or black—when they saw one. Sociocultural survival guaranteed that blacks had
a keen ability to judge political motive.

Hamer closes her raucous speech at the Holmes County Courthouse by ad-
dressing, ever so subtly, the thorny matter of gender and politics. Recall that
Hamer, Canton's Annie Devine, and Hattiesburg's Victoria Gray were the public
and national face of Mississippi racial politics in 1965. That same year in an oral
history conducted by Stanford University undergraduates, Hamer claimed that
Mississippi women were overrepresented in the movement primarily because
black men would simply get killed attempting to do the work that she and other
women did. Four years and many victories later, Hamer urges her black brother
to "go ahead," as the women had done their "thing" to "get it prepared"; now it
was his time to "come on and do yours."

*   *   *

Thank you very much, Mr. Guyot. Good evening, ladies and gentlemen. I
know it's getting late but, you know, we've had quite a bit of very beautiful
talks tonight, and I want you to know something; honey, don't *nobody* feel
comfortable when I leave the building because I'm going to tell you where
it's at. I don't want you to start thinking that you're going to feel comfortable
around here with me talking, and I don't want you to think that I'm going to
stop talking about black folks and where we are today because I'm going to
tell you where it's at, children. And I think this minister is really together back
here. This man [Reverend Warren Booker] is beautiful. You know, this man
said so much tonight, that's the first time I felt like just picking a man up in my
arms and kissing him, you know, because you see, in the first place, our folks
done got tied up on compromising too much with this white man that's done
done all this damage to us.

Now, some of you all is going to be scared because you was scared when
you got here. That's all right, too. I'm going to tell it like it is. Now, I'm not going to be up here no hour, but I'm going to tell you what we have to do at this
time, and I'm about to tell you something about people talking about black
men and young white men being angry all over this country. We got to think
about the Holy Bible. I think that when Christ said he would raise up a nation
that would obey him—I can see why these young mens are angry because
they're going to make democracy work, or we ain't going to have nothing.
And I'm grateful to them for it.

You see, I heard them say a long time ago, said, "Only way, this country,
this world is upset, and the only way we going to have a change throughout

this country is [to] upset it some more." You see, I am sick to see, and I want white America to know, and my white brothers and sisters to know—and you just can't say that I'm not your sister because the seventeenth chapter of Acts in the twenty-sixth verse says, "He has made of one blood all nations." So I don't care if you're white as your shirt or black as a skillet, we are made from the same blood, brother. And you're going to have to deal with it.

You know, and I'm sick of seeing, these white people becoming so conservative today that they say, you know, one man asked me a little while ago, said, "Fannie Lou, ain't you afraid of your kids going to school with mine?" I said, "Unh-uh, and you ain't afraid of yours going to school with mine. You is afraid of your wife's kids because you got them in every schoolroom." See, what this man has been trying to put over to us and I want you to know that we know it, brother if you hadn't have been doing with your thing what you was doing, we wouldn't have all these light-skinned folks here tonight. I know you're going to say that white and black men didn't do it. And you would go right now and hang a man up to a tree here in Lexington, and would go to bed with a black woman if she let you share her room. You see the whole enslavement and I'm telling you where it's at. And I can challenge any white man anywhere on the face of this earth because God knows he made a mistake when he put me behind. I watched him, now I know him; he doesn't know me. You know that, baby.

See, I would like to tell you a little story. You know, I got to tell you where it's at. I was working on this plantation. So this man, they didn't want me to eat at the table with them. So what I would do, I would get that spoon, every spoon they were going to eat out of, and I would eat out of that spoon *first*. And I would watch that cat when he'd eat behind *me*. You see, I just want white folks to quit tying up themselves like everything, man, you think we ain't had, we done already had it. Even when you didn't let us back in your bathroom, while you was out, we got in it and used that perfume, too, because when you got back home, you couldn't smell mine because you had it on you.

So, I'm trying to tell you, you been acting stupid, and we know it because black people is some of the greatest actors in the world. I used to watch this man come to the field, and I would place this grin on my face. You know, he was coming out. I could have called him everything while he was on his way, but when he gets close enough, I change it to a grin. So this was a shock in Mississippi white people when you all said, "They wouldn't have *never* done that if those outside agitators hadn't have come into Mississippi." But that's a lie, baby; we been dissatisfied a *long* time.

When you were saying we were satisfied, we were getting to each other raising *all kinds* of hell. And it's a beautiful thing, you know, to see these black men and black women—I'm not ashamed to call you black, baby, because if you're not white, you're black. And I'm glad to see you running for public office because it's one thing about it: I am getting sick and tired of seeing the power structure talk about qualifications. And I ask one question: what in the hell has he done with his if he had it? See, I want *every* person in this building, honey, to really win come May 13, because if we would run candidates in the ruralest of the rural, poorest of the poorest, USA, Sunflower County, the home of Senator James O. Eastland, that was paid $255,000 to let his land waste while we starve, you certainly can do your thing here because you own property here in Holmes County.

These people have been trying to trick us a long time. A few years ago, they were shooting us; so what they decided to do is to starve us out of the state. So overnight, after they redistricted us and done all this kind of crap, they decided in Sunflower County to give us stamps. Now, they know if a man wasn't able to buy, goes to pick up his free food with fifty cents, how in the world can he buy a stamp? So this is another kind of oppression. So what I'm telling this man: if he eats, I'm going to eat. I'm not going to starve. And if he's sick of looking at me in Mississippi, pack his bags and leave because we going to stay. And the thing that's got white people shook up all over the country is not really what we're doing. This man is scared to death because of what *he* done done. Now, he make out like he doesn't believe all these things, but when he goes to the book of Ecclesiastes, preacher reads that little scripture that says, "Be not deceived, for God is not mocked. For whatsoever a man soweth, that shall he also reap." And that scared the hell out of him. Do you think that we would have problems if the white people in Mississippi didn't think that we would do them the way they have done us? We wouldn't be having problems. They're frightened of what they think that we'll do back to them, which I call "guilty conscience."

But I want you to know something tonight. I wouldn't drag my moral and my dignity low enough to do all the things to us the things to *you* that you've done to us. And I'm not fighting for a black Mississippi; I'm fighting for a people's Mississippi. I'm not fighting to seat an all-black government in the state of Mississippi, but I want you to know something, white people, it certainly ain't going to be an all-white one, either. And these people have a right, they have a reason, and God knows I hope they win, because all over this country, Dr. Aaron Henry says, all over this country we are having problems.

But we got to think about even this report on civil disorder that talks about it was racism that started the disturbance in the cities. They didn't do anything about the racism, but they armed them with more tanks and guns.

And I want you to know something: when he talked about John R. Lynch we had a chance of knowing something about John R. Lynch when we was in our challenge from the state of Mississippi in Washington, when we was challenging the five racist seats from the state of Mississippi. We found during the time that we was doing our challenge that John R. Lynch placed this same type of challenge before Congress almost a hundred years ago, and he succeeded. Nineteen sixty-five, we failed. People always talking about we're having so much progress in America, but when we think about that those five wasn't unseated in 1965, but Adam Clayton Powell was unseated in 1966, there's something wrong with America. America is sick, and man is on the critical list.

The whole world is watching us today, and I want you to know something, black *and* white, especially to white America: you can't destroy me to save your life without destroying yourself. From 1962 through 1964, forty-five churches was bombed and burned in the state of Mississippi. And I want you to know something: every time a church was bombed and burned in Mississippi, it was a little piece of church falling off of every church in America. It makes me think of the man that was possessed with devils. He was so possessed with devils, he had to go out in the cemetery and live out there and just cut and gash hisself up. But he cried out with a loud voice to Christ to cast them legions of devils out of him. After He had cast out the legions of devils, they went in a herd of three thousand swine. The community should have been glad that a human being's life had been restored to normal, but they told Christ, said, "Get out of here; you've destroyed our pigs."

Today people are so concerned and hung up about what they got, they don't understand why young black men, young white men is angry. Young black men and young white men throughout the country and Mississippi, too, is angry because they found out that what's been in the books hadn't been functioning like it's supposed to. And they found out that somebody has been lying. And that's why they're angry.

And I want you to know something. Any man on Tuesday, or any woman on Tuesday, that will sell his right to the white power structure in Lexington or any other place in the state of Mississippi, any man that will sell his right, or woman, they're not fit to even go inside of their own house. If we think about the things that have happened to us in the past, if we think about the lynchings, the mobbings, and all of the things that have happened throughout the state of Mississippi, and we don't have enough dignity to walk up and vote for our own people, there's something wrong with us.

When he talks about Marcus Garvey, I thought about . . .

[tape lapses]

. . . I received a call when I was in Atlantic City, telling me to go back to Africa. Cute, wasn't it? Go back to Africa. I said, "OK, baby," wherever I see any white folks there, I said, "Let's make a deal," I say, "after you've sent all the Jewish people back to Jerusalem, the Koreans back to Korea, the Australians back to Australia, the Chinese back to China, you give the Indians their land back, and you get on the *Mayflower* from whence you come and there wouldn't be too many of us at home." I'm not going anyplace; I'm going to fight for my rights in the state of Mississippi, and by getting my right, I won't only free myself, but I will help to free the white man because no man is an island to himself. And we have to know that and quit talking about qualifications.

You know, a few years ago, the teachers wasn't participating. They wasn't participating in nothing. We got a few here today; really beautiful folks that I know are here in this building, really from the Delta, we don't have them all over the state. But honey, I'm going to tell you something about these cats, now: everywhere you go these cats was after me because they feel like *their* time ain't long. And you see, I don't believe in, and I'm not the kind of person that believe in compromising a principle. I don't believe in compromising. Because if it's something supposed to been mine a hundred years ago, don't offer me a piece of it now. I want every bit of it yesterday.

And I got to let you know something before I close; I'm not going to talk too long, but I got to let you know something, baby. We are not fighting men today; we're fighting with the devil himself. Sixth chapter of Ephesians, and eleven and the twelfth verse say, "Put on the whole armor of God that he may be able to stand against the wiles of the devil." The twelfth verse says, "For we wrestle not against flesh and blood, but against power, against principalities, against the rulers of darkness of this world." "Spiritual wickedness in high places"—that's when the minister will stand behind the podium and sell you out. But I got a little song we sang for men, not a minister. Now, some of them said we're going to boycott the meeting, but the Baptist people have had a nice singing, "Shall We Gather at the River?" Now, we decided to gather at the river with some of these cats and leave them in there, if necessary. Because I'm sick and tired of hearing these ministers, these chicken-eating ministers, some of them. I'm not saying all of them because this man [Reverend Warren Booker] is really together, but I'm talking about the ones that's dumb. I'm sick and tired of seeing these cats telling me that I should expect milk and honey—I can't drink sweet milk, and I don't eat honey—when I get to the other side, and him riding in a good car. This ain't going to work no more, honey. You know, and I'm tired of being fed, "He said, 'Thy will be done on earth as it is in heaven.'" Now, I know some of the stuff that's going on down here. God don't want this stuff in heaven. That means, we're going to have to push these men and these women and put them in office. And, baby, you're going to be beautiful.

You see, a few years ago, if you hadn't of quit, the white folks wouldn't even been here, tonight. Now, it reminds me—I'm not calling you a snake, but if you feel like one I'm going to say, then you remind me of a man one time—you know, our folk have always been kind saw a snake in the road, froze almost to death. This man picked the snake up and put him in the bosom, and he began to warm the snake up. And he rubbed the snake and rubbed it, and finally the snake began to waddle about, you know what I'm saying? So this man looked down in his bosom at the snake, and the snake said, slapped out his tongue. So the man said, "Now, would you bite me? And I picked you up when you was *froze* and warmed you up."

He said, "You knew I was a snake before you put me in your bosom."

So we have to be mindful, people, because somebody going to sweet-talk us, and we get them warmed up, they been in our bosom, but as soon as they get us where they want us, they're going to let their tongue out again. I want you to know that, baby. And you're going to have to fight for what you don't want for your children. I don't want my children to come through what I had to come through. I want to make Mississippi a better place for *all* the kids, not only for the wealthy white kids.

It reminds me of the principal calling me one day, and he told me that my little girl had been stealing—she was in the white school. I said, "Well, can you really show that she been stealing?" He said, "Yeah, she been stealing." I said, "Well, you better know what you talking about, Mr. Principal, because I'm going to carry it to court."

He said, "Well, I ain't sure she stole it. But she did help to spend it, what the other girl stole. I'm going to tell you something, Fannie Lou."

I said, "What's that?"

He said, "Two things I hate."

I said, "What is that?"

He said, "A liar and a thief."

I said, "Well, do you know it's your folks that you hate?" I said, "You don't hate mine stealing," I said, "because if your folks hadn't have lied and cheated and stole all my people had, we would own Sunflower County." So you see what I'm saying? That we going to forgive our white brother for what he done in the past, but I'll be doggoned if he going to do it to us again.

I'm not compromising, and I'm not saying we're trying to do it because we are not going to put up with it, and we going to free you, and we going to have you doing the same thing that the politicians are doing in Sunflower County. I see more of them folks now, visiting us in a litter, the same folks that said "old Fannie Lou Hamer," saying "Miss Hamer." The same folks that said "nigger" is saying "nigra." You know, they're saying that over here, too. But I just want you to know, honey, you have to have your thing together, and we got to put these folks in office. Now, this is going to be a beautiful thing.

I often brag on Holmes County, and I wasn't bragging on it on account of the power structure. I'm bragging on it because some black folks have got together and decided to put some folks in office, and if we have any trouble over here, we can bring a bunch of folks over here and stay as long as you want us and sit in, lay in, wallow in, and do whatever is *necessary* because if we win, honey, we going to fight. Now, I'm not the kind to say, "I'll back you." I'm sick of people telling me that, "I'm going to be behind you." They're a hundred miles behind, but, honey, I'm right there patting you on the shoulder saying, "Go ahead, brother," because a few years ago these brothers couldn't do it. And most of the women ought not to done it, but women always have had their role to play. Even Esther was told one time, "you don't go out there"; say, "I ain't going either." So we had to do our thing to get it prepared so you could come on and do yours.

So as I close tonight, I'm going to close this little thing that I've said in supporting these candidates. Don't worry about what the world say about you, and don't worry about what the power structure going to say about you because right now, whatever you do, if it's anything, you going to beat what he's already done. And don't worry about the qualifications because my husband was arrested in Drew, Mississippi, and the chief couldn't give him his ticket till they had a trial because he was too dumb to write it out. So, I want you to know that all these white folks that you hear tell of ain't smart, either. And don't worry about the qualifications because just like they learned it, you can, too. And you go on up there trusting God and be able to sing this old hymn we used to sing, "Should earth against my soul engage, and fiery darts be hurled, when I can smile at Satan's rage, and face this frowning world." Thank you.

Testimony Before the Democratic Reform Committee, Jackson, Mississippi, May 22, 1969

Not long after the disappointed members of the Mississippi Freedom Democratic Party (MFDP) left the 1964 Democratic National Convention, an interracial coalition of Mississippi politicians including Charles Evers, Pat Derian, and Hodding Carter III came together to ensure the success of the 1968 challenge to seat an integrated delegation from their state. By stringently adhering to the national Democratic Party's guidelines and by gathering a broad base of support from local branches of the NAACP, the American Federation of Labor–Congress of Industrial Organizations, the Black Prince Hall Masons, and the Black Mississippi Teachers Association, the group dubbed the Loyal Democrats of Mississippi succeeded in their 1968 challenge to be seated in place of the all-white delegation.

Many original members of the MFDP did not fold seamlessly into the Loyalist coalition, however. At issue was not just the feeling of displacement; there was also a fundamental clash of principles. Faltering resources and waning support eventually led the MFDP to officially join the Loyalist coalition, but Freedom Democrats like Lawrence Guyot, Fannie Lou Hamer, and Unita Blackwell continued to advocate for more than the safe and expedient issues that would lead directly to the seating of the integrated delegation. These members of the MFDP also worked tirelessly to infuse policies like comprehensive health care, free higher education, land grants, subsidies for co-ops, and a guaranteed annual income into the party's platform. According to Hamer, these concerns were largely overlooked—not only by the leading members of the Loyalist Party, but by the larger national Democratic Party as well. What's more, Hamer suspected that members of the MFDP were being closely monitored to ensure that they would not disrupt the convention.

Considering the violent handling of the Vietnam war protestors outside the convention and the virulent censoring of the more radical voices inside, Hamer contended that the 1968 Democratic National Convention represented the "funeral

of the Democratic Party." She was given the opportunity to share these senti-
ments several months later when the Democratic National Committee elicited
suggestions for reform at hearings held throughout the United States. Hamer's
testimony at one such hearing held in her home state reveals her grave dis-
appointment with the party, even as the address captures her vision of "true
reform—for a true Democratic Party." Of particular note here is Hamer's use
of pronouns, which shift in this speech delivered not long after her speech on
behalf of the Alabama delegation. Whereas she attached herself to the national
Democratic Party before, urging its restoration in her 1968 DNC address, here
she offers the Democratic Reform Committee suggestions as to how they *ought*
to improve their *party. Both the tenor of her message and the use of third-person*
pronouns indicate a critical transition, signaling that though Hamer was willing
to lend her perspective to the party, she would exert her activist energies outside
its confines.

* * *

I didn't think that a Democratic convention could be so outrageous until
Chicago.

The people were left out of any real say-so on the crucial issue. The chair-
men would ask for "yeas" and "nays" and a few people would say "yea" and the
majority would say "nay" and the chairman would say, "Yeas have it."

It was just like back in Mississippi. Chicago was so much a part of Mississippi that I could laugh at one minute and cry the next. I told a congressman
that I was at the funeral of the Democratic Party; that's how sick the convention was. I think that it was a vicious way—our convention, our conventions—
was closed to the people.

I had a funny feeling going there, like I was fenced in. And despite all of the
power the party gave to Daley, the party still lost to President Nixon. So many
people throughout the country knew what was going on because they saw it
on television. And I would just like to say what the people saw on television
they've been told that they didn't see it. So, we lost the election because of
Chicago and what Chicago and Mayor Daley and our party stood for. And the
party was naked for all to see and now maybe because [of this] you will start
talking about principles and not just how many votes that Mayor Daley or any
man at the top can steal for the party.

We been to a convention in the name, but that's all. We the same poor folks
we've always been. The way I see it we need to get these things straight for true
reform—for a true Democratic Party. Control with the people, for the people,

and by the people. You see I'm against seeing people picked from the top because grassroot people in Mississippi and nowhere else in this country—whether they're white, black, or polka dot—hadn't been represented. And it's time that these people should have a voice and young people have a voice in the government, if we are to have a real change.

I know it's people have talked about destroying my life and they've talked about me as being from the far left. One man told me, he said you will admit "you are from the far left." I said, "I admit I'm from the far left. To be exact I am four hundred years being far left. I don't think it could be any further."

[tape lapses]

Something disgusting to me when one of the women that was with us at that convention, one of the black womens that we thought was with our delegation, was not only flanked at that convention, but three security agent stamps was put on her bag. We was watched, some of us, like we was criminals. We know some of the thing that happened at that convention. We still talk about democracy in our country. We talk about the change that we should have. We get angry when the young whites and the young blacks is trying to tell us something, but God bless them because they are the people that's going to bring a change; because they don't believe in hypocrisy—and I don't either; because we know that our *Loyal* Democratic Party is not really up to par, because some of them voted down some good things that was happening.

We will have to—you will have to—do something with the Democratic structure because, you see, I know it's something wrong when we was accepted, it was like a woman that's nursing a baby and don't have time to really give him what he need, but to put a pacifier in his mouth. And that's what we have today—something that really didn't do us any good, but just get us to hush.

It's time for some real changes. And if we're going to make democracy work—this all boil down to the problems that we are having in Mississippi today—if we could elect the people that we desire to be in office, people wouldn't be starving in the Delta where we outnumber the white in places five to one. They wouldn't have to starve, hungry white children, hungry black children. People is unrepresented in the nation; it's time to do something about it. We would like to have some change.

I would like to say one other thing in closing. One other thing that really struck me was the thirteenth of May when we was not only running a black slate—we had three black men running in Ruleville, along with the two white that we could support. That day, the man that had been expert on tallying the votes was a black man. He wasn't allowed to tally the votes because the same

Democratic machine is allowed to get away with all the thing they've ever got away with. Whatever money come into the state come in through these same folks that's got me crippled today because I believe in a principle. I believe in a principle that until this nation wake up and see that it's something wrong and without some straightening out being done, we are on our way out. It have to be with the people, for the people, and by the people. Right now, I don't say "put a half a million dollars in Mississippi to do voter registration"—we need a million dollars to do voter registration on. And let some of the grassroot people have a chance—we never get any kind of recognition.

[tape cuts out]

"To Make Democracy a Reality,"

Speech Delivered at the Vietnam War Moratorium Rally, Berkeley, California, October 15, 1969

In 1965, when Fannie Lou Hamer first began speaking out about U.S. involvement in Vietnam, hers was among a small chorus of bold voices to challenge the war. By 1969, however, there was a widespread shift in public sentiment— opinion polls indicated over half of the country felt that the United States should have never intervened, and antiwar protests began to grow in both participation and frequency. The first major demonstration to protest the Nixon administration's handling of the war was organized by the New Mobilization Committee to End the War in Vietnam (New Mobe) and held on October 15, 1969. New Mobe's Vietnam War Moratorium Rally incited millions of Americans to take the day off from school or work and participate in demonstrations held in cities across the country.

Hamer elected to participate in the nationwide rally by addressing a crowd gathered at Lower Sproul Plaza on the University of California at Berkeley's campus, a school well known for its free speech and antiwar demonstrations. On that particular October afternoon, Hamer shared the podium with members of Berkeley's city council, the university's student body president, and a representative from the group GI's Against the War in Vietnam. Her speech echoes others delivered that day in its call to "bring the boys home," but it stands out from the rest as she grounds her opposition to the war in a variety of her lived experiences. For instance, Hamer exposes the interconnection between U.S. foreign policy and domestic civil rights abuses, which lead to unrepresentative representatives—Senator James O. Eastland is her case in point—who then fashion policies that run counter to the interests of the constituents they should be serving. Continuing in that vein, Hamer underscores the need for domestic programs to meet the basic entitlements of American citizens, reasoning that instead of fighting for democracy abroad America should redirect its efforts to feed those "suffering from malnutrition" as a first step to *"make democracy a reality for all of the people of this country."*

As the impassioned applause and shouts of *"right on"* suggest, Hamer's speech was well received by the West Coast students and activists she addressed. More than evidence of her continued ability to rouse a crowd, though, this speech also reveals that Hamer never lost her faith in the potential for institutions to effect the type of social change she desired; she reasons here that, unlike scores of former civil rights activists who, by the end of the decade, were saying, *"Well, forget about politics,"* this was a piece of instruction she found impossible to heed because *"baby, what we eat is politic. And I'm not going to forget no politic. Because in 1972, when I go to Washington as Senator Hamer from Mississippi . . . it's going to be some changes made."*

Although Hamer never made it to Washington as a senator, she continued to exemplify her faith in the American system of politics by running for Mississippi's state senate in 1971 and by honoring her commitment as a delegate to the 1972 Democratic National Convention.

*   *   *

I really feel grateful that what has happened here is something I said in front of Lafayette Park in Washington, D.C., in 1965. After I had sent President Johnson a telegram telling him to bring the people home from the Dominican Republic and Vietnam—and I said to President Johnson at that time, "If this society of yours is a Great Society, God knows I would hate to live in a bad one."

But at that time, at that time, we felt very alone because when we start saying, "The war is wrong in Vietnam," well, people looked at us like we were something out of space. But when they talked about the other day of the Gallup Poll being 58 percent of the people against the war in Vietnam then we see if you are right, you have to stand on that principle and if it's necessary to die on the principle because I am sick of the racist war in Vietnam when we don't have justice in the United States.

I've heard, I've heard several comments from people that was talking about with the people, for the people, and by the people. Being a black woman from Mississippi, I've learned that long ago that's not true; it's with the handful, for a handful, by a handful. But we going to change that, baby. We are going to change that because we going to make democracy a reality for all of the people of this country.

A couple of Sundays ago, I was in Washington at the cathedral there and I read in the *Post* magazine that here was Secretary of Defense Melvin Laird's son had been classified as 4-F. And he had been classified because he had a tendency of a purine malatibination that would sometimes result in the gout. I said, "What in the world is the gout?" So we got the dictionary and looked this word up and what it was saying, sometimes his joints might swell up and resulted in a painful swelling of the big toe. Now ain't that ridiculous? Look it up, "the gout," that's what the man had. And it didn't say he would have it, said he may have it.

And you see the strange and the awful thing about it, the people that's conducting this war in Vietnam don't have sons to go do it. And we are sick and tired of seeing people lynched, and raped, and shot down all across the country in the name of law and order and not even feeding the hungry across the country.

There's something, there's something else funny too. There's something very funny when a man like Senator James O. Eastland, the biggest welfare recipient in the whole country, there's something wrong when he can help to set policies for Vietnam and own fifty-eight hundred acres in the state of Mississippi and people on the plantation suffering from malnutrition. There's something wrong with that.

And we got to go a long way back, people, and talk about real conspiracies because it was something wrong in New York City when Malcolm X was shot down through conspiracy. It was something wrong in America when again—Kennedy hadn't been a very liberal man, but when he seen there was so much wrong that he had to do something about it—he was shot down. And again, on the fourth of April a couple of years ago, one of the most nonviolent souls of our time—Dr. Martin Luther King—was shot down through conspiracy. I want you to know what's happening to us today, America is sick and man is on the critical list.

We want a change throughout the country, and the only way we can have a change is to bring those men home from Vietnam. People have been greatly punished—they have been criticized—because we are in a racist war that don't give a man a chance, that carry him to Vietnam. And I don't believe, you know, the first escape boat this country got to get away on is *communism*. Now, I know as much about *communism* as a horse know about New Year, but nobody and that mean nobody, have to tell me that it's not something wrong with the system. And no communist have to tell me that I'm without food and clothing and a decent place to live in this country.

And I think that charity really begin at home. And we are not dealing, you know, some people don't like for you to call him a devil, but we are not dealing with men today. The sixth chapter of Ephesians and the eleventh and the twelfth verse say: "Put on the whole armor of God. That he may be able to stand against the wiles of the devil." The twelfth verse say: "For we wrestle not against flesh and blood, but against powers, against principality, against the rulers of darkness of this world—spiritual wickedness in high places." That's when the ministers would stand behind the podium and make a deal with the power structure. So we are telling the ministers, we are going to start singing some songs for them and some of the songs is going to be "Shall We Gather at the River," and we going to leave them there!

Because people now no longer believe in a lot of the stuff they been reading. You know, I was really shocked, I got to go into a lot—a little of our history to come back to Vietnam and our policy. The truth hadn't been told to us no way. Because I was really shocked when I found out that Columbus didn't discover America, when he got here it was some black brothers said: "Get on off, honey, and tell us where you want to go."

You kept too many things hidden, not only from *my* kids, but you kept them from *your* kids. That's the reason why your own kids is rebelling against you because of a sick system. But we want the boys—you know I don't think that we have time to say, "Well, we can get them out after another million is killed." We want the fellows to come home, now!

And you know I do believe with this kind of audience, and I think it's this kind of audience in other places, I think a man should be impeached when they are not really dealing with the people.

And I want to say, I want to say to you, white America, you can't destroy me because I'm black to save your life without destroying yourself.

[Member of the crowd shouts: "We don't want to destroy you."]

All right, well, we want to have peace, we want to have peace, and the only way that we can have peace is to bring the boys home from Vietnam, start dealing with the problems in the United States, stop all of this urban renewal and model cities that's pushing people out of a place to stay and start dealing with facts of life.

It's a lot of people, it's a lot of people that said: "Well, forget about politics." But, baby, what we eat is politics. And I'm not going to forget no politic. Because in 1972, when I go to Washington as Senator Hamer from Mississippi, you going to know it's going to be some changes made. Because we are going to change Mississippi.

Even a storm, a person is mistreated in a storm. When we had Camille in Mississippi, the government sent for the refugees. The black people was put in Jackson State College, the white people was put in Robert E. Lee Hotel. When they started sending the people out, the white people was put in trailers. The black people was put at Camp Shelby. The National Guardsmens was caught looting. The National Guardsmens is what we call the "draft dodgers." They are not going to do anything at home, but beat the people down that's trying to bring a change in this country.

And, people, whether you believe it or not, you better remember this to-day: a house divided against itself cannot stand. A nation that's divided against itself cannot stand. And it's two past midnight and we are on our way out. But we have to have a change. And the change is going to first start in bringing the boys home from Vietnam.

And I don't want you to think that you have to pick out a way for me to exist in this society. You know, black people is caught a lot of hell too. We first been told that we wasn't fit into—we got the kind of education to fit into this society. But as sick as it is, I wonder do I want the kind of education that's go-ing to really rob me of having real love and compassion for my fellow man? We got to start, we got to start in every institution in this country because the history that we been getting, baby, had never happened and it never will. And we got to change some curriculum and in making the change, we can have more peace, and real democracy when we bring the boys home and some of the billions of dollars that's being spent in Vietnam can go into rural areas like Mississippi.

And I want you to know something—don't kid yourself, baby. You can say up-South and down-South. The only difference in Mississippi and California, Berkeley, is we know what them white folk think about us and some of you don't know what they think about you here. They will shoot me in the face there and as soon as you turn around they'll shoot you in the back. So you ain't doing no big thing here. The problem here is like the problem all over the country and decent people—I'm not talking about I'm going to attack some-body because it look foolish to me to come out of my house and throw a bottle at my brother's house—I'm not talking about that kind of crap, I'm talking about some real changes that's going to help people throughout the country and the only way we can do that is stop engaging ourselves—and I have to say "us"—in this racist war.

We watched what happened in Chicago last year when they had this Na-tional Democratic Convention. Tell you, I was a delegate there. And they had a little blue-eyed guy assigned to me. I made his life miserable because I learned to dodge, you know, when I felt like it. But they must have told him, said, "Don't you let that woman get out of your sight." But some of our bags was flanked and things was taken out of our bags—thank God we didn't have nothing. So, they was looking for us, you see, to do a big thing there. They planned to kill a lot of us, but we'd done our homework. Told our black brothers, said: "Don't you go out there, because they're planning to get us, man." So, they didn't go. But they was so determined to do something they beat you kids nearly to death.

Now a society is sick when a convention would have to be held with fixed bayonets. And that mean, stick you if you stand there and shoot you if you run. But we need a change and the only way we're going to have a change—don't you think that this is not important—one man's feet can't walk across the land, two men's feet can't walk across the land. But if two and two and fifty make a million, we'll see the day come around.

And we keep on saying we're against the war. One crowd of people can't change the status quo, but if two and two and fifty make a million, we'll see the day come around that we will have our boys home. And we'll be able to stand and fight together for the things that we rightfully deserve, not in Vietnam, not in Vi-Afra, but right here in the United States to make democracy a reality for all of the people of the world regardless of race or color. Thank you.

"America Is a Sick Place, and Man Is on the Critical List,"
Speech Delivered at Loop College, Chicago, Illinois, May 27, 1970

Fannie Lou Hamer traveled north to Chicago's Loop College in the spring of 1970, as part of its "Decade of Civil Rights History, 1960–1970" speakers' series. The college, which was founded in 1962 and today bears the name Harold Washington College, also honored Hamer with a Citizen's Achievement Citation for her civil rights activism. No doubt Hamer was also doing some fundraising for the recently launched Freedom Farm Cooperative, which she founded in 1969 to help Sunflower County's most vulnerable feed, clothe, and shelter themselves. While Hamer continued to have a national presence in civil rights circles, increasingly her work and her extensive travels were geared toward helping the impoverished in her home county. That work and travel had grown more urgent by 1970: just two years earlier her adopted twenty-two-year-old daughter Dorothy had died from causes related to malnutrition.

Instead of beginning her remarks to this interracial gathering with the gravity of her failed attempt at voter registration in August 1962, Hamer starts much more playfully as she recounts daily acts of resistance to Mississippi's Jim Crow way of life. Whether it was wearing the white women's clothes she was laundering, luxuriating in their bubble baths and perfumes when they were away from home, or surreptitiously providing sharecroppers with a fair cotton weigh-in, Hamer's activism did not suddenly emerge after civil rights workers spoke at her small Ruleville church; rather, she sensed something was wrong with the myriad inequities she witnessed daily, on and off the plantation.

The physical violence she encountered following her failed first attempt at voter registration and the abuse nine months later in Winona do get emphasized in this speech—but with an even more disturbing detail: one of the white law enforcement officials directing the beating felt under her clothes after he lifted her dress over her head. Over the years, Hamer had only hinted at the sexual violence she encountered in the Montgomery County Jail—typically by mentioning the lifting of her dress and the number of men alone in the room with her. Before her Loop College listeners, and for the first time in her public speeches of which we are aware, Fannie Lou Hamer explicitly details her sexual assault on June 9, 1963.

*   *   *

Thank you very kindly. I'm happy to be here tonight. One of the funniest things that happened to me today that I guess never happens: I left Mississippi—it was very hot—so I wore a short-sleeved cotton dress. You know, looks kind of thin. So when I got to the airport, didn't have a sweater, didn't have a coat but I had this dress in my overnight bag. The only thing I could say is that somebody got to get me a sweater or loan me something to wear tonight. So you can imagine what it was to me, to walk out tonight in a storm for the first time in low-heeled shoes.

But I'm very glad to be here, and if we are going to talk about "from 1960 up until 1970," I'll have to talk about what was happening to me in 1960. In 1960, I was a sharecropper on a plantation four miles east of Ruleville, and I had been a sharecropper and a timekeeper at that plantation for some time. I was always mad out in the field because, you know, I had some funny feelings about my work in the field because I would always see the landowner always end up with what was happening and we knew it would be horrible in the winter. So 1960, I was mad. Sixty-one, I was mad. Nineteen sixty-two, and I get out in the field and I tell folks and I say, "Look folks, don't you know the white folks is using us?" I said, "You see? Now, there is no way in the world, they could tell us they are not getting anything out of cotton, but this is impossible, they got two or three cars—the wife got a car, the landowner got a car, the son got a car, and we have to thumb a ride." I said, "Now something wrong." You know, I said, "Something wrong with this." And I've been thinking it a long time.

So, as I was in charge with keeping up with the cotton weights on this plantation, this landowner not only would rob us economically through the cotton, but I would have to weigh the cotton and keep up with the weight and this man had the nerve to have a "p" [a device used to weigh cotton], a p to weigh the cotton lower. So I would always carry my p to the field and I would use my unloaded p until I would see him coming. And when I would see him coming at us, I'd switch p's and use his loaded p, but it would always, you know, give us a few pounds.

I had a lot of gripes because, you see, not only was I keeping up with the time on this plantation, keeping up with the cotton weights at this plantation, but when it would rain and when I couldn't be in the field, I had to be in this man's house. Now one thing that would really bug me was when they would tell me that I couldn't eat at the table with them; I would have to wait for all them finished. So, what I would do was eat first. I would just eat and have myself a time. And maybe some of the things I'd done wasn't right because I would eat out all of the spoons and watch them eat behind me. And then whenever they would leave home, I would get in that bathtub, because I didn't have one. I would get in that bathtub and I would take me a bubble bath. And I would put some of everything on me that they had been using because—one thing about it, you know, just like a man who drinks whiskey: if you drink, you can't smell mine because you already got some in you. So they couldn't smell this perfume because they had some on them. I would walk out feeling very proud, I just carried my little own protest, you know. So I had to wash the clothes; I had to iron the clothes—I wore them clothes, too. I would wear them clothes, you know, if they was having a party in ten miles I would show off one of them dresses because I had them at my house. I would wear it and I would look at them, you know, the next day wearing something that I had been wearing. And you just don't know. And that's why it's so, it's so funny to see people today saying what we can't do, when we've already done it.

You know, I used to watch my mother. She would help the white people kill hogs, and they would give her what people call "soul food" today. They would give her the chitlins, the head and the feet. I hated chitlins. So, when I started helping to kill hogs, I would go to the landowners and I would help to kill the hogs, and I would have that five-pound, that five-gallon can full of pork chops and put chitlins in the trough. So, I could do my own little thing in my own way.

So in 1962, I was really fed up. So one day I went to church, a little Baptist church in Ruleville, the church was named Williams Chapel. I know that little church, it was once out on W. O. Pepper's place, plantation. So Ida Winters here, we went to school together in Ruleville, Mississippi, so she know what I'm talking about. But anyway, they had a meeting one Sunday, on the fourth Sunday at this little church, and the pastor announced at the end of the services, he said it was going to be a mass meeting that Monday night, and everybody was invited. Now up until 1962, I had never attended a mass meeting in my life. So I wanted to go and I did go. My husband—you know, in the South people have to work very hard. Right now they don't have to work very hard because there's no jobs available and people are just there starving—so in 1962, that Monday night after the fourth Sunday, I went to this mass meeting, after my husband told me, "Well, I tell you what," said, "I'll carry you out to that mass meeting tonight if you pick three hundred today." So you don't fool around when you pick three hundred pounds of cotton, you have to really roll and there's an art in that just like people have, people say "those people are uneducated," but you couldn't do it if you didn't really have the art to do it. So, I picked the three hundred.

So then that night we went to the church. James Bevel was there from the Southern Christian Leadership Conference. Mr. Amzie Moore was there from the NAACP. Dave Dennis was there from the Congress of Racial Equality. Jim Forman was there from SNCC.

James Bevel preached that night from the twelfth chapter of St. Luke, and the fifty-fourth verse: "Discerning the Signs of Time." And after he preached this sermon, he talked about how a man could look at a cloud and predict the rain and it would become so. And today men cannot discern this time; it was a beautiful sermon. After James Bevel had preached, Mr. Moore, Dave Dennis and some of the others talked, and then Jim Forman from SNCC got up and talked about how it was our constitutional right, that we have a right to register and vote. And he talked about, you know, what we could do if we had the power of the vote. And during the time Jim Forman was talking about how it was our right and how they'd passed the Fifteenth Amendment that I'd never heard of, I was one of the persons that made up my mind that this was something important to me. And it seemed like it was something that I wanted to take a chance on.

So they asked at the end of the services who would go down that Friday to try to register to become a first-class citizen. I was one of the eighteen persons that went to the county courthouse twenty-six miles from Ruleville. We went with a black man that owned the bus, the old bus from Bolivar County. And this bus had been used year after year to haul cotton choppers, and cotton pickers to Florida where they could try to make enough money to help their families exist through the winter months. So we've never had any trouble with this bus, but the thirty-first of August when we went to the courthouse in Indianola, 1962, twenty-six miles from Ruleville.

When we got there it was eighteen of us. We got off the bus and we went on inside the courtroom and the circuit clerk's office and he asked us what did we want.

And we told him we were there, I said, "We are here to register."

And he said, "All of you will have to get out of here except two." So, I was one of the two persons that remained inside. Mr. Ernest Davis stayed inside with me and he was giving us literacy tests that consist of twenty-one comments and questions like: write the date of this application, what is your full name, by whom are you employed—meaning we'd be fired by the time we got back home—where's your place of residence in the district—this mean you would be giving your address to the White Citizens' Council and the Ku Klux Klan. And then it said that if there's more than one person of the same name in your precinct, by which name do you wish to be called? And then it asked if you, are you a minister of the gospel in charge of an organized church or the wife of such minister?

Then the registrar brought out a huge black book and he pointed out a section to me with the sixteenth section of the constitution of Mississippi and he told me to copy that section, and it was dealing with de facto laws. And I knowed about as much about a de facto law as a horse knows about New Year's. I copied it exactly like he asked me to copy it. After I had copied the section, the sixteenth section of the constitution, he told me to give a reasonable interpretation—"tell the meaning" and I guessed, good God! He told me to tell the meanings of the section that I had just copied. Quite naturally, I flunked the test.

By the time the eighteen of us going in two by two had finished taking the literacy test—now there's people, mind you, there that day with guns, dogs, and rifles. Some of them looking exactly like Jed Clampett with the *Beverly Hillbillies*, only they wasn't kidding—so after the eighteen of us had finished taking the literacy test, it was almost four o'clock. We walked out and we got on the bus and started back to Ruleville. On our way back to Ruleville, we were stopped by a state highway patrolman and a city policeman. They ordered us to get off of the bus, we got off of the bus, and they told us to get back on. We got back on the bus and they ordered the bus driver to turn around and carry us back to Indianola. We was carried back to Indianola and there the bus driver was fined a hundred dollars for driving a bus that day with too much yellow in it. They finally cut his fine down to thirty dollars. The eighteen of us had enough to pay this fine. And then we continued our journey to Ruleville.

When we got to Ruleville, Reverend Jeff Sunny—another minister there who had gone down that same day to register—he carried me out in a rural area where I had worked the eighteen years as a timekeeper and sharecropper. My oldest daughter met me and she told me that the landowner was very angry. And she said, "Mama, I just don't know what's going to happen because this man has been raising Cain ever since you went to the courthouse today."

During the time she was talking, my husband came and he told me the same thing. I walked on in the house because, as I was going in the house and my husband was telling me what the landowner had said, I was thinking about how unjust the boss was being to me because this same man when he was in service, I was taking care of his kids while his wife was out bowling. But because I wanted to do something for myself . . . I just couldn't understand why.

Then, during the time my husband was talking, the landowner walked up, and asked my husband, said, "Has Fannie Lou made it back yet?"

And you, any of you from the South know what I mean when they say, "Yes, sir." My husband said, "Yes, sir." "But did you tell her what I said?" He said, "Yes, sir."

He said, "I mean that, she'll have to go back and withdraw her registration, or she'll have to leave."

And I got up from on the side of the bed, and I walked out on the porch so I could just look at him when he said that. And he said, "Fannie Lou," said, "I got three calls while you was in Indianola, and they going to worry hell out of me tonight and that mean I might have to worry the hell out of you," said, "But you got a choice you either go back and withdraw your registration or you'll have to leave this plantation."

I said, "I didn't go down there to register for you, I went down there to register for myself."

I had to leave that night. I went to the home of Mr. and Mrs. Robert Tucker, the thirty-first of August 1962. The tenth of September, I know all you read about it in *Jet* magazine, and other news media. The tenth of September, 1962, sixteen bullets was fired into the home of Mr. and Mrs. Robert Tucker where they'd shoot in there to kill me because I'd refused to go back and withdraw my registration. That night in Ruleville, two girls was shot. They were shot at Mr. Herman Sisson's. They also shot at Mr. Joe McDonald's in Ruleville. My husband become very upset and he told me it wasn't safe for me to stay there in Sunflower County. So he asked me then to go to one of my nieces in another county in Mississippi, which was Tallahatchie County.

I went to Tallahatchie County, my husband wanted to leave the plantation, and the landowner told him, said, "If you leave this plantation you not going [to] get a rag out of this house. You will have to help harvest in what we have before we give you anything." So I went to live with a niece in Tallahatchie County. I had the two children with me at that time. And we was some time, it was raining we didn't have food to eat. We didn't get a chance to pick cotton much because we could pick enough cotton to kind of feed us, if the weather had permitted, but it was very bad.

So one Saturday out in the field, it was in October, I told my niece that I was staying with, I said, "I'm going back to Ruleville today."

And she said, "Please don't go back," said, "because anything can happen."

I said, "Well, it can happen if I don't go back." I said, "I'm not a criminal; I hadn't committed a crime, and I don't have no right to be dodging nobody. And I'm going back to Ruleville, and if I'm killed in Sunflower County I'll still be a part, but I'm not running any further."

I did come back to Ruleville that Saturday night, but when I got there they had guys call my husband, they called some of those people into town where they did have telephones, because we didn't have telephones where I had been living. And they told him about one of his cousins had been blown up in a plant in Argo, Illinois. So I left that same night, coming into Chicago. I came to Chicago and I was here in Chicago two weeks. And I said, "I've had it, I'm going back to Mississippi."

I went back to Mississippi and I went to live with my sister about a mile and a half east of Ruleville. And I began to look for a house because I didn't intend to run any longer. But it was December third before we found the place, a old three-room, run-down dilapidated shack at 626 East Lafayette Street in Ruleville, Mississippi. When my husband got ready to move—we didn't have nothing in the first place—most of that had been taken. So we moved to this address, 626 East Lafayette Street, one Sunday the third day of December.

On the fourth day of December, 1962, I went back to the courthouse, and I told the registrar that he couldn't have me fired again because I was already fired. I said, "I won't have to move because I'm not living in a white man's house." I said, "I want you to know something, Mr. Campbell: you will see me every thirty days until I become a registered voter."

This time he gave me the forty-ninth section of the constitution of Mississippi, was dealing with the house of representatives. It was a funny thing because when I went back to check the second time, I had passed the literacy test. But the thing that was so crucial about this, the registrar that was giving the test when the Justice Department and Civil Rights Commission came to Mississippi and, you know, gave them some of the same literacy tests, they flunked it too.

So, then, after I'd become one of the first black women in Sunflower County to become registered, it was like I become a hunted person, criminal. I remember one morning in February of 1963, there was a knock on our door. At five o'clock that morning, my husband had gone in the washroom, and when he walked to the door to open the door, it was two armed cops, flashlights in one hand, guns in the other hand, and they wanted to know what my husband was doing up that time of morning. Now one of these mens was called "Sundown Kid," and he looked it. The other one was S. L. Milam—S. L. Milam might not mean much to some of you, because some of you are too young. But S. L. Milam was J. W. Milam's brother, one of the brothers that helped to lynch Emmett Till, the little kid from Chicago that came to Mississippi to visit his grandparents, and a white woman passed and he whistled, and it was called the "wolf whistle." He was lynched in Sunflower County, carried to Leflore County, and the weights from a cotton gin was put on his body, and he was put in Tallahatchie River—this was the beginning of the harassment. Later on in 1963, I went up to the city hall to tell the mayor it was impossible for me to use nine thousand gallons of water when I didn't have running water in the house. I said, "Now I just want you to know that I know better." I said, "I'll pay it, but I want you to know that I don't owe you." My husband was arrested as a result, and he was jailed. Later on in 1963, my oldest daughter, Dorothy Jean, was arrested.

Then on the ninth of June 1963, I had gone to a voter registration and a voter educational workshop, to be taught the sections of the constitution of Mississippi, then we could go back to Mississippi to teach other people how to pass the literacy test. On our way back to Mississippi, we stopped—we was riding on the Continental Trailways bus—we stopped in Winona, Mississippi, and four people got off to use the restaurant, and another person got off to use the washroom. And I was looking out the window of the bus when I saw the people, when they rushed out of the terminal and the girl rushed them around the bus terminal where she had gone to the washroom, and I stepped off of the bus to see what had happened.

And as I stepped off of the bus, Miss Ponder said, "Mrs. Hamer," said, "it was some policemen inside, and they began to tap us on the shoulder with billy clubs, and ordered us to get off, get out of the restaurant." Now, this was after the ICC ruling, that you had a right to go in any of the places to eat. So I said, "Well, Miss Ponder"—Miss Ponder was a Southwide supervisor for the Southern Christian Leadership Conference—I said, "Miss Ponder, this is Mississippi."

So, I went to step back on the bus, but as I was getting back on the bus and looked out the window, they was putting the five people into a state highway patrolman's car. Again, I stepped off of the bus to see what had happened, and the patrolman screamed from the car he was in and told another man, said, "Get that one there!" And this police jumped out of a two-colored car, it was beige and brown, and it was two of them in the car and he jumped out of the car and he said, "You are under arrest." He opened the back door and as I went to get in the back, he kicked me. I was carried behind the five that was in the patrolman's car to the county jail.

When we got to the county jail—they had cursed me all the way to jail, asking me questions about what was we trying to do and when I would start answering they would tell me to hush—so when I got there and got out of the car, as we walked into the booking room, one of the policemen that was about six feet [tall] jumped up on the black guy's feet. And then they began to place us in cells.

I was placed in a cell with Miss Euvester Simpson and they left other people out in the booking room. And I began to hear some of the saddest and some of the loudest screams and sounds I'd ever heard in my life. And finally they passed my cell, with the girl, was June Johnson, fifteen years old. Her clothes was torn off of her waist, and the blood was running from her head down in her bosom, and they put her in a cell. And then I began to hear somebody else when they would scream and I would hear a voice say, "Can't you say 'yes, sir,' nigger?"

And I understood Miss Ponder's voice, and she said, "Yes, I can say, 'yes, sir.'"

"So why don't you say it?"

And she said, "I don't know you well enough."

And I don't know how long they beat Miss Ponder, but I would hear her body when it would hit the floor, and I would just hear the screams, and I will never forget something that Miss Ponder said during the time that they was beating her. She asked God to have mercy on those people because they didn't know what they was doing. And finally, they passed my cell, and they had Miss Ponder, her clothes were ripped from the shoulder down, one of her eyes looked like blood and her mouth was swollen almost like my hand. And they carried her to a cell where I couldn't see her, and the only way she was holding up, was by propping herself against the brick walls. She wasn't even aware that she had passed my cell.

Then three white men came to my cell and they asked me where I was from. One of these was a state highway patrolman, and he had an insignia across his pocket that said "John L. Basinger" and on his pocket, on his arm was a brown signal that said "State Highway Patrol." And he asked me where I was from and I told him I was from Ruleville. And he said, "We are going to check that." They left out of the room and when they came back he said, "You are from Ruleville all right," and he called me a name that I wouldn't mention in this room, but he said, "We are going to make you wish you was dead."

I was led out of that cell into another cell, where they had two black prisoners. The state highway patrolman ordered me to lay down on the bunk bed on my face, and he ordered the first prisoner to beat me. The black prisoner said, "Do you want me to beat this woman with this?" It was a long leather blackjack that was loaded with some kind of metal, and he used a curse word and he said, "If you don't beat her," said, "you don't know what we will do to you."

The first prisoner began to beat me, and he beat me until he was exhausted. I was steady trying to hold my hands behind my back to try to protect myself from some of the terrible blows that I was getting in my back. And after the first prisoner was exhausted, I thought that was all. The state highway patrolman ordered the second prisoner to take the blackjack. And the second prisoner began to beat, I began to work my feet and I couldn't control the sobs then because I was screaming and couldn't stop. The state highway patrolman ordered the first prisoner to sit on my feet—that had beat me. And during the time the second one was beating, he would hit so hard with this leather blackjack that my dress worked up real high behind my body. And I had taken my hands and smoothed my clothes down because I had never been exposed to five mens in one room in my life, because one thing my parents taught me when I was a child was dignity and respect. And during the time my dress worked up and I smoothed my dress down, one of the white men walked over and pulled my dress up, and in the process from the prisoner beating me, one of the white men was trying to feel under my clothes.

They beat me, they beat me, and I couldn't hush. And then one of the men, the plainclothes white man, walked over and began to beat me in the head. I remember wrapping my face down in a pillow, just burying it down in the pillow, where I could muffle out the sounds. I don't know how long this lasted, but I remember raising my head up and the same cop was standing there cussing, telling me to get up.

At first it didn't seem like I could get up because at this point my hands was navy blue, and I couldn't even bend my fingers. And he kept telling me to "get up, bitch. You can walk, get up, fatso!" And he kept saying, "Get up," and I finally got up, by straining every muscle in my body. They carried me back to my cell where they had brought me from, and just to bend my knees forward, you could hear me screaming I don't know how far.

They got us up at night with their guns to try to make us sign a statement they hadn't hurt us. I wasn't able to walk to my trial, they had to carry me. When I got to my trial, I was charged with disorderly conduct and resisting arrest. I really thought that somewhere there, that some of those people might tell the truth. And I looked over at the man that had arrested me, and carried me to jail, and I said, "Would you tell them the truth? Would you tell them that I hadn't done anything to resist? And what have I done, if so?"

Said, "Oh, you did, you just ran, and you cut up sideways."

And I said, "Well, you might kill me today, but I'm innocent, I'm not guilty, and I will never say I'm guilty." That was on Sunday, the ninth of June 1963.

I was in jail without any kind of—the rest of us, all of us had been beaten, was in jail without any kind of medication. And I was in almost a stone wall, buried with bricks, you could just see the windows, one window and it was down.

Lawrence Guyot heard about us being in jail and he came to see what had happened. They almost beat him to death. They carried him to another jail in Carrollton, Mississippi. They had taken paper to burn off his private. They opened the jail cells to give him a chance to escape. He refused to leave jail because he knew that was giving them just excuse to kill him. So we was in jail from Sunday until Wednesday without any medication.

When we got out of jail that Wednesday, after I had walked about six or eight feet, James Bevel was the one that come to bond us out of jail, and Reverend Andy Young from the Southern Christian Leadership Conference and Dorothy Cotton. And when we was about six to eight feet from the jail, after we'd been bonded out, they told us about Medgar Evers, had been shot in the back.

I didn't go home because I didn't want my family to see the condition that I was in because at that point, my body was hard as wood, it was hard as metal. And I'm just one of the few that have suffered this kind of harassment in the state of Mississippi because I know some of the people here know about a black man with nine children, Herbert Lee, that was doing voter registration work and was shot down in Amite County, a place called *Liberty*, Mississippi. He was shot down by a state representative, in Mississippi. Reverend Lee of Belzoni, doing voter registration work, supposed to have a crash. And when the doctor, Dr. Battle, that they framed not too long ago, and put him in the mental hospital because he had dared to tell the truth, when he came back to Mississippi to do practice, he was sent to Whitfield and that hadn't been three months ago. But he told them, said, "This man didn't have a wreck, this man was shot with buckshots." He had to leave Mississippi, and he worked for a long time at Meharry Medical Center with Dr. Walker, Matthew Walker.

But this was just the beginning because after then, a person to come to my house, I remember one evening that Larry Steele from *Jet* magazine came to my house, and he got a ticket after he left there for drunken driving because they said he was driving too careful. People that would visit my house, they got a ticket. But not only am I concerned about getting the black people registered in the state of Mississippi, but it's poor white people that's been taught that they are better than I am because of the color, the pigment of their skin. But when I see the suffering in the state of Mississippi, I know that I can't just pin the fight down just for black people, because due to all of the suffering that I have gone through in the state of Mississippi, I refuse to bring myself down to the depths of hell to hate a man because he hated me.

I've seen what hate, and we all see what hate is doing to this whole sick country at this moment. America is a sick place, and man is on the critical list. But we are determined to bring a change not only for ourselves, but I believe that we are some of God's chosen people, you know a lot of folks say, "Well, I don't believe in God," and a lot of young people said that, "I don't believe in God," but the reason they said, they see so much hypocrisy in the churches [inaudible]. But I believe in God and I believe in the beautiful passage of the fortieth chapter of Isaiah and the fourth verse that say, "The valleys will be exalted"—and that's people. "The mountains and the hills would be made level, and the crooked roads be made straight." We tried to go from the level of voter registration and getting people registered—and I want to tell you something about this county I'm from. It's what you call the ruralest of the ruralest, poorest of the poorest, U.S.A. This is the home of Senator James O. Eastland that in 1967 received $255,000 to let his land waste, while people on the plantation suffered from malnutrition. So this is a sickness that's not only occurring in Mississippi, because you have a hell of a lot of problems in Chicago.

We tried to go into the regular Democratic Party, in the state of Mississippi. I remember it was eight of us went up to the first precinct meeting there. And when they had the doors locked in our face, we held our *own* precinct meeting. We elected our own secretary, our delegates, and our alternates, and we passed a law of resolution, and we went from there to the precinct level to the county, and from the county, district, from the district, county, county to the state, and on up. And on the twenty-sixth of April 1964, the Mississippi Freedom Democratic Party was organized in the state of Mississippi.

And you remember what happened to us in Atlantic City, New Jersey? When we went to the National Democratic Convention in Atlantic City when they offered us two votes at large, we refused to accept the compromise, and they had never dealt with the new breed we got, they having to deal with now. So I was saying in 1964 that something supposed to been mine a hundred years ago, don't offer me a piece of it now, give me all of it or nothing!

We refused to accept the compromise. We went back home, without any power. We went back home and we tried to get on the ballot again, to run for Congress. They refused to put my name on the ballot to run for Congress, and we conceived of our own Freedom Ballot, to prove what it would mean if we had the power of the ballot. And I ran on the Freedom Democratic Party ticket and I received 33,009 votes against my opponent's 49 votes. I'm not talking about 49,000—49 votes. This is what made us go to Washington in 1965, to go before the door of Congress and challenge the five representatives' seats from Mississippi, and this is the reason I know people listen, this is not Mississippi's problem alone, this is America's problem.

We was told in Washington, D.C., that we couldn't go into the House of Representatives unless we was a congressman or congresswoman. So we told him to give us a chance to prove that we had been right. We asked lawyers from all over the country to come to Mississippi, and to help us prove that we had been right with our challenge. We had lawyers to come from all over the United States, including Chicago, and we were able to gather fifteen thousand pages of evidence that the five congressmens shouldn't be in Congress. They still there though.

The thirteenth of September, 1965, we had a hearing before the Subcommittee on Elections. They called me in Mississippi, and asked us to be in Washington. This hearing was closed to the press, but they told us in Washington at that time, said, "We won't say that you nigras are not right"—well, that's the way they say it when they don't want to say "nigger," but it's still nigger, folks. That's the reason I'd rather for them to call me black, and they don't have any trouble saying that—"We won't say you niggers are not right, but if you get away with this kind of challenge, they will be doing it all over the South." So we said that, if we throwing out all over the South, then we will throw them out all over the South.

On the seventeenth of September 1965, we watched this challenge being dismissed. During the time we was doing research for this challenge, we found that another man, a black man from Mississippi almost a hundred years ago, had placed this same type of challenge before Congress and succeeded. Almost a hundred years later, we failed. See, this brings me up to the *progress* in America, because then in 1966, Adam Clayton Powell was unseated. Now Adam Clayton Powell, what he had done wasn't no more than none of them other folks there. The only thing that was different, he was black. And they wasn't unseating Powell, they was unseating us. But we still, regardless of all that pressure, we have elected ninety-one black people to office in Mississippi, and we are going to turn the tide in Mississippi.

We know it's rough as hell now, but we are going to come out in the lead in Chicago, because I was here in '68 at that convention, and I wondered: was I in Mississippi? That's the first time in my life that I enjoyed on the radio,

"I wish I was in Dixie." Because you know, people, there is something very wrong, when a convention is held with fixed bayonets. You see what the fixed bayonets was there for, they was there to kill a lot of black folks, but we had done our homework. I said, "Don't you cats go out in the streets." I come up here, you know, we got quite a little while before the convention and I talked to them cats and I said, "Don't y'all go out there in the streets because they're after us." So after they didn't have none of us to beat, they beat their own kids.

See, you know, there is something wrong in a country that they tell us we have a right to speak out, the freedom of *speech*, and shoot you if you speak. Do you know there's something wrong, people? There's something very wrong in a country that people can go in because I was so upset and some of you going to be upset when I say it tonight, but I was so upset, when they killed the Panther brothers in the bed because when I watched that on TV there ain't never been a black man shooting at no white man laying down! See, and all I want you to know is to know that we know, now I know there's FBIs in this building, Central Intelligence Agents, stool pigeons.

I was in New Haven, Connecticut, a few weeks ago just before a demonstration for the Panther brother Bobby Seale, and somebody, the press every time they would walk up to me they would want to know one thing: "What do you think of the Black Panther Party?"

I said, "Hold it, just a minute." I said, "What do you think of the White Citizens' Council? What do you think of the Ku Klux Klan? What do you think of the Mafia? What do you think of the Minutemen? What do you think of all of these things that not only killing people in this modern time?" I said, "We talked about what happened under Hitler's administration that killed six million Jews, but have you thought about how they wiped out forty million black folks?" And people will say that they can't understand a hippie, a yippie, a Black Panther, a nationalist. All I'm saying to you tonight, whatever you have, you help to make them that.

But what I'm trying to say to you tonight, we are faced with some difficult days ahead. And I hope white America learns to love, before they teach every one of us to hate. This is what is happening in this country. And you see I couldn't tell anybody in my right mind that I am fighting for equal rights because I don't *want* any. I'm fighting for human rights, because I don't want to be equal to the people that rape my ancestors, dead, kill out the Indians, dead, destroyed my dignity, and taken my name.

I remember when I was walking the streets of Africa, in 1964. I went to a palace—and as we know most of our people came from the West Coast of

Africa—and walking the streets of Africa I saw a lot of people that looked a whole lot like my grandmother. And I wept like a baby because I said, "Now, right here—just like I'm living in America. And the black people over here is my own people. I can't even speak the language because you've taken it from me." They didn't know me, and I didn't know them.

White America, we know that the problem today is grave. But I want you to know something. What's happening in this country at this point is not bravery. People in this country today is scared as hell that they is going to reap what they've sown. And we are not even, we are not even wrestling with men today because I believe in God, but the sixth chapter of Ephesians and the eleventh and twelfth verse said "Put on," the eleventh and twelfth verse said, "Put on the whole armor of God, that he may be able to stand against the wiles of the devil." The twelfth verse said, "For we wrestle not against flesh and blood, but against principalities, against powers, against the rulers of darkness of this world, spiritual wickedness in high places"—that means no-good, chicken-eating ministers will go up to the man and make a deal about you know who.

But the reason we are going to survive, if I told you tonight that I hate you I would be lying to you, because I see what hate had done to you. And I am going to do good, where you have done evil about me. I'm going to do good. And I know it worked because in Ruleville, Mississippi, it was a time that people couldn't drive up to my house and they couldn't stop. If they stopped for any length of time, they was arrested. But I remember a man, the mayor told me one time, said, "Fannie Lou, if you're really tired of what's going on in Mississippi," said, "you ought to leave."

I said, "Well, I'll tell you what, mayor, if you sick of looking at me in Ruleville, then you pack your ass up!"

So the fifth Sunday in March, it was Easter Sunday, was called "Fannie Lou Hamer Day," and I received a letter from this same mayor—because I don't care how high you go, you got to come down to the ground if you're going to eat—and this man wrote a letter, and said, "You know it's been people decorated for bravery, and battles won where they didn't really face danger." He said, "This is not true in your case. You faced ever-present danger but you taken your troop and you walked them to the captain enemy." He said, "And your name is going to be in history." He said, "Now, I know you're concerned about the tangible things"—and I am concerned about the tangible things, because I'm concerned is when I went to this White House conference on nutrition, the president said they didn't have enough money to feed us. But a couple of weeks later, saying, they put twenty-five million dollars into Vi-Afra and what I been saying, "Vi-Afra brothers don't take it because they're trying to get their hands on something over there." See what I'm saying?

Now there is something wrong when they can spend billions of dollars to put a man on the air—because I don't know whether he went to the moon or not—but we can send a man up, and can't feed people on earth. Then there's something wrong that in 1967, when I couldn't get a doctor for my daughter, Dorothy Jean, and I watched my child hemorrhage. And by the time we drove 119 miles to Gadsden Hospital, it was too late. My twenty-two-year-old daughter died and left two little girls and a husband. And the part that's so wrong about that, today that man is in Vietnam fighting for what we don't have.

You see, I know, it's, you know, when I first in 1965 stood in front of Lafayette Park, and said President Johnson bring the folks out of the Dominican Republic and put them in home, because I know then people attacked me in a *Newsweek* magazine, they called me "demagogue," which a lot of people say is wrong now. But you know I know if Stennis and Eastland had something to do with it, then it damn sure had to be wrong.

But we are going to make this place a better place for all of us. I think about in Mississippi, I'll be going into court—if somebody don't shoot me while I'm up here, because I feel safer in Mississippi—but on the eleventh of June, we going into court. We going into court because they are talking about desegregating the schools. And as I told the superintendent of education in Sunflower County, I said, "The most beautiful thing about this county, we have more black children in Ruleville than you have in the county, white children, that's pretty, ain't it?" Just little black children, when I look at that county map it was the most beautiful thing I'd ever seen.

So we got all kinds of children, and I'll tell you the next thing that I don't buy, I don't buy distributing birth control pills and legalizing abortion, because they're talking about us! If you want to abortionize somebody, do it to yourself because [I'm] going to try to keep the children. Because you see my whole hang-up with that, if you can bring folks over here from everywhere else, and then two years they have a better position than we have, then you got room for these folks here. Because I know that's the reason I can *stand* up, and look at that flag with pride, because every red stripe in that flag represents the black man's blood that has been shed.

And what kids are saying to you throughout the country is why didn't you tell us that we have the longest history of civilization of mankind? And why didn't you tell us it was a black man that made the alphabet? And why didn't you tell us it was also a black man that discovered science? And why didn't you tell us something about Dr. Drew, the man that learned to save blood plasma that died out in a hall because he couldn't get a blood transfusion? And all we want to know now is all that stuff that you've had hid from us, bring it out, because you see, this is where your children is rebelling, because you told your children that we were dumb, we were ignorant and we couldn't think. And you see, honey, we would be in your house thinking. And as Jerry Butler said, "Only the strong survive."

You know of all of the things that have happened to us in this country— rape, lynching, murder, hanging, shooting, and killing, we still got it, black doctors, black professors, black scientists. So you can't take it from us. So what you're going to have to do is remember these words: a house divided against itself cannot stand. A nation that's divided against itself cannot stand. And I want to say to you today, whether you're white and black, or white or black, we are divided, but if we were to come out of this situation where we can go to college campus—and that's the next thing that make me so mad, is seeing the National Guard go to the college campus and shoot down innocent kids, and they're the draft dodgers that's dodging the army, then go to the camp where folks hang out on the street there. And I think about those kids that was killed in Jackson, Mississippi. You see, we know there are problems, and we know without you saying that somebody going to snipe you, nobody has ever caught the sniper, because that's something that didn't really exist. Six months after the thing in Newark, New Jersey, they found that it wasn't any sniper.

Folks, you better straighten up and fly right because at this point on out people all over the world hates us. They hate us and don't you, you might feel like that you got it made, but as you carry me down, I'm going to bring you down with me. And if you stand up, you can't stand up to save your life, without letting me stand up too. As I told them in Mississippi, you know, when I was talking about school situations, the mayor asked me, said, "Now look, Fannie Lou, do you really want your kids to go to school with mine?"

I said, "Look, fellow, you're not afraid of your kids going to school with mine. You're afraid of your wife's kids going to school with mine, because you got them in every damn school in the state."

We are going to make things better, and we are going to straighten out the crooked roadways, not only in Mississippi, but throughout this country. As I close I always like to think about a song my mother used to sing, a lot of people is ashamed of this old Baptist teachings, but my mother used to sing a song, it was a hymn that said, "Should earth against my soul engage, and fiery darts be hurled, when I can smile at Satan's rage, and face this frowning world." Thank you.

"Until I Am Free, You Are Not Free Either,"

Speech Delivered at the University of Wisconsin, Madison, Wisconsin,
January 1971

Of her scores of speaking destinations, perhaps none was visited more frequently by Fannie Lou Hamer than Madison, Wisconsin. Not only was Madison home to many progressives within a progressive state, but Hamer received significant and regular support for her Freedom Farm ventures from Measure for Measure. The organization was founded in 1965 by Madison residents, who had traveled south to forge contacts with rural blacks in Mississippi and Arkansas. Hamer first met with Measure for Measure members during a visit to Madison as part of her Office of Economic Opportunity training in 1966. In 1968, the organization brought thirty-five hundred pounds of clothes to Ruleville, and later in the same year they raised five thousand dollars to help residents of Sunflower County purchase food stamps. Measure for Measure would also be a frequent contributor to Hamer's Freedom Farm Cooperative as it sought to purchase land, farm animals, seeds for crops, and farm machinery.

Before a predominantly white audience at the University of Wisconsin, one that had likely heard her speak before, Hamer strays from her autobiographical calling cards of August 31, 1962, and June 9, 1963. Instead she ranges broadly across several topics, including birth control, black power and black separatism, the story of Freedom Farm, foreign policy, federal bureaucracies, the interrelationship of all classes and races, and the importance of young people to a progressive political agenda. Of note also is the relative absence of religion, specifically the interanimation of movement goals with Old and New Testament parallels. Such an omission was not new for Hamer: often when speaking before northern progressive audiences, she would de-emphasize her literalist and occasionally apocalyptic reading of Scripture.

For one of the first times in her speechmaking, Hamer calls attention to her manner of delivery: she did not work from a manuscript because she liked to "tell it like it is" to "folk" like her in the audience. A detailed manuscript was a fiction, an elaborate and artificial rhetorical gesture that inhibited her ability to connect with audiences. Public speaking was always personal and imbued with the spiritual for Fannie Lou Hamer. As someone who had spent all of her religious life in the rural southern black church, she understood intimately the power of the impromptu word to connect with listeners—white and black. As such, while a manuscript might mask some of her educational limitations, it would also profoundly interfere with her ability to inspire and move total strangers to action.

*   *   *

Thank you very much, Martha Smith. I don't know whether I'll have to holler or not because I am just used to talking loud. So, I don't have too much trouble having to carry my voice. But with this kind of introduction—Martha Smith is a very good friend of mine. I remember going on educational television with Martha here about two years ago here at the university in Wisconsin and honest to God this woman tickled me to death. You know, I had all kinds of trouble, but she just brought all of that out and for a while I could relax, just doing this show with Martha Smith. I would like to say this a beautiful audience out here to me this afternoon because I always like people. A couple of weeks ago I was doing a show in New York City for NBC on the role of a black woman and somebody asked a question during the time we was on this panel: how did I feel talking to a lot of people?

I said, "I feel like I always feel because I know out there in front of me is just some more folk," you know. So, you don't have to worry about other people—no, you get up and tell them the truth.

Now, you might be expecting me to have a long essay written down and I would have to use my glasses every time—[indicating] this and this way. But I don't carry around a manuscript because it's too much trouble. I'm just up here to rap and tell you what it is and to tell it like it is.

As Martha said, I was born fifty-three years ago in Montgomery County. Now Mississippi, you heard about this twister the other week, but it was already a disaster area before the twister. And it's been a disaster area fifty-three years and I know people is older than me said it's been a disaster area before then. Now I was born fifty-three years ago to Mr. and Mrs. Jim Townsend. And I am the twentieth child. And so help me God, I respect my mother so much that they didn't have them birth control pills because if they had them I probably wouldn't be standing here today. So as I made that narrow escape to be here, I fight for the other kids too to give them a chance. Because if you give them a chance they might come up being Fannie Lou Hamers and something else.

But during the time I was a child my education was very limited because I had to start work when I was six years old. I remember one day I was playing beside a gravel road and the landowner asked me could I pick cotton and I told him I didn't know and he told me he wanted me to go to the field that week and pick thirty pounds of cotton. I went to the field and I did pick thirty pounds of cotton, but the next week I was tasked sixty pounds of cotton and by the time I was thirteen years old I was picking two and three hundred pounds of cotton.

My family was some of the poorest people that was in the state of Mississippi, and we were sharecroppers. Now sharecroppers is really something; it's out of sight. Number one, what I found since I been old enough, it always had too many "its" in it. Number one, you had to plow it. Number two, you had to break it up. Number three, you had to chop it. Number four, you had to pick it. And the last, number five, the landowner took it. So, this left us with nowhere to go; it left us hungry. Because my family would make sixty and seventy bales of cotton and we would pick all of the cotton and then, after we was finished picking the cotton, we would sometimes come out in debt. We never had so many days in my life that we had cornbread and we had milk and sometimes bread and onions. So, I know what the pain of hunger is about.

My father and mother finally got enough money out of one crop to buy some livestock when I was about thirteen years old. And a man went to our lot one night—and he wasn't black—and he take about a gallon of Paris Green and stirred it up in our livestock's food and killed everything we had. At that point my parents had bought three mules and two cows. Ella, Bird, and Henry was the mules and Maude and Della was the two cows. And they killed everything that we had.

I used to watch my mother when she would come out of the fields and she would have a big bundle of things by her side and she would mend our clothes over and over. And I watched her when she would wear things that was so heavy after she had mended them time after time looked like she would have trouble carrying them. At first I couldn't understand why this just always happened to black people so I asked my mother one day how come we wasn't white. The reason I asked her that was because we worked all the time, the white folks never worked and they had everything. Now, this was really curious to me, as it still is. So my mother told me: number one, she wanted me to remember to respect myself as a black child and as I got older she told me to respect myself as a black woman. And she said, "Maybe you don't understand what I am talking about now, but one day if you respect yourself other people will have to respect you."

My grandmother was a slave—Liza Bramlett—Liza Gober Bramlett. She had twenty boys and three girls. And I know what has happened to us in the past, but after I become about thirteen years old and find out how mean that people could be to people, I said that I was going to do something about what was happening in Mississippi. So that's the reason I become involved in politics in 1964.

But it had been other things in my life that I had done that some of the white people don't know that I'd done yet. Because number one: I always had to work at their house. So they would tell me that I couldn't eat with them or I couldn't bathe in their tub so what I would do was eat before they would eat and bathe when they was gone. I used to have a real ball knowing they didn't want me in their tub and just relaxing in that bubble bath. Then I would fill up with everything they put on them and walk out and they couldn't smell mine because they had the same thing on them. So when they was saying that I couldn't eat with them, it would tickle me because I would say to myself, "Baby, I eat first!" And one of the other things I'd done when I was a kid and after I had grown to be a woman—you know we had to wash, Martha, you know how people had to carry clothes home to wash for the white people—and if they had a dance in fifty miles, I wore the best dress because I wore their clothes. You know—we had—I was rebelling in the only way that I could rebel.

So, what I am saying to you, white America, please don't say what black people can't do because some of the things we've been already doing. The sad thing that has been in the whole country is what white America done to us and how we can forgive. When I think about the question that comes up so often about how six million Jews was destroyed under Hitler's administration, I felt a kinship because it wasn't six million of my people destroyed; it was forty million of my people destroyed as they was bringing my ancestors here on the slave ships of Africa.

When I think about the crime that's been committed against us, as human beings and as people, I can forgive *easy* for a lot of things, but when white America taken my name, that was a crime. I went sometime ago to Charleston, South Carolina, and I looked at the documents there and some of the documents there would say—would call the name of the person and said, "She doesn't have any education, but she's a good breeder: twenty-five dollars." I saw where my people had been sold as things and not human beings.

And I think about some of our past history when you never taught us, white America, that it was a black doctor that learned to save blood plasma to give a blood transfusion—you never taught that in the institution. And you never taught us that the first man to die in the Revolution was Crispus Attucks, another black man. And so many other things that I found out.

And so many things that I found out about the church—if you really want to see some hypocrites—if you *really* want to see some hypocrites, go at eleven o'clock church service throughout the country. Not only in the black churches, but in the white churches. While they would tell us, and tell you as kids, "Well, those people are all right, but just don't bring them home with you." But the contribution that we have made in the past—and we know as well as you know—that this country was built on the blood and the sweat of black people. And all we are saying to you today—now, what you have done in the past, you've done that—but we can't let you get away with just trying to wipe us out as human beings.

And some of the black folks have got so confused they talking about setting up seven states with us, which I refuse to let them do. Setting up seven states with us and one night the White Citizens' Council, and the Klu Klux Klan, and the Birchers, which you have here, could wipe us out. And I am not going in seven states by ourselves, we plan to be in this country with you whether you want us here or not. And we plan to make this a better place for all the citizens, both black, red, whites, and browns and we want you to understand this.

I never been hung up in all of my work in just fighting for the black. I've never been hung up in that because I know that a lot of black people have given their lives. But I also know it was people like Andy Goodman, Michael Schwerner, and James Chaney that gave their lives in the state of Mississippi so that all of us would have a better chance. And when they died there they didn't just die for me, but they died for you because your freedom is shackled in chains to mine. And until I am free, you are not free either. And if you think you are free, you drive down to Mississippi with your Wisconsin license plate and you will see what I am talking about.

These are the kind of changes that we have to have and these are the kind of changes we are going about. In 1964, when we went to the Democratic Convention in Atlantic City, and challenged the seating of the representatives of the delegation from Mississippi, when they turned us down and told us to accept two votes at large, I told them at that time, sixty-eight people was there in that delegation and all of us are tired. In 1968, we came back to Chicago and we won our seats. Sixty-four I was in the convention—out of the convention—wishing I could go in. In 1968, I was in there wishing I could get out. I composed a song when I was there: "Jingle Bells, Machine Gun Shells, Convention All the Way!" Because I had never in my life seen in the land of the free and the home of brave—which we have translated in Mississippi to the land of the tree and the home of the grave—I had never seen a convention that had to be held with fixed bayonets [inaudible]. That mean, they would stick you if you stand there and shoot you if you run.

I was in that convention and I made, I made some of them guys they had trailing me, I made their lives miserable. I don't know what he was an FBI, a Central Intelligence Agent, or what in the hell he was, but he was there. See, what happened all my life, I've been behind white people and I watched them. See, that's where you made your mistake, white America. You put us behind you and we watched you and now we know you and you don't know us. So, I watched this guy while he be watching me and whenever I got ready to dodge him, I'd put this dodge to him. And they must have told him, "You better not let her get out of your sight," because this little man had some of the saddest little blue eyes, and he'd be jumping through that convention and I'd be standing there laughing. And after I would let him go through total hell, I would step out where I could see him and you could see him just relieve all over.

You would have to be in that convention to know what we are faced with today when we say "with the people, for the people, and by the people." That's a lie. It's "with a handful, for a handful, by a handful." Because I know sometime when some of the votes would come up and they said all in favor of so and so happening say "aye." Ten people would say "aye," there were a few say "nay," half a million said "no," and they say "ha, ayes have it" and so it's carried. Some convention. But we had to give up because with the young people of today, we are going to make democracy a reality for all of the people.

And I don't want you telling me to go back to Africa, unless you going back where you come from. I got a note one day telling me to go back to Africa and ever since that time—it's been three times a week, I say it, when I am in a white audience—I say we'll make a deal: after you send all the Koreans back to Korea, the Chinese back to China, the Jewish people back to Jerusalem, the Koreans back to Korea, and you give the Indians their land back and you get on the *Mayflower* from which you come, [inaudible] right? You don't agree, but as we all here on borrowed land, then we have to figure out how we're going to make things right for *all* the people of this country.

And we know what has happened in the past with food stamps, welfare, and all of this kind of stuff. And it is not only in the South—it's up South and down South—where our people have suffered from malnutrition. One of my daughters stayed in the hospital six weeks, suffering from malnutrition. And I remember other things with other people where kids literally starved almost to death. And then I start traveling throughout this country to try to do something about the problem. So, I would come to Madison, Wisconsin, New York City, California, and all over the country trying to raise funds to purchase food stamps. But the real crime, I think it's a crime, that if a man and woman is hungry, that they have to pay for the food stamps when thousands of people in the state of Mississippi have made less than five hundred dollars in 1970.

So one day, a man called and said he had some land. He had forty acres of land and he wanted to sell the forty acres. So I called a very small organization here in Madison, Wisconsin, called Measure for Measure. Martha Smith is a part of that organization. Jeff Goldstein, Sarah, "Broccoli." And it's a small organization, but I called them and told them about the forty acres of land. And if we could get the forty acres of land to grow our own vegetables, and to grow our cabbage, and to grow our pork, we could wipe out hunger in Sunflower County. I called another friend of mine was at Harvard University—in charge of the political science there—and he also started raising money too. We finally succeeded in getting forty acres of land. And this land is organized and founded in '69 is called Freedom Farms Cooperative. Last summer we fed a lot of people there, but then we needed more land. So it was a man told me one day that he would sell 640 acres of land.

[break in tape]

And, you know, it was just like I'd been hearing in the past, that "ah, there ain't nothing to that, we might get two or three dollars, but we'll have to try." Last April, we were able to put $20,000 up for the auction on the 640 acres of land. Then on the fourteenth of January 1971, we finished the down payment of $65,500 on 640 acres of land and we had enough from that same march out of Madison, Buffalo, and Milwaukee to do that. And we also have about sixty-eight people that's living in decent homes. We put the down payment on that land. So now what we plan to do is to grow our own vegetables, is to grow our own cattle, and to grow our own pork and have a hundred houses in that area. Now it's no way on earth that we can gain any kind of political power unless we have some kind of economic power.

And all of the qualifications that you have to have to become a part of the co-op is you have to be poor. This is the first kind of program that has ever been sponsored in this country in letting local people do their thing theirselves. Because I've seen government-funded programs with cooperatives and after you get through making the proposal with a stack of paper this high and after you finish paying all the administration from twenty-five thousand dollars to twelve thousand dollars it would be exactly two dollars to go to the program. The only person that's paid at this point is the secretary.

And you can't—you don't—tell me that you can't change a man's mind by not hating. We have gone through all kinds of pressure, but I refuse to hate a man because he hate me. Because if I hate you because you hate me, it's no different: both of us are miserable. And we going to finally have something in common: hating. But as a result of what I can give of myself that I can love you if you hate me, we have poor whites that's coming into this organization and we're going to feed not only the black people of Sunflower County, but all of the people that's hungry regardless of color.

And the young people are the people that's made this possible for us. You know, I just about fell out with all of the people my age—I am fifty-three— and most of them my age are hopeless cases. But I am fifty-three, but I think nineteen. I catch myself sometimes when I am talking to the young people and they're talking about how old people can't relate to them, I said, "You're not kidding. I don't understand what's wrong with those people!" Because I am not going back with every step, I am going forward.

And it's been a sad thing that happened in Mississippi recently. We had a twister that hit several counties in the state of Mississippi. The Red Cross came and after they was there two days I told them, "If I go to Heaven and see the Red Cross sign, I will tell the administration to let me go back home." Because they were a hopeless case. People are suffering because it didn't just only kill people, but it's people now that want to put the trailer houses where they don't have any kind of sewage.

But you got to care enough to do something because what you do here in Madison, Wisconsin, at this university—you are not only doing this for us in the South, but you're doing it for yourself. I noticed what was happening with the Young World Development with the walk, the walk that would be held on the eighth and ninth of May. I see this as a opportunity of bridging the gap between young people. Bridging the gap because not only do I think that white children and young white men and young white women should walk, but I think it's the responsibility of the black people to walk here, too. And if they walk throughout this country with 350 walks in this country and 40 other countries funding it—sponsoring the walk it would be millions of people walking throughout the country—out the world. Because one thing I found out: that it's not only hungry in the state of Mississippi, but two-thirds of the people in the world are hungry. And we have to be concerned. And you have to be concerned here. Because we know with the administration that we have today it's not too many people going to eat.

But I want you to know one thing—that President Nixon wasn't no fool when he got Agnew because that's his safety. Nobody is going to hurt President Nixon and leave us stranded with Spiro Agnew. But all of you here have to be concerned. Not only do we have to be concerned about hunger, but we also have to be concerned about peace in this country. You know it's something strange to me when they tell me that we are over there in Vietnam fighting for the rights of people to elect their government and all of this kind of crap with Eastland in the Senate helping to make policies when we can't do it in Mississippi. And you young people are going to have to help make this change. Because we can't continue in the same way—expanding the war in Vietnam, killing the people over there. And people being shot down in the streets throughout this country, sometime in the name of law and order.

I've been to jail. And I've been beaten in jail till my body was hard as metal. And I've been charged with disorderly conduct and resisting arrest and there's a lot of other young people throughout this country that has been beaten down, but I want you to know something in this audience today—a house divided against itself cannot stand. A nation divided against itself is on its way out. We are going to have to stand up and make demands that will make this country worthwhile. Because I have trouble today and I've had trouble in the past few years. When I got out of jail and couldn't hardly sit down and a man carried me to see the Statue of Liberty and a woman standing with a torch and facing another problem. I told the man that I was riding with that day, I said, "I would like to see this statue turned around to face her own problems. And the torch out of her hand with her head bowed because we have as many problems in this country as they trying to point to in other countries."

I can't stand today, not with dignity, and sing the national anthem. "Oh say can you see by the dawn's early light what so proudly we hailed . . ." Poor oppressed people throughout this country don't have anything to hail. And I just think that in my own way when I have to stand and sing that song, because you know as well as I know that America is sick and man is on the critical list and when people can be shot down at a college like Kent and at a college like Jackson State College by people that's dodging the army. There's something very wrong. I call the National Guard draft dodgers. Not only have they dodged being drafted, but they was caught looting in southern Mississippi after the storm.

We have to work to make this a better place and we have to deal with politics and the history of this country that's not in the books. You know we've been reading about what was in the book, you know about "Columbus discovered America." And when he got here there was a black brother walked up there and said, "Let me help you, man." And there was some Indians here too. So how could he discover what was already discovered? The education has got to be changed in these institutions. Because it wasn't many people realize with our challenge in 1965—the congressmen from Mississippi—that we were able to gather fifteen thousand pages of evidence and they still there and the same kind of challenge had been done almost a hundred years ago and they succeeded. But in 1966, Adam Clayton Powell was unseated and he hadn't done any more than any congressman there, the only difference: he was a black man. We got to tell the truth even in these institutions because there's one thing about it, folks—you elderly folks my age is almost hopeless—you got to know now that the children know what's going on and you not going to be able to fool them any longer.

Before I close, I would just like to say that I believe in God and He said He would raise up a nation that would obey Him. So the young people that's out here today, that's fighting for justice for all human beings, I believe are the chosen people that's going to lead this country out if it's not too late.

I have one announcement and then I'll close, the community club of the Third World Development starts March the eighteenth at seven a.m., St. Francis House.

These are the young people that some of you sponsored, that made it possible for us to have today 680 acres of land. Are enabling us to determine some of our destiny. And is enabling us to stand up as human beings. Not to try to take the state of Mississippi, because tonight I figure if the state of Mississippi would become 100 percent black, I would be on my way out. But to make it a state where all human beings will have a chance.

And as I close I would like for you to take a look in the mirror and ask yourself—as we have paid such a big price—ask yourself: "Must I be carried to the sky on flowery beds of ease while others fight to win the prize and sail through bloody seas?" Thank you.

"Is It Too Late?,"

Speech Delivered at Tougaloo College, Tougaloo, Mississippi, Summer 1971

When Fannie Lou Hamer spoke at Tougaloo College in 1971, she was follow-ing in a long line of modern civil rights advocates—from Robert F. Kennedy to Stokely Carmichael—who had addressed this private historically black liberal arts college tucked away on the northern edge of Jackson, Mississippi. This was not her first address to the school where her long-time political ally Reverend Ed-win King served as chaplain, and where student activists such as Anne Moody first became involved with the civil rights struggle. Throughout the 1950s and 1960s, Tougaloo College became a hub of civil rights movement activity—its politically active students led demonstrations against discrimination in Missis-sippi's capital city, and civil rights workers like Bob Moses and James Lawson came to campus to offer workshops on nonviolence and voter registration. At the end of the decade, moreover, the school recognized Mrs. Hamer's contribution to the movement with an honorary degree.

In this particular speech, Hamer carries a message of both hope and convic-tion. She acknowledges her charge—"to attempt to deal with question and the topic of 'Is It Too Late?'"—to which she ultimately responds that it is, in fact, not too late; "there is still time for America to change." To do so, however, re-quires grappling with a host of pressing problems. In a relatively short speech, Hamer assesses the nation's health by considering such controversial and emo-tionally charged topics as the war in Vietnam, birth control, race riots, and the assassination of political figures. Her consideration of each of these concerns is both connected to, and simultaneously dwarfed by, her advocacy of black male leadership.

While she proposes collaboration between the sexes, designating a special sec-tion of her message for her "black brothers and sisters," Hamer also unabashedly places black women in a subordinate position with regard to curing the societal ills she explicates. This aspect of her address undoubtedly surprised some of her auditors at the time and certainly holds the potential to startle contemporary readers. Her remarks with regard to gender relations can be better understood, however, in light of such contextual factors as the 1965 release of The Negro Family: The Case for National Action. *In what became known as the "Moynihan Report," Senator Daniel Patrick Moynihan argued that the destruction of the black family was the primary impediment to the black race's progress in both the economic and political arenas. Furthermore, he reasoned that the matriarchal structure of the black nuclear family was at the core of black men's inability to function as leaders in their communities. Although Hamer virulently contested Senator Moynihan's assertions, exclaiming elsewhere that "you know that Moynihan who wrote about black matriarchal society knows as much about a black family as a horse knows about New Year's," she also acknowledged the dearth of male leadership in black communities by the late 1960s, and she sought to rectify that deficiency through her insistent promotion of black men. So, while Hamer disagreed with Moynihan's assessment of the cause of black male inaction, she shared his concern for the effects of such inaction and, thus, she would commonly tailor her addresses to encourage a more engaged role for men in the black community. Hamer's speech conveys her faith that greater involvement of black men would not only benefit black communities, but that the "salvation of the nation" lies in their hands as well.*

* * *

I am here tonight to express my views and to attempt to deal with question and the topic of "Is It Too Late?"

First, as a black woman, fifty-four years of age, a mother and a wife, I know some of the suffering and the pain mothers must feel for their children when they have to face a cruel world both at home and abroad.

In the streets of America, my home and land where my fathers died, land of my family's pride, I have taken a stand for human rights and civil rights not just for my sake, but for all mankind.

I was born and raised in a segregated society, beaten for trying to act like all people should have a right to act, denied access to the ballot until I was fifty years old, but things are a little better now. God is in the plan; He has sounded the trumpet and have called the march to order. God is on the throne today; He is keeping watch on this nation and marking time.

It's not too late—there is still time for America to change. God have delayed destruction on this nation to test the hearts and the consciousness of us all. Believe me there is still time.

The war in Vietnam must be ended so our men and boys can come home—so mothers can stop crying, wives can feel secure, and children can learn strength. Because in men, the strength of this nation lies.

I am a woman, strong as any woman my age and size normally, but I am no man. I can think, but I am still a woman and I am a mother, as are most women. I can carry the message, but the burdens of the nation and the world must be shouldered by men. Decisions concerning life, comfort, and security must finally rest in the hands of men. Women can be strength for men, women can help with the decision making, but men will ultimately take the action.

The methods used to take human lives, such as abortion, the pill, the ring, et cetera, amounts to genocide. I believe that legal abortion is legal murder and the use of pills and rings to prevent God's will is a great sin.

As I take inventory of the past ten years, I see the many tragedies of this nation: Medgar Evers's death in my state, John Kennedy, Malcolm X, Martin Luther King, Jr., Robert Kennedy, and more recently Jo-Etha Collier in Drew, Mississippi, and countless of thousands in Vietnam and in the streets of our larger cities and towns. For these sins this country should pray, because we have been spared a little longer. Miles of paper and film cannot record the many injustices this nation has been guilty of, but there is still time.

Maybe if all of the ministers in this nation—black and white—would stand up tonight and say, "Come, earth's people, it is not too late. God have given us time!" Perhaps we could speed up the day when all men can feel as I do. I am not afraid tonight. Freedom is in my soul and love is in my heart.

While here tonight, I have a special message to my black brothers and sisters. As we move forward in our quest for progress and success, we must not be guilty of misleading our people. We must not allow our eagerness to participate to lead us to accept second-class citizenship, and inferior positions in the name of integration—too many have given their lives to end this evil. So stand up, black men, this nation needs you, mothers need you. In your hands may lie the salvation of this nation.

The Bible tells us that a good name is rather to be chosen than great riches, love and favor rather than silver and gold. I call upon all men and women to stand up with pride and dignity, but especially black men.

"Nobody's Free Until Everybody's Free,"

Speech Delivered at the Founding of the National Women's Political Caucus,
Washington, D.C., July 10, 1971

As the 1960s drew to a close, black women and white women were both in-
spired and disenchanted by the movements for social change that surrounded
them. Their experiences within civil rights, Black Power, and newly formed stu-
dent organizations reinvigorated the centuries-long struggle for gender equality.
Though the inception of both black women's and white women's movements for
social change have been traced to the period between late 1967 and early 1968,
and while many of the movements' initial leaders had worked alongside one
another in the earlier part of the struggle for black freedom, black women's and
white women's particular life experiences informed their respective demands and
belied an unconditional unity. Nevertheless, the radical way in which women of
all races sought to reconfigure relations between the sexes as the basis of a more
egalitarian society contributed greatly to the larger climate of social change.

Core aspects of the women's liberation movements in their varied instanti-
ations—black, white, middle-class, revolutionary, reform-oriented, young, and
old—did not sit well with Hamer. Because the second wave of feminism flowed
from the civil rights movement of the 1950s and 1960s, Hamer's background
could have secured her a prominent position of leadership among the ranks of
the 1970s feminists. To assume such a post, though, would have meant making
ideological compromises to fit within the confines of popular belief systems that
did not comport with Hamer's lived experience. Specifically, Hamer objected to
many feminists' one-dimensional view of relations between the sexes; she took
issue with feminist stances on birth control and other aspects of reproductive
rights; and she argued that the banner of sisterhood belied significant racial and
class tensions between and among women. To be clear, she was neither anti-
feminist nor against coalition building between women. What Hamer fought
against was an over-eager and all-too-simple push for unity amidst difference.
To Hamer, difference had always mattered, and now the differences she saw

between herself and various strands of feminism functioned not necessarily as impenetrable impasses, but certainly as vital issues that demanded attention before collaboration could ensue.

Hamer gives voice to these and other seemingly divergent concerns at the founding meeting of the National Women's Political Caucus. Her speech clearly acknowledges the momentous occasion—Hamer enlists the Book of Esther to convey the significance of being present "for such a time as this." She also pays tribute to white women who recently "woke up" to myriad instantiations of white male patriarchal oppression, and to black women in Mississippi who "started the ball rolling" with regard to civil rights activism. Pushing past the conventional components of the address, Hamer's speech also reflects her ability to connect a wide array of issues back to a common theme. She moves from marking the historic occasion and celebrating the accomplishments of women to harnessing their political strength for causes beyond their immediate gendered purview. Hamer speaks out about the war in Vietnam, malnutrition in Mississippi, and the "dope" pandemic ensnaring the nation's youth, all the while challenging her audience to recognize the strength of their coalition in a manner that empowers more widespread change.

*   *   *

Thank you very much. It's a great pleasure for me to be here today for the National Women's Political Caucus. And listening to different speakers, I've thought about if they've had problems, then they should be black in Mississippi for a spell.

Now we've had it and we're not going to stand idly by and let the same thing keep happening in Mississippi that has happened in the past. That's one of the reasons for the organizing of the Mississippi Freedom Democratic Party in the state of Mississippi. And when one of the speakers talked about how the white male rulers of this country would be coming to talk to women, you wouldn't believe the hell that I've gone through in the state of Mississippi. The white politician, male, is also bringing cards to my house. One man wrote me a letter and told me if I would just support him he would do in the future what he has done in the past. And I said, "That's the very reason don't look for my support."

Now, we talk about the liberation movement—that of the white women in this country have known for years that they aren't free. But for so many of them it was a rude awakening, a few years ago when they woke up, and found out that not only were they not free, but that they had a whole lot of problems not like mine, but similar to mine. But somehow we're going to have to bridge the gap.

And I'm not fighting to liberate myself from the black man in the South because, so help me, God, he's had as many and more severer problems than I've had. Because not only has he been stripped of the right to be a politician, but he has been stripped of the dignity and the heritage and all the things that any citizen of a country needs.

As I stand here today my mind goes back to the problems that we have had in the past. And I think about the Constitution of the United States that says, "with the people, for the people, and by the people." And every time I hear it now I just double over laughing because it's not true; it hasn't been true. But we are going to make it true—this business, "with a handful, for a handful, by a handful."

But if women had more power in this country we wouldn't have the young people dying in Vietnam that we have dying there today. We wouldn't have the young people dying in the United States that we have today. Because I think about, it wasn't too long ago at Kent College in Ohio that kids were shot down because they wanted a taste of peace and freedom in this country. And then I think about not long after that, we had the same problem at Jackson State College, and two kids were shot down. And I have the mother with me today of a young girl that was coming out of high school in Drew, Mississippi—there's a lot of us [mothers] in this building today—because of so much racism and hate, as this young girl walked away from school, from the commencement exercise, holding her diploma to her chest, she was shot down.

Now, something has got to break in this country. We have got to have some changes and we can't keep standing around waiting for the white male, because that's what we are saying. We talk about the percentage of women in office, but we don't have too many blacks in office either.

Now, we've got to have some changes in this country. And not only changes for the black man, and not only changes for the black woman, but the changes we have to have in this country are going to be for liberation of all people— because nobody's free until everybody's free. And as I wage the fight in the South, and as I move across the country in helping political people get in office, and as I look at the South and I think about the kind of things that have gone on in the South—right after I voiced my opinion about what had happened to Jo-Etha, the insurance was canceled on my house. On the twenty-eighth of January 1971—not '61, people—after all of the working and all of the trials and all the tribulations that we've had in Mississippi, on January 28, 1971, my house was bombed.

You know, I couldn't say today that I'm fighting for equal rights. I don't want it. I've passed equal rights and I'm fighting for human rights, not only for the black man, for the red man, but for the white man and for all the people of this country. Because America is sick and man is on the critical list.

When people can make decisions and don't even pay us any attention—not only the black people of this country, but the white people of this country also—when people can just walk out, when one man becomes so powerful that we have the kind of war that we have going on today, and as many people as are getting killed in an undeclared war, we might think that we are doing something, but we are on our way out.

And that's the reason, folks, not only will I be running for senator this year, but I will also be running for the United States seat of a senator next year. Because we plan to bring some changes in the South. And as we bring changes in the South, the northern white politician won't have any excuse and nowhere to hide. Because what we have today is up-South and down-South. The politicians in the South will shoot us in the face, and if you are a minority you'll get shot in the back when you turn around anywhere in the North.

So, women, honey—this hasn't just started. I heard one of the speakers talking about Congressman Emanuel Celler. I never will forget one time I almost split my sides talking to this man. I had gone to him asking him for support. This was the time we was trying to get support to silence the representatives from the state of Mississippi. And he made it very clear to me that what he'd done was the Voting Rights Act in 1965. I said, "Well, Congressman Celler, if this meant something, we wouldn't have to have a Voting Rights Act in 1965 because we were guaranteed that right almost a hundred years ago." I said, "What I'm saying is, if you support me now—" So, just as he was fixing to throw me out of his house, because that's where I was, as he was planning to throw me out of his house, we had petitions from people in his district—thousands of signatures on these petitions that supported me. And when he saw this and saw that I had support from his district, you should have seen his changing and becoming a very intelligent man. So, this is the kind of power that we have to deal with.

But we're going to bring a change. And you know, I don't look for television coverage because any time I get out and start stating facts, you can see them doing this [indicating]: cut her off now, because she's going to tell too much.

But you know, a house divided against itself cannot stand and a nation divided against itself cannot stand. And that's what we have today, people: a divided, sick nation. We're always talking about how strong we are. But, you know, I think it's so utterly ridiculous that people can spend billions of dollars to send a man to the moon to pick up a few rocks to carry them around the country to pass out—passing out those rocks, and he could get plenty of them down there in Mississippi. I think then you know it's time for change. If we can pick up rocks, so help me, God, and let children die from malnutrition and not getting the proper health care, and not getting anything that children need throughout the country.

And if we talk about minority groups—somebody's trying to fool us, you know, to make you think that because we are a minority, then there's just no power there. But if you think about hooking up with all these women of all different colors and all the minority hooking on with the majority of women of voting strength in this country, we would become one hell of a majority. And this is something that should have been done for a long time because a white mother is no different from a black mother. The only thing is they haven't had as many problems. But we cry the same tears and under the skin it's the same kind of red blood.

So, as this congresswoman spoke from New York, talking about the things that we have to have, she doesn't have to worry about me because we are going to be fighting in the South. And it was women that made what little progress we have had. It was women in Mississippi that really started the ball rolling.

And one of the things that I can't say yet, whether I'm a Republican or a Democrat, I went to a meeting a few Sundays ago in Jackson and people there were pledging their loyalty to the Democratic Party. I refused because I said the Democratic Party hasn't been loyal to me at all. So, I'm going to be running as an Independent.

We have to have changes. And we can't wait too long. The longer we wait, the more problems we are going to have. And I do know in this audience there must be some people here that talk about not wanting our kids to go to school together. But I want to know something—the problem we are having in this country today with all of these kids, they're getting hung up on the same thing and that's dope. We've got to think about that, people, because these young people are just about ready to write us off. Because the things that you have taught them, they see in reality are not true. So, we're going to have to work together.

But if I've done all that I could in the past fifty-four years to help bring a change and to help make this country a better place to live, then I'm concerned now when the white man asks me for my vote in the South, because he says we do need some changes. I'm going to say, "If you want to see this, you can support me because I'm going to be the next one running, baby." These are the kind of changes that we need throughout the country because when women team up together we can do a whole lot of things.

And going back to what Congressman Celler said and to the Bible, it brings up the Book of Esther in the Bible. And by her being there at the right time, at the right place, married to the right cat, she was able to save her people that would have been destroyed. So, I'll close by saying one of the things that her uncle told her when he told her to look out: "They might get me, but you're one of us too."

So, I'm saying to you today, "Who knows but that I have cometh to the kingdom for such a time as this." Thank you.

"If the Name of the Game Is Survive, Survive,"

Speech Delivered in Ruleville, Mississippi, September 27, 1971

As voting rights laws evolved after passage of the 1965 Voting Rights Act, many blacks in the South entered the world of electoral politics, especially in areas where blacks outnumbered whites. Considering that she was a woman who marked her entry into civil rights activism on the single issue of voting, it was no surprise to find Fannie Lou Hamer running for elected office in 1971; it would prove to be her third and final attempt. Based on the encouragement of Charles Evers, Medgar Evers's older brother, and the continued injustices she witnessed in her own community, Hamer ran for the Mississippi Senate as an Independent against two-term Democratic incumbent Robert Crook. Twelve other local black candidates ran as a slate called the Concerned Citizens of Sunflower County to Elect Black Officials (CCSCEBO).

Hamer ran a spirited campaign despite little money, crisscrossing the state with out-of-town national figures such as Betty Friedan as well as more regional SNCC friends such as John Lewis and Julian Bond. Hamer was also known to travel with Gussie Mae Love, the mother of Jo-Etha Collier, who had been gunned down on May 25, 1971, in front of a Drew, Mississippi, grocery store by three drunken white men. Collier had been celebrating her high school gradua-tion, which had taken place just hours earlier, when she was fatally shot in the back of the neck.

None of the thirteen candidates comprising the CCSCEBO won their races, including Hamer, who was defeated by Crook, 11,770 to 7,201. Even in her home-town of Ruleville, Hamer lost badly, 720 to 434. White turnout proved to be very high as many locals feared what might happen should a black governing coalition control Sunflower County politics. Hamer and others also cited voter fraud and voter intimidation to account for the seemingly lopsided loss. Across the state, even though whites beat blacks in 259 out of 309 races, blacks now held 145 elected positions—more than any other Deep South state.

Hamer spoke very rarely from a manuscript, but before a Ruleville audience in late September, she relied on written remarks—which we've represented below with all their original emphases—to convey a righteous anger, but also the hopes of an interracial future. Long an admirer of Malcolm X, Hamer borrows from one of the Muslim militant's favorite alliterations: "the ballot or the bullet." Racism would be dealt with by "men and government" or by "men and guns," and while Hamer favored the former, she did not believe that nonviolence was the only way; in her house were several loaded weapons—which she and her family knew how to use. Like Dr. King, Hamer glimpsed a future of racial harmony, but one premised on blacks and whites working together at the most local of levels; it was also premised on whites aiding blacks in economic development. This latter point is underscored by Hamer's reference to James Forman's "Black Manifesto," a controversial reparation plan aimed at white churches to the tune of $500 million. While Hamer lent her name to the manifesto when it was made public in May 1969, its Marxist-inflected discourse conflicted with her own deeply Christian sensibilities. Even so, confronting Christians with their own hypocrisies was very much in keeping with Hamer's longstanding critique of the church—black and white.

*   *   *

I expect a drastic change to occur in this country, particularly in the Deep South, as blacks become more aware of the importance of entering into politics and developing the skills necessary to find the solutions to the problems of "mass confusion." I believe there will be more interest generated for politics at the grassroot level by the everyday kind of people who lost confidence in the *democratic process* because of corrupt politicians and their desires to perpetuate themselves in office while causing the "masses to suffer."

I would not advise blacks in the South to migrate to the North to change their situation. As a believer in God, I keep struggling with the belief that the situation in the South CAN and MUST be changed as more and more blacks become registered voters; and as more and more blacks become registered voters the "old line white racist politician" will begin to feel uncomfortable, because he will feel threatened at the thought of *Black Power*.

I consider the state of Georgia to be the most advanced in the area of politics. Here we have a deep southern state with more black members in its state legislature than there were blacks in the United States Congress. Too many of the so-called liberal northern states are second to the state of Georgia, particularly the city of Atlanta, Georgia. However, in my opinion, race relations in the Deep South have not improved to any great degree.

Some people, it seem, will never change. Why just a few months ago in the state of Mississippi, a young high school girl, who attended a white high school in Drew, Mississippi, was shot down as she stood looking at her hard-earned diploma a few hours after her graduation. She was a child who completed the first step toward the American way of "survival." Of course I will agree with the late Dr. Martin Luther King's "nonviolent approach" in some cases, but in other cases, one has to take a more militant approach and I am not referring to turning the other cheek.

The new militancy on the part of blacks and many young whites have caused, not only in the Deep South but the North as well, to realize that racism is an unnecessary evil which must be dealt with by "men and governments" or by "men and guns." If survival is to be the name of the game, then men and governments must not move just to postpone violent confrontations, but seek ways and means of channeling legitimate discontentment into creative and progressive action for change.

Politics will occupy the attention of the nation in the '70s as the black man makes his reentry into the political arena. Step by step he will achieve many victories as we have seen in our northern big cities. While this is important, I believe that the key to real progress and the survival of all men, not just the black man, must begin at the local, county, and state levels of governments. While politics will not cure all of our ills, it is the first step toward erecting a representative and a responsive government that will deal with the basic needs.

Land, too, is important in the '70s and beyond, as we move toward our ultimate goal of total freedom. Because of my belief in land reform, I have taken steps of acquiring land through cooperative ownership. In this manner, no individual has title to, or complete use of, the land. The concept of *total individual ownership* of huge acreages of land, by individuals, is at the base of our struggle for survival. In order for any people or nation to survive, land is necessary. However, individual ownership of land should not exceed the amount necessary to make a living. Cooperative ownership of land opens the door to many opportunities for group development of economic enterprises, which develop the total community, rather than create monopolies that monopolize the resources of a community.

Community living and group decision making is local self-government. It is this type of community self-government that has been lost over the decades and thus created decay in our poor rural areas in the South and our northern ghettos. This is what we have seen played back to us time and time again, first as peaceful demonstrations, and most recently in the form of violence and riots. If this nation is to survive we must return to the concept of local self-government with everyone participating to the maximum degree possible. This is not to say, however, that we should not have a strong national or federal government, because these branches too must be responsive to the needs of all local and state governments through true representation of all men and women who have *total commitment* to a true *democratic process*.

As the black politicians return to the scene of politics from years of deprivation, he must bring these Democratic principles because the "white racist politicians," in his effort to control the minds of the blacks and poor communities, have lost these principles. So it seem to me that the salvation of this nation, in more ways than one, rest in the hands of the Almighty God and the *black striving politicians* attempting to save His people and thus free the world.

Economically, the black community is crippled, mainly because of noncapital. The black community does not have access to small business loans, local credits from banks in any sufficient amount and/or private or individual grants. This is due solely to the fact that the black community have been powerless, and not only "not represented," but in many instances, "misrepresented." If the black community is to thrive economically there must be more unity and honest leadership by the black appointed and elected officials. I have high hopes in the young peoples of this nation, both black and white, because I believe that they are concerned that their children live free from the grandfather clause, which said that unless your grandfather was rich and powerful you must be a slave to the grandsons of those who were powerful.

In the near future, the South will be a much better place to live than any place in the North. There is already a move on the part of the blacks, who migrated to the North during the "milk and honey era," to return to the South. Many of these blacks have acquired professional and technical training, which will be of a great asset to the black community as they seek to develop economically. Of course the economic development of the South will depend largely upon the speed with which *real communication and race relations* develop. The black community must depend to a large degree on the white community and the presently established institutions for the resources necessary to establish black community-based business enterprises. The white community must see this development as an attempt to put the black man on his feet: for example, several blacks have recently demanded large sums of money from the white churches. This demand was called the "Black Manifesto," which in essence says that the church owe to black development capital to be used as "seed money."

Since the church for hundreds of years have collected these large sums of money and used them for literally nothing, hopefully some of the demands will be met and the necessary "seed money" will be obtained. As this economic development is taking place, black economic leadership must be developed. The black community must have trained economic heroes as it has black political heroes. *These men MUST must know economic.* They must have the vision to plan ahead for ten to twenty years at a time, so that as the black community grows, its economic enterprises will also be adequate. But until communication and race relations improve and the total community becomes united, then we will not see a real change in the South. However, at the rate race relations and communities are improving, many of us will be long gone before complete progress in this area has been made.

As did Dr. Martin Luther King, I too have a dream that one day our children will live together, both black and white, and not be ashamed to look each other in the face as human beings. God has blessed the black man to endure more than three hundred years of suffering and today he stands at the crossroads of the greatest period in American history, not as a slave, but as a man claiming full rights to all privileges to which this nation has to offer, having made his contribution to every stage of development that this country has had. The history of this period will record those valuable contributions, those successes, and those failures, and yes, our struggle to survive.

I do not know what President Abraham Lincoln had in his mind when he said that "all men were created equal," with certain inalienable rights, but to me it simply meant that we all have a right to a decent life.

Seconding Speech for the Nomination of Frances Farenthold, Delivered at the 1972 Democratic National Convention, Miami Beach, Florida, July 13, 1972

By all medical rights, Fannie Lou Hamer should not have been in Miami Beach, Florida, in July 1972. But at the behest of her political friends and allies, and by virtue of being elected as a delegate, Hamer traveled to the Democratic National Convention; it would be her last appearance before the quadrennial gathering. Hamer was increasingly burdened by failing health, and her speaking appearances dwindled, even as her stature locally, regionally, and nationally was coveted.

Hamer's health took a turn for the worse in early January 1972, when she collapsed from "nervous exhaustion" as she walked a picket line near her home. She eventually retreated to a hospital in Nashville to escape the onslaught of visitors at her hospital room in the all-black community of Mound Bayou. For the next seven months she convalesced, venturing out only to receive an honorary degree at Howard University and to attend the Democratic National Convention.

For her many admirers and political supporters in the Delta, the timing of her illness could not have been worse: Hamer had promised to run in 1972 against the long-time incumbent, archsegregationist, her frequent rhetorical foil, and resident of Sunflower County, Senator James O. Eastland, in the Democratic primary. While Hamer would have most likely lost the race, her campaign speeches would have been a damning indictment of eighty-plus years of Jim Crow white supremacy, Mississippi style. No doubt her campaign would have also attracted a large national press following. Instead, Hamer was largely confined to bed rest in Ruleville where hypertension, diabetes, and depression wore her down.

Hamer's one "speech" we recovered from this period is not much of a speech at all; rather, it's a blessing, a seconding vice presidential nomination for Texas's Frances "Sissy" Farenthold. While Hamer, and many others, would have much preferred the candidacy of Shirley Chisholm, the first black woman to ever run for the presidency, Chisolm was not willing to have her name placed on a ticket with George McGovern. Ever the stalwart, Hamer labored to the podium to second the nomination of Farenthold, instead. It was a final eloquent and embodied gesture by a woman who knew more than most what it meant to have a "place" in the national body politic.

*   *   *

MR. LOPEZ: Fellow Democrats, amigos, my name is David Lopez, a Chicano, a union member, and a delegate from the state of Texas, a state whose citizens believe in social justice and have learned to make their tacos with cauliflower instead of lettuce.

A great American wanted to precede me to this microphone tonight to second the nomination of Sissy Farenthold, but though her heart is strong, her body has temporarily given her a little trouble. I refer to that courageous Democrat from the state of Mississippi, Fannie Lou Hamer.

Let me read to you what she wanted to say. "This has been a good week for all Americans. This week the people, the people of our country, have been represented here by their own kind—other people just like them. Many of us have worked for many years for this week. Now I ask you to make it all very real. Help to be born tonight a new America. It is struggling to be born. Help it. Vote for my fellow southerner and a fine human being, Sissy Farenthold of Texas."

That, fellow Democrats, is a message from Fannie Lou Hamer.

MRS. HAMER: Madam Chairman, fellow Democrats, and sister Democrats, I am not here to make a speech, but just giving support and seconding the nomination of Sissy Farenthold for vice president. If she was good enough for Shirley Chisholm, then she is good enough for Fannie Lou Hamer. Thank you.

Interview with Fannie Lou Hamer by Dr. Neil McMillen, April 14, 1972, and January 25, 1973, Ruleville, Mississippi; Oral History Program, University of Southern Mississippi

Of the many interviews Hamer gave during the last fifteen years of her life, this oral history interview—conducted by Dr. Neil McMillen, professor of history at the University of Southern Mississippi—is distinctive. While several newspapers and magazines published interviews with Hamer throughout the 1960s, by the early 1970s the nation's gaze followed the civil rights workers out of the Mississippi Delta and toward urban centers where race riots and antiwar rallies raged. This shift in focus left many Americans in the dark about the local work Hamer continued to do in her community. Most regrettably, information about her Freedom Farm Cooperative, which secured food, shelter, and jobs for the Delta's poor, is not widely known. McMillen's two-part interview with Hamer, conducted at her Ruleville home in April of 1972 and January of 1973, helps fill this gap in knowledge about Hamer's local activism with her own commentary about Freedom Farm, in addition to the school integration and voting rights struggles she continued to wage.

The later period in Hamer's activist career, during which this particular interview occurred, is also significant, as the lapsed time imbues Hamer's memories of her most well-known struggles and popularized experiences with additional perspective. McMillen prompts Hamer to reflect upon the Mississippi Freedom Democratic Party's 1964 challenge, their subsequent relationship to the Loyalist delegation, the 1972 Democratic National Convention, her trip to Africa, and much more. Through the process of sharing these memories, Hamer explores her past and present relationships with local and national politicians as well as civil rights leaders; and, in so doing, she fashions an aperture through which to view the alterations in her activist ideology over time.

*   *   *

Part I

McMILLEN: Mrs. Hamer, why don't we begin with something about your childhood life? Where were you born and what was your life like when you were a little girl?

HAMER: Well, I was born fifty-four years ago on a plantation in the hills, the kind of place that's something similar to Hattiesburg, the place where you are from. In fact I was the last child of twenty children, six girls and fourteen boys. I'm the twentieth child of a very poor family, sharecroppers [who] never had anything—family life, didn't hardly have food to eat. My family moved to Sunflower County when I was two years old; that's fifty-two years ago they moved here to Sunflower County, so I was mostly raised here in the Delta. In fact, from two years old up until now I've been in the Delta. My family moved here, and we moved on a plantation; the landowner was named Mr. E. W. Brandon. So we lived on his place until I was grown, but it was just hard. Life was very hard; we never hardly had enough to eat; we didn't have clothes to wear. We had to work real hard, because I started working when I was about six years old. I didn't have a chance to go to school too much, because school would only last about four months at the time when I was a kid going to school. Most of the time we didn't have clothes to wear to that; and then if any work would come up that we would have to do, the parents would take us out of the school to cut stalks and burn stalks or work in dead lands or things like that. It was just really tough as a kid when I was a child.

McMILLEN: What subjects did you like when you were in school, Mrs. Hamer?

HAMER: I loved reading when I was in school. When I was a child, I loved to read. In fact, I learned to read real well when I was going to school. I never had a chance to go to school too long—about six years—but I believe I can compete today with a kid now that's twelfth grade at least.

McMILLEN: So how did you spend your life then from when you were finished with your six years of school?

HAMER: Well, that was just in and out of school—in and out of school, until I was grown. I'd just have some months I'd be in school and some I wouldn't.

McMILLEN: Then you worked, of course?

HAMER: Yes.

McMILLEN: Did you work in the fields?

HAMER: Yes, I worked in the fields. In fact, all the kids around in this Delta worked in the fields. Wasn't no other work to do. They didn't have no such thing as factories; these factories are something new. They didn't have any factories; wasn't nothing to do but fieldwork. That's all you had to do, though. This time of year, well, when there was no cotton to chop, we would be raking corn stalks or doing something like this. But there was never, never a time in April that kids would be in school when I was a kid—never a time that a kid would be in school in April.

McMILLEN: Of course not at all in the summer.

HAMER: Not at all in the summer. But they worked because there was much more work to do at that time than there is now because they don't let the people work in the fields now. But at that time you didn't get nothing for it, but you could work steady, because when the cotton got up big enough to chop, you—we called it "hoeing the cotton," because it wasn't chopping— after you hoed the cotton about two or three times, then you would call what they called chopping because it wouldn't be bad then. We would just go over it from three to four, sometimes five times. I remember during the time I was a kid, and since I've been grown, some people would be in the front with the hoe chopping cotton, and the other people would be behind them in about a week with a sack picking cotton. They just worked from one season to the other one. There wasn't no such thing as a period where they had a lapse between there. They just chopped cotton, chopped cotton, over and over. When they'd go over it one time, if they finished up about Monday, sometimes they'd have a week out, and then they'd be right back in the field and go over that cotton again. They would keep doing that, and then when time came to harvest the crops, there wouldn't be grass and stuff in it. They could pick it, and it would be clean because it wouldn't be like it is now; they use chemicals and all that. But they didn't use chemicals then; people used hoes to clean that cotton out.

McMILLEN: Let's move forward in time, Mrs. Hamer. When was the first time you really wanted to vote?

HAMER: That was 1962.

McMILLEN: Tell us about your efforts to vote.

HAMER: Well, I didn't know anything about voting; I didn't know anything about registering to vote. One night I went to the church. They had a mass meeting. And I went to the church, and they talked about how it was our right, that we could register and vote. They were talking about we could vote out people that we didn't want in office, we thought that wasn't right, that we could vote them out. That sounded interesting enough to me that

I wanted to try it. I had never heard, until 1962, that black people could register and vote.

McMILLEN: Never heard that in your life?

HAMER: I'd never heard that; we hadn't heard anything about registering to vote because when you see this flat land in here, when the people would get out of the fields if they had a radio, they'd be too tired to play it. So we didn't know what was going on in the rest of the state, even, much less in other places.

McMILLEN: When you were a child at school, did the books you have say anything about voting or democracy?

HAMER: Never! I'd never even heard that that was in the constitution. I never heard anything about it. In fact, the first time I was aware that Mississippi had a constitution was when I tried to register to vote, and they gave me a section of the constitution of Mississippi to write, to copy, and then to give a reasonable interpretation of it. I didn't know that we had that right.

McMILLEN: When you were growing up, did you know about politics nationally? Like, would you know who the president was? Were you in touch with [that]?

HAMER: We would hear about the president, but it was kind of far-fetched from us. I remember one president, looked like he kind of stands out was President Franklin Delano Roosevelt, was a president that kind of stands out. I remember him putting people on jobs they called WPA and all that, when I was a kid.

McMILLEN: Did you think of him as a friend of the black people when you were growing up? This would be in the Depression.

HAMER: Well, I kind of thought it from my parents—I'd hear my father talking about—and I'd hear him talk about, sometimes, Republicans and Democrats, but I didn't know, wasn't aware too much of what it meant.

McMILLEN: When you first tried to vote, where was that? Was that in Ruleville?

HAMER: When I first tried to register?

McMILLEN: Yes, ma'am.

HAMER: Well, when I first tried to register it was in Indianola. I went to Indianola on the thirty-first of August in 1962; that was to try to register. When we got there—there was eighteen of us went that day—so when we got there, there were people there with guns and just a lot of strange-looking people to us. We went on in the circuit clerk's office, and he asked us what did we want; and we told him what we wanted. We wanted to try to register. He told us that all of us would have to get out of there except two. So I was one of the two persons that remained inside, to try to register, [with] another young man named Mr. Ernest Davis. We stayed in to take the literacy test. So the registrar gave me the sixteenth section of the constitution of Mississippi. He pointed it out in the book and told me to look at it and then copy it down just like I saw it in the book: put a period where a period was supposed to be, a comma and all of that. After I copied it down, he told me right below that to give a real reasonable interpretation then, interpret what I had read. That was impossible. I had tried to give it, but I didn't even know what it meant, much less to interpret it.

McMILLEN: Lawyers don't know what it means.

HAMER: Well, I didn't know.

McMILLEN: So what happened then? You were arrested, weren't you?

HAMER: Well, when we got started back to Ruleville, we were stopped by a state highway patrolman and the city police, and they ordered us to get off of the bus. We got off of the bus, and then they told us to get back on the bus and go back to Indianola. We got back on the bus and we went back to Indianola. When we got back to Indianola, they arrested one of the men that was with us, which was Mr. Lawrence Guyot. They arrested him, and then they told this man who'd drove us down there that his bus had too much yellow on it. They fined him a hundred dollars, but they finally cut his fine down to thirty dollars. We got enough to pay his fine and come on into Ruleville.

McMILLEN: But you didn't spend time in jail that time?

HAMER: I didn't go to jail even, that time. We just went back. It was just one of the people arrested and that was the man that was with us.

McMILLEN: Now let's go back a little bit to when you first heard about voting. Was that Mr. Robert Moses and the Student Nonviolent Coordinating Committee people?

HAMER: That's right.

McMILLEN: I see. He [Moses] was there in person, that's where you [met him]?

HAMER: I was with them on the bus the day that we went down to register.

McMILLEN: With Robert Moses?

HAMER: That's right.

McMILLEN: Now when you heard about it first, though, in the schoolhouse back before you tried to register, when you first heard about voting—

HAMER: At the church?

McMILLEN: Yes, at church. Did you hear it from Robert Moses?

HAMER: I heard it from Robert Moses and another man named Jim Forman. He was from the Student Nonviolent Coordinating Committee. He told us that we had a right. There was another man from CORE, Congress of Racial Equality, and his name was David Dennis. All of them talked about it that night, and after they talked about it, it just made enough sense to me that I wanted to try it.

McMILLEN: Did he tell you it might be dangerous in Mississippi to try to vote?

HAMER: They didn't tell us that it might be dangerous.

McMILLEN: Did you think it was dangerous that first time you tried?

HAMER: I had a feeling that—I don't know why, but I just had a feeling because the morning I left home to go down to register I carried some extra shoes and a bag because I said, "If I'm arrested or anything, I'll have some extra shoes to put on." So I had a feeling something might happen; I just didn't know. I didn't know it was going to be as much involved as it finally was. But I had a feeling that we might be arrested.

McMILLEN: What happened when you got back? Did anything at all happen? Did you lose your home?

HAMER: Well, when we got back I went on out to where I had been staying for eighteen years, and the landowner had talked to my husband and told him I had to leave the place. My little girl, the child that I raised, met me and told me that the landowner was mad and I might have to leave. So during the time that my husband was talking about it, I was back in the house. The landowner drove up and asked him had I made it back. He [my husband] told him I had. I got up and walked out on the porch, and he [told] me did Pap tell me what he said. I told him, "He did." He said, "Well, I mean that, you'll have to go down and withdraw your registration, or you'll have to leave this place."

I didn't recall myself saying nothing smart, but I couldn't understand it. I answered the only way I could and told him that I didn't go down there to register for him; I went down there to register for myself. This seemed like it made him madder when I told him that.

McMILLEN: So you had to leave right away?

HAMER: I had to leave that same night.

McMILLEN: Your husband stayed on to finish the crop?

HAMER: He stayed on because he [landowner] told him the next morning that if he left he wouldn't give us any of our belongings. But if he'd help him harvest the crop, well, he'd give us the rest of our things.

McMILLEN: Had this planter been fair to you before, or not?

HAMER: Not too fair, that's one of the reasons it was important to me to try to register, because he hadn't been fair. Now we had worked on that—I had worked on that place for eighteen years. My husband was there before I went there. We had worked awhile with his father, but his father seemed to have been a better man than the son.

McMILLEN: What kind of work did you do on that plantation?

HAMER: Well, I was a timekeeper and then a sharecropper, too.

McMILLEN: Where did you go then, Mrs. Hamer, after you had to leave the house on the plantation?

HAMER: I came out here to town, right across from the main highway, and I started staying with some people, Mr. and Mrs. Tucker. Then my husband got frightened and carried me to my niece's. And after he carried me there, then they shot in that house that I was staying with those people—they shot in that house.

McMILLEN: The Tuckers' house?

HAMER: In the Tuckers' house.

McMILLEN: So you were turned down then; your registration effort failed?

HAMER: It failed.

McMILLEN: When did it finally succeed?

HAMER: Well, after coming back to Ruleville, I went to Tallahatchie County and stayed awhile. After my husband got so frightened, I went to Tallahatchie County and stayed awhile. When I came back, we moved here in Ruleville to 626 East Lafayette Street. We moved in on the third of December, and I went back on the fourth of December to take the literacy test again.

McMILLEN: Nineteen sixty-two?

HAMER: Nineteen sixty-two, on the fourth of December. That was one Monday. And the registrar gave me another section of the constitution, was the forty-ninth section of the constitution of Mississippi, dealing with the house of representatives. He told me to copy that down and to give a reasonable interpretation. I copied that, but we had got hold of the constitution of Mississippi and had been able to study it. Some of the people from the Student Nonviolent Coordinating Committee would help us to try to interpret it, so that time I gave a reasonable enough interpretation. When I went back to see about it in January, I had passed that literacy test. So I didn't take the test but twice.

McMILLEN: I see. So then you voted. When did you first vote?

HAMER: Well, the first attempt that I tried to vote I didn't really get to vote. I went up to vote—that was in a primary election because it was in August. We went up to vote that day, and I didn't have two poll tax receipts. I hadn't been paying poll tax, and I didn't have two prior years. They told me I couldn't vote because I didn't have two poll tax receipts.

McMILLEN: So you couldn't vote that time. When did you finally cast your vote?

HAMER: The first vote I cast, I cast my first vote for myself, because I was running for Congress. The first vote, I voted for myself.

McMILLEN: Oh, is that right? That was what year?

HAMER: That was in 1964.

McMILLEN: And who were you running against?

HAMER: Jamie Whitten.

McMILLEN: Jamie Whitten, 1964. When did you get involved actively in the civil rights movement, other than simply trying to vote? When did you become a civil rights worker?

HAMER: Well, all of that went together, because as soon as I was fired from that plantation, I started right away then working on voter registration. It just kind of materialized together. I didn't have anything else to do.

McMILLEN: Did you work for SNCC?

HAMER: I worked for SNCC. In fact, I worked not only for SNCC, I worked for COFO, Council of Federated Organizations, so all organizations were together. But I was first hired to work for SNCC.

McMILLEN: And that was ten dollars a week if they had ten dollars?

HAMER: If they had the money; that's right.

McMILLEN: Did SNCC often have the ten dollars?

HAMER: Not when I first started.

McMILLEN: How did you SNCC fieldworkers survive with so little money?

HAMER: Well, it was really survive, because so many times we didn't have nothing. A few friends would help kind of tide us over; and this man I was talking about you doing an interview with him, he was like a real father to me, because they would try to keep our gas bills and important bills paid.

McMILLEN: His name was?

HAMER: Mr. Amzie Moore.

McMILLEN: Mr. Amzie Moore. Talk about your activities as a voter registration worker in the early period.

HAMER: Well, it was rough because we would go to places, go in to do voter registration in places, and we talked to people. We would walk the streets in different little areas, and we would tell them we were coming back the next day. And by the next day somebody would be done got to them, and they wouldn't want to talk with us, and this kind of stuff. Some days it would be disgusting, some very disappointing. Some very disappointing. Then we'd go to churches, and occasionally along, they was burning up churches. These are the kinds of things we faced.

McMILLEN: Who would get to the people you talked to?

HAMER: Well, you know, like the landowners. The white people would get to them, and then they would tell them. We would work on them with food, too. We were trying to get people to get commodities; all of that went together, because at that point it was really rough.

McMILLEN: What about the Citizens' Council? What activity did they pursue to prevent you from voter registration, or weren't they active then?

HAMER: Well, they was active. Of course, we couldn't tell what group was doing what. We just knew we would be harassed, and we knew cars would be passing the house loaded with white men, and trucks would be passing there with guns hanging up in the back. They would walk the streets sometimes with dogs. And we knew it was something, but we didn't know what group it was.

McMILLEN: You didn't really have much luck in those early years of voter registration, did you?

HAMER: No, it was really rough.

McMILLEN: How many people do you think you carried down to register?

HAMER: Not too many, but it was a few that would go. We carried some down, and then they would be pressured, and they'd go back and withdraw theirs. Occasionally along we [would] carry some down that would refuse to go. And they made a kind of what I would say was an example of those of us that did say we weren't going back. We were punished to the fullest to keep other people disgusted, to keep them from going.

McMILLEN: Who felt freest to go among the black people, was it the old people or the young people or the self-employed?

HAMER: Well, in this area it was more people my age than it was young people. It's always, the movement in this area has always been grown people. We've never had a strong movement with youngsters here and still don't have. The folks mostly that go out in the front are older people.

McMILLEN: Why do you think that's so?

HAMER: I really don't know, but from the beginning of the movement here, like Brother Joe McDonald, he's dead now, and Mr. Herman Sisson, Mrs. Hattie Sisson, Mrs. Joe McDonald; all of them was elderly people. They're older than I am, but they were the ones that stood up in the front and stood there. People like Brother Joe McDonald stood there until he died, with all kinds of pressure, because the night they shot in the Tuckers', they shot in his house and the Sissons', too. Two girls were shot that night at the Sissons' house, but they stood their ground. And it was older people.

McMILLEN: I didn't expect that; I thought mostly it was the very young.

HAMER: No, young people worked with us, the SNCC workers. But all the work [that] was going on was carried out by grown people in this area.

McMILLEN: Were most all of the SNCC workers in those early years black, or were there some white SNCC workers?

HAMER: At the beginning they was all black. Then the whites began to come in, so it was blacks and whites.

McMILLEN: You've mentioned COFO. We associate COFO with the Freedom Summer, but COFO actually got started before then, didn't it?

HAMER: It did. It got started before then.

McMILLEN: Do you know anything about the origin of COFO and how it got started and when it did?

HAMER: Well, I don't know exactly when it got started, what time it got started, but I know it was organizations like the Student Nonviolent Coordinating Committee and the NAACP and the Congress of Racial Equality that decided to get together and form COFO as an umbrella for all of the organizations; so it just wouldn't be in one name. At that point SNCC was doing most of the work anyway.

McMILLEN: Usually, COFO was SNCC.

HAMER: That's right; that's right.

McMILLEN: It's been said that most or many SNCC workers, and many COFO workers, too, thought that the Justice Department under Bobby Kennedy was going to offer protection for civil rights workers and voting rights workers. Did you have that understanding, that the people from the Justice Department would keep the white police and the Klansmen and the Council people away and offer protection during your voting rights efforts?

HAMER: I thought that, but we never did get no protection. You know, we would file suits when people would be harassed to go to jail. We'd go in the court and all of that, but nobody was never really—but the FBI. I guess you know about them, too. That was the only people they would send in [to] investigate something, after something been done happened.

McMILLEN: I know about the FBI, but for the record, was the FBI the friend of the black people, or would you say they were more the friend of the white establishment?

HAMER: I feel like they were more of a friend to the white establishment than they were to the black people. I still feel that way.

McMILLEN: You still feel that way. But originally, you thought as a voter worker that Justice would offer some support or some help and that John Doar or Mr. Marshall—

HAMER: Yes, in fact, we'd get in touch with the Justice Department, Mr. John Doar, and the attorney general at that time was Senator Kennedy. I really believed that—I believed with all my heart—that they would protect you. Until a certain length of time. So much went on that nothing was done about, and I had a kind of little leery feeling: would they really protect us or not? But that didn't stop us from doing what we felt that we had to do.

McMILLEN: Yes. Among yourselves, how did you explain the reluctance of the federal government to come in and support you in your efforts to get your rights of a citizen of the United States?

HAMER: Well, we would just talk about it among ourselves, and some of them would finally just give up on it and say there wasn't nothing going to be done. That's when I've seen a lot of people, black young people and white young people, become disgusted and disillusioned with the whole setup, you know. They said, "There ain't nobody going to do nothing," and all of that.

McMILLEN: Yes. What about Freedom Summer? What were you doing during the summer of 1964? What was your activity like? Just talk generally about that summer in Mississippi.

HAMER: Well, that was doing the same thing, voter registration and having mass meetings trying to get more people involved and bringing more people out—adults, because at that time, there was no such thing as the eighteen-year-old vote. We were trying to get as many adults as we could to register as possible. And that's what we worked on mostly that whole summer: voter registration and getting as many people as we could involved.

McMILLEN: You had Freedom Schools, too?

HAMER: Yes.

McMILLEN: What did you do in the Freedom Schools?

HAMER: Well, they'd teach because there were lot of people that couldn't [read]. I didn't go much to the schools because I was out on the road most of the time, going to mass meetings in different areas and different places. Like they'd want me to come from place to place to speak, and that's what I was doing.

McMILLEN: Yes, but Freedom Schools taught about the constitution and about citizenship and voting?

HAMER: That's right.

McMILLEN: They had community centers, too, didn't they?

HAMER: That's right; they had community centers, and some of the white kids, and the blacks, was teaching in these Freedom Schools and holding citizenship education classes because in this Delta it's a high rate of illiteracy. It's a lot of people still here that can't read and write.

McMILLEN: Did you know Andrew Goodman or Michael Schwerner or James Chaney?

HAMER: I knew Michael Schwerner and James Chaney real well. I didn't know Andy as well as I knew Mickey and James Chaney.

McMILLEN: Did you see them shortly before they were killed?

HAMER: I had been to Meridian to go to a meeting that they invited me to a couple of weeks before they went to Oxford, Ohio.

McMILLEN: Let's rest a minute.

Part II

McMILLEN: Mrs. Hamer, let's begin with your trip to Africa. How many trips have you made, and what did you do in Africa?

HAMER: Just one. You know, I had never been out of the states in my life, and after the convention in 1964 we needed rest. It was people like Harry Belafonte, and I don't know who else was involved, who supported [us] making it possible for eleven of us to go to Africa. Just to see Africa and try to—we had learned and heard so many things about Africa. I wasn't sure whether I would be frightened or what, because what little we had read about Africa was just wild. We didn't know really; we really didn't know that they were our people. Although we realized they were our ancestors, we didn't know how they act. So to get to Africa, we stopped [at]—I think it was Dakar. We got on a Ghanaian flight, and went to Conakry, Guinea. And it was—I had never seen a black stewardess on a plane. When I saw a man come out of the cockpit who was black, right away then this meant that it was going to be different from what I had been [used to], what had been taught to me. It was something different. Well, when we got to the airport there stood President Sékou Touré, and they had a delegation to welcome us there. After we had got situated where we were staying [as] guests of the government—after we got—everybody got a bath and changed, the government was there, and the president was there in less than an hour after we got there. It was just remarkable.

I saw some of the most intelligent people, you know, because I had never in my life seen where black people were running banks. I had never seen nobody behind a counter in a bank. I had never seen nobody black running the government in my life. So, it was quite a revelation to me. I was really learning something for the first time. Because then I could feel myself never, ever being ashamed of my ancestors and my background. I learned a lot. It taught me a lot while I was there. Because the welcome, and even the shame that we have here in this country, they don't have it there. In performing and all that kind of stuff, we have been made to feel ashamed of so many things that they're not. And it's not unclean, it's just innocent people, you know, just pure innocence, and people almost as true as our little children. Because that's just about the truest thing that we have in this country at this time is little children. [They] don't tell tales. If they think you're ugly, they'll tell you. And if they think you've made a mistake, kids speak out. It was this kind of—well, it was real honesty.

McMILLEN: Natural.

HAMER: Natural, just being their real selves and not having to pretend to be somebody else. And that was really beautiful to me.

McMILLEN: I'll bet it was a very emotional experience for you.

HAMER: It was, I felt sometimes, you know—well, we would go in at night because they had a two weeks' program at what they called a promenade, or something like that, and we would go in and sit down. Then when the president would come in at night to seal this friendship, whether it was a man or woman, you know, he'd kiss them on each side; kiss them on one side and then kiss them on the other side. If a man would kiss a man here, you would hear all kinds [of things], but they pay it no attention. I really was proud to see that kind of honesty in men sealing the friendship of men, you know.

And I just thought that Sékou Touré was one of the most fascinating guys I've ever met. When he was talking—I couldn't understand French. But Bob Moses and also Jim Forman were steady translating, and we could understand what they were saying. The whole thing, when I would go out where we call the rural area here—we'd go out there and there was always something that we had in common. Africa to me, before I left, was like going on Greasy Street in Ruleville.

McMILLEN: Is that right?

HAMER: You know just like—

McMILLEN: You were at home?

HAMER: Yes. You know, it was just like—I got friends over there and I could argue with them and we didn't know what each other was talking about! But you know we could communicate. And I loved it; I really loved every bit of it. But one thing I thought about while I was there. I thought about just like I'm living here in the United States, some of my people could have been left and are living there. And I can't understand them and they don't know me and I don't know them because all we had was taken away from us. And I become kind of angry; I felt the anger of why this had to happen to us. We were so stripped and robbed of our background; we wind up with nothing. You know, because after we got here we were in a sense neither white nor black and that put us in the center of being Negroes. We just don't know anymore about ourselves than the names that the slave owners gave us, and you know that was a real crime.

McMILLEN: So, you have no notion of what part of Africa you came from?

HAMER: Don't know any part of it. I knew that my mother—my grandmother was a slave. But I don't know any parts of Africa. But this don't mean now, what I'm saying, that if I ever get a chance that I'm going back to Africa. I'm going to stay in this country because I'm a part of this country. But I just think that somewhere along the line it would have been a nice thing if they had made slaves out of us, but still kept up with this background of ours. Because you can't ever tell, Miss Gentz over there could have come from a king, a family that was a king in Africa. And that was the part that I felt a little upset about, that here I had people somewhere there and might have been my real people. I had a guest visit me once from Sierra Leone, Africa, and she just kept pointing out that "you act just like my mother, you act just like my mother," and it's something about it binds you.

McMILLEN: If you don't want to stay, you certainly wouldn't mind going there again for a visit.

HAMER: I've always wanted to go back. It's like I'm visiting some of my people, and it is my people.

McMILLEN: It is. What did the people in Africa that you met, your new friends there, what did they know about the United States, and what did they think about the United States?

HAMER: Not much of nothing, because them translating—they're talking the language that they were talking—it was as though everything was okay in the United States; that we was happy and didn't have any problems. Another thing that I saw there, I saw a book—now that was 1964—and this book had Bob Moses and another man sitting at a counter, and that was showing how the South had progressed in integration. You wouldn't believe it, see, people be brainwashed there. I'm not kidding, they be brainwashed there like we've been brainwashed here.

McMILLEN: So the people in Africa don't know how things are?

HAMER: They didn't. They don't know it, and they were running up and show-ing us this picture. And when Bob Moses saw that picture, you know, he was just mad enough to just—it made him very angry. Because at that time you know how it was.

McMILLEN: I do.

HAMER: You know how it was in 1964. Though last night I kind of—couldn't hardly believe it—I went to a parent and teachers' conference last night. And there was a large-size group of whites, right in the middle of Central High—a black principal—there sitting down together. It showed that it can be done. And it was small children there, and it was grown children there, and the parents was out there last night. So, I do know if this country, if they would just, you know, if they would leave the kids alone it would be a lot better. It would be a lot better. These kids have got to be taught to hate!

McMILLEN: Like in Memphis. The children are not permitted to go to their new schools. They like their new schools, but the other children can't, their parents won't let them.

HAMER: And there are always going to be a few of those standing out there and say, "That's right and I'm not going to do any different." Just like it is here at Ruleville schools. Now, I'm not saying that everybody around Ru-leville and Sunflower County goes to Ruleville schools, but it's quite a few parents that's there and was with their kids last night. They had sent this letter out for all the parents to come, and teachers were going to meet, to have a conference, to ask questions, to visit their rooms, talk to the teach-ers. And I think that was really good.

McMILLEN: What has happened in the Ruleville schools? Have most of the white children—

HAMER: Left.

McMILLEN: They've left and been—

HAMER: Most of them have left.

McMILLEN: Are some coming back now?

HAMER: Some, I believe, are coming back. I hadn't seen, I've never seen that many parents, white parents, at a PTA meeting.

McMILLEN: What went on at this PTA meeting?

HAMER: Well, they had a speaker that wasn't so hot. He was an army guy. One of the things that maybe, that I wouldn't say was so hot, I don't think too much about the army. I think we've done a lot of things that we didn't have to do. And he made a speech, he made a talk, and he showed a film. After that—they had a sergeant—some of the black teachers and the black principal, they, you know, got up and said something. But the guy just wasn't no speaker; he wasn't no speaker at all!

McMILLEN: What questions did the white parents have about the school?

HAMER: Well, what had happened: after the conference was over last night, then they asked you to go with your child—each to where his teacher was. And you had a chance to go, and here was a black teacher and a white teacher. And you had a chance to talk face to face with the teacher about your own child. Then the one program—the oldest little girl of mine down there is kind of slow. I think what really happened, right at the time she needed me most I was on the road a lot. And it's just not like, leaving a child is not like having somebody there to steady be with him. So, she was slow, but she has moved—she's in a Distar program, but she's not retarded. She was just slow because there wasn't nobody at home to do too much teaching. And they were telling me and I looked at her progress report— now, she went there, you know, and she didn't know how to spell her name, or none of that kind of stuff, and she's moved now to the top two. They've got five levels, and she's at the top now, and they said they hoped they could keep her next year, but they might put her in the public part and she wouldn't be in this Distar. But I actually believe it would have been good if a lot of other children had gone through that Distar program. But they really teach those kids something.

McMILLEN: Now, what is this Distar?

HAMER: It's called Distar, D-I-S-T-A-R, Distar. And you know, there's three teachers with not a lot of children, and they just have the time, the courage, and patience, and they've got time to deal with those kids.

McMILLEN: So they can really do something?

HAMER: They can do something and this little girl now sits up and reads the things coming on television, and she knows all these letters, and she's good in her arithmetic. They just said that she was very good in her arithmetic.

McMILLEN: How does she like *Sesame Street*? Does she watch that?

HAMER: She watches *Sesame Street*, but it was a long time before we could get *Sesame Street*. And after it got to Jackson—see, people in this area can't get *Sesame Street* unless they're on a cable and everybody don't have the cable. But *Sesame Street* is a very good program.

McMILLEN: We've had trouble with my little four-year-old. He wouldn't sit still long enough to watch it until the last couple of months. But I think he objects to being tricked into learning. You know, he's there to be entertained and then all of a sudden they teach him how to spell or they teach him numbers and he wonders if that's right!

HAMER: Yes, most kids pick up these kind of things. But I think *Sesame Street* is one of the best programs they've ever had on television. I really think so.

McMILLEN: Let's go back a little bit to the Credentials Committee in 1964. You testified.

HAMER: Yes.

McMILLEN: What, in essence, did you tell the Credentials Committee? Could you sort of summarize what your testimony was?

HAMER: Well, the whole thing was around what had happened to me when I tried to register. The whole thing, that's what it was about. The whole speech was centered around me trying to register and what had happened to me after I tried. That's what I was talking about.

McMILLEN: And you told me in an earlier interview and there's several interviews, one with Miss Ponder, I believe—

HAMER: Yes.

McMILLEN: And that's basically what you told—

HAMER: That's what it was.

McMILLEN: I see.

HAMER: When I testified—

McMILLEN: There's no point in our going into that more. Why didn't you accept what Dr. King and A. Philip Randolph and Hubert Humphrey and everybody else wanted you to accept? Why didn't you accept those two seats?

HAMER: Well, to me—you know, it might sound funny and strange, but to me that wasn't nothing!

McMILLEN: I agree with you.

HAMER: You know it wasn't nothing; and that's the beginning of my learning of politics. Now, I learned politics at its fullest—well, that's where politics was in 1964 in Atlantic City, New Jersey. I will never forget what they put us through. You see, by me being a Mississippi housewife and never exposed to politics, or nothing else too much, because I was just a housewife, a farmer, and they couldn't understand why that we had to—we didn't feel like that we had to take other people's word. So, they first began to kind of drill us on this when they told us, you know, that Dr. King—now Dr. King, this was funny, too, because at first he had said that what we were doing was right and he'd help us carry it out. But it began to be pressure brought about on different people, you know. Like President Johnson, I would hear them talking about all of this big funeral of his, but I'll never forget him either. Because the time I was testifying, it was a man there, very close, that told me that he said to get—told them people with the cameras "to get that goddamn television off them niggers from Mississippi" and put it back on the convention, because, see, the world was hearing too much.

McMILLEN: Did Johnson say it?

HAMER: President Lyndon Baines Johnson. I've got a book somewhere here on it. But it was somebody very close that knew what was going on that said he said, "Take them cameras off"—see because, I found out after then women and men from over the country wept when I was testifying—because when I testified, I was crying too. But anyway after that time, I think the president became very angry, especially with the black delegation, and a lot of the stuff they covered up. But we've been victimized so much that we didn't watch what was going on. So, they carried me to one meeting and at this meeting they told me if we didn't compromise for the two votes at-large, that the vice president—see, Johnson had put Humphrey on the spot and told him that if he couldn't calm us down then he wouldn't let him be his running mate for vice president. This is the kind of politics we were exposed to. Then they had a big meeting of everybody else except us in Mississippi and just decided they were going to tell us what to do. And when we came back to this church, at this meeting at this church, they were saying what Dr. King, James Forman, Roy Wilkins, and it was other big people, and Senator Humphrey.

McMILLEN: Randolph?

HAMER: Yes, and Bayard Rustin. And I says, "I don't know nothing about them people." But we felt that we had a right—as it was us, as it was our own delegation, and the delegation was from Mississippi—we had a right to make our own decisions. Not them! They couldn't understand it when we rebelled and we refused, you know, because if we got two votes at-large we didn't have nothing.

McMILLEN: Of course. It wasn't a compromise at all.

HAMER: It was just nothing. So, we almost fought there at one time. Because I told Dr. Henry, if he didn't tell them that we wasn't going to accept no compromise, I, you know, would do something to him. So, he come on out—and he didn't have no other choice because the sixty-eight of us, you know, including him and myself, was just mad enough that we weren't going to let them do us like that, and I felt better.

McMILLEN: Yes, what was Dr. Henry's position first? Was he inclined to compromise?

HAMER: Yes, Dr. Henry—after, you see, they couldn't handle me, they got Dr. Henry and Reverend Edwin King. And they were going to accept this. They were going [to go] out there and accept it!

MᴄMILLEN: King was willing to accept it, too?

HAMER: Yes.

MᴄMILLEN: Edwin King?

HAMER: That's right. You know, I looked in 1972 at that National Democratic Convention in Miami, Florida. I was very disgusted. I felt disgusted because the people they had pulled in with the Loyal Democrats don't know what suffering is and don't know what politics is about. This is the new group of people. Because, you see, right now the best thing that could happen in the state of Mississippi is the Freedom Democratic Party, and in some areas, they do have it—like Holmes County. They have the Freedom Democratic Party. But it's the only solution that's going to do anything for us in the South. And that's not only blacks, that's blacks and whites. Because it's the kind of politics that's going to be clean, and, you see, this country is not ready for that.

MᴄMILLEN: Yes. What about the Loyalist faction now? You think they're just too white-oriented or too willing to compromise?

HAMER: Really, honest to God, when I was at that convention, in that fall, in Miami, Florida, all I watched was the Regulars who had been replaced with another group of 99 percent white—because I watched it. I watched the whole thing and I, you know, I say, "Well, I've been sick so I could be imagining things." So, then I called Representative Clark. I said, "Representative Clark, I would like to know what you think, really honest to goodness, about this convention. If I'm suspecting something, I'm just, being just, if my mind is making me think that I see what I'm seeing."

He said, "You're not telling no lie!" He said, "This is their convention." And I watched. It was Watkins, it was Hodding Carter, it was Jan Watkins and her husband, and Hodding Carter. I watched the whole thing and then before they left when they had the conference it was just, had been orientated into another thing. So, at first, I really couldn't understand Cleve's positions, but Cleve McDowell—

MᴄMILLEN: Cleve McDowell?

HAMER: Yes. I couldn't understand his position, but now that I know where he stands I respect him so much.

MᴄMILLEN: He's a Regular Democrat, isn't he?

HAMER: Yes, I respect him so much. Because if you're not ruled by one, you're ruled by the other one. And, if you noticed there wasn't any black people had nothing to say at that convention from Mississippi. Hodding Carter made one of these big, flamboyant speeches. Well, I like Hodding. And then I just watch how they run the show, and they might not really be doing this intentionally. But it's there!

McMILLEN: Why did they organize the Loyalist Party in the first place?

HAMER: I think the whole thing was to break down the Freedom Democratic Party, because we had a certain position, you know. From the beginning it was organized with grassroots folks. We was against the war; we was against everything that we thought wasn't right. And for this reason they're making and passing that resolution that they had to seat somebody in 1968. Well, again, this was the thing that hung up in between there, you know. Because it's never been really represented right. When we went to Chicago in 1968 for that convention, I told Charles Evers that, number one, Charles Evers wasn't here to do none of it. Charles Evers rode to fame on his brother's name. But anyway, in 1964 when we went to that convention and didn't accept that compromise, they have to have something to do all they could to crush the Freedom Democratic Party. So, when they went back in 1968 it would look more decent. So, out of that comes the Loyal Democrats. And I mean they talked to me as though I wasn't in the first founding of the real political thing. And they told me that if I made any kind of speeches up there that don't speak for the Loyalists, speak for the Freedom Democratic Party—and I'm telling you—

McMILLEN: That's in 1968?

HAMER: That was in 1968. I'm telling you some things I heard from Watkins and some of those people that was up there was really sickening to me. So, I can't just have the love for the Loyal Democrats that I have always— whatever, if it's just a splinter of the Freedom Democratic Party, I'll always be there. It's something that was bringing clean politics with people, and that's what I think we need. We've had bad politics too long, and it's a lot— you know, it's a lot of young people now want something different, and that's what we was about.

McMILLEN: Yes. Do you think that Hodding Carter and—what's his name— Earl Watkins and the other whites involved in the Loyalist Party were just afraid that the MFDP would become like the Panther Party in Lowndes County, Alabama?

HAMER: No, I don't think that they thought that, but I think they thought that it would be too much recognition for a bunch of niggers. So, why not step on the bandwagon and take it over. You know what I'm saying? That's what I think that was about. Because, you know, I'm not the kind that—and I'm going to whale on about this—not the kind what would have just kept going alone and by ourselves. It would have had to have been other people. So, this wouldn't have been a Black Panther Party; this would have been a real political force.

McMILLEN: Would you have accepted whites into it?

HAMER: Certainly!

McMILLEN: So, it wasn't racial exclusiveness?

HAMER: No, it wasn't racial exclusive because we tried to include poor blacks and whites and any other body that was really concerned about real changes. Because, you see, to have a real change, we can't do the same thing that they've done in the past, right? So, it would have to be a change from that. But that's what I've seen as far as the Loyalists. I went to this convention, I observed, I looked at it, and I talked to other blacks in Mississippi, from Jackson; it was the same kind of exclusion that it had been in the past, only it was the Loyalists. But they had their own thing going on. There just wasn't enough of our folks speaking out. Because you see, when we went to Chicago they give the white 50 percent of the delegation. The white wasn't over 10 or 15 percent. I said, "Now, I don't mind giving the whites what they got, but don't give them over what they got," I said, "because they never give us nothing. So, if they have 10 percent of this delegation, set that 10 percent, and let that other 90 percent that was black go on up there." But see, this would have been too much. Like the schools when they call them integrated and have five whites and two thousand blacks. That's not integrated, you know. So that's what it's about. That's what the Loyalist was about.

McMILLEN: Have you, do you think, a lot of black voters feel that way, that they just don't want to integrate?

HAMER: Well, a whole lot of them don't even know.

McMILLEN: I see.

HAMER: You know, there's a lot—you know, I think about sometimes that we're so far, some of us, ahead of people in Mississippi, of knowing what's going on and being there and seeing the change made. If you weren't there sometimes you just wouldn't figure out what was happening.

McMILLEN: Yes. You wouldn't know. What about voter registration? Can black people go down to the courthouse in Clarksdale—

HAMER: Indianola.

McMILLEN: In your case, Indianola, can they go down without fear to register today?

HAMER: They can go down. But the thing about it is so sad, they ordered us— we had, you know, thousands of people on the books—but they ordered us to reregister. Now we've got to go from scratch. See, this is the thing that's disgusting and disillusioning, you know, the people. Now, he'll question, "Why do I have to register?"

MCMILLEN: Did that affect how many blacks ended up on the rolls? Did you lose a lot of black voters?

HAMER: We've got to register voters. We don't have many now. All of this has happened since you were here before. A reregistration!

MCMILLEN: You have to just start all over?

HAMER: Start all over again.

MCMILLEN: No federal registrars?

HAMER: No federal registrars. I talked with this guy Barry from the Justice Department, and I finally told him I wasn't looking for them to help me, not from Nixon's administration, and I wasn't. So, we've got that to start over again.

MCMILLEN: Now, Dr. Henry told me about a court case, that was started in Clarksdale, that got a court order that all blacks had to go back on the books who'd been registered before. That doesn't apply to Sunflower County?

HAMER: Well, it hasn't. I'll get in touch with Dr. Henry and find out, so maybe all of our names will be put back on there.

MCMILLEN: He's under the impression that this court case would apply, and he thought that after this court case had come up and had been decided that most of the blacks finally got back on the rolls. But that's not true in Sunflower?

HAMER: No. You know, they said that we could vote in November, but if [you] hadn't voted, after November in [the] same length of time, then you couldn't vote in 1973 unless we had reregistered. So, I'm going to check this out because if that is true where we won't have to reregister it would mean a whole lot to us; because I just don't see all these people, some of this they went through before, they ain't going to do it again.

MCMILLEN: Yes, it's a great hardship.

HAMER: Yes, it is. You're going to Indianola, and thousands of people ain't got nothing to do. So, how do you get down there? And they had them here, they put the books in Ruleville for awhile, but the majority of the people that live out in the rural area didn't even know that folks was registered in town. So, we just missed it.

MCMILLEN: They didn't advertise it?

HAMER: It was advertised, like people go up there in a store and you would see, saying, "You can register in so and so many days." The average person passing that sign didn't see it.

MCMILLEN: Yes, people just didn't know—

HAMER: That's right.

MCMILLEN: —to reregister. Well. But do planters tell their black hands, "Don't register." Do they say that anymore?

HAMER: I don't think they tell them that anymore. I really don't think they tell them that.

McMILLEN: People aren't afraid then?

HAMER: They're not afraid. They're really not afraid—not of the landowners telling them that now. I haven't heard nothing like that in a long time.

McMILLEN: Nobody gets arrested or shot at or things like that?

HAMER: No, that hasn't happened in a long time. It's been quite a while. They're having a school trouble up at Drew.

McMILLEN: Yes. What about white officials who manipulate the black voter? Do whites take advantage of illiterate blacks in the polling booths?

HAMER: They do!

McMILLEN: How does that work?

HAMER: So help me they do!

McMILLEN: Well, how does it work?

HAMER: Like some of the kids that we had poll watching have seen them just taking ballots, stuffing them, where there wasn't a machine, just stuff them in the box when they came out. There is just no way in the world that you can handle [that].

McMILLEN: This is evidence that things have changed in Mississippi—the fact that blacks aren't intimidated anymore when they try to register.

HAMER: No, they're not intimidated.

McMILLEN: How else have they changed in the last, well, seven or eight years? You've seen incredible changes, I think.

HAMER: I've seen incredible change, some of it, some people really are trying to make the change. Some of them is rats, thoroughbred rats, would do the same thing they done in 1964 or '63. But they've got sense enough to realize what power means, and they've got sense enough to know that people can move them with the vote. That means make them act sometime what they really are not. You know, I've seen some of the fishiest things happen in the past two years in this town that I've ever seen. But the guy, when you meet him, he's got a big smile on him and you just think he's almost a saint. But you know he's doing some tricky things. And that's the kind of stuff; they're doing a lot of.

McMILLEN: People haven't changed their minds, they've just changed their outward behavior. Is that it?

HAMER: That's right, that's right. Now, I've seen, with some people, I've seen the change. I never will forget, there's one man in this town was about as worse as anybody I've ever met. And he changed. Now, I couldn't say that for a bunch of them, but I watched that man change.

McMILLEN: What about the Citizens' Council? Is it active anymore?

HAMER: It's probably active because right up there on the highway, on forty-nine, they've got a Mecca. Of course it's been almost burned down. And I was just laughing one day, we were going up the highway, and I said that's funny, they didn't allow no black folks around then and they might get a black cook, but you couldn't get nothing about as far as going in that place. But the other day they had black folks repairing the place. What it means, regardless of what they do or how they act, we really need each other. You know, a lot of folks say, "I can make it without them." We got to have each other and they know that, but they hate to admit it. They hate to think to themselves that they need us. But you know, if some of us wasn't in that black school, you know, that integrated school they call it, they couldn't get all the federal money. So, they need us. That's what happens.

It's not all these people, it's some of them—well, there's some I didn't even know about have wished me well through the whole fight. Like a guy came here and he was sick—and that's been about a year ago—but anyway, my husband had to help him up the steps, an old man. And he came to the table on Christmas Day, and he thanked me for what I was doing, said he really appreciated what I was doing. Well, you wouldn't have looked for that from a man that old. Then later on he stopped and asked me did I read *Reader's Digest* and I told him I did. He said, "Well, you know, I'm having a year's subscription mailed." Now, he's saying what he feels. He appreciated me doing what he was afraid to do. There ain't no telling how many sleepless nights he slept not wanting things to be like they had been all the time. So, that's the price for freedom, too. He is not free until I am free.

McMILLEN: It liberates both.

HAMER: Yes, as I liberate myself, I liberate him.

McMILLEN: Yes, I see. What about local officials? Are there black local officials now in Ruleville?

HAMER: Yes, and I have to give them credit for this. Now, that's one thing, we've got a real change in the police officials. You know that, don't you [speaking to another person present]? Because some of this time I think I might react different to the way they act. I don't think at this point they could be any better, because brutality is really not in Ruleville. You don't have that! And if something or other comes up, most of the time, whether it's a young black or a young white, they have gone to such extremes, they can expect something, but the kind of beating and all that kind of stuff, they don't have any of it.

McMILLEN: The law enforcement has changed, then.

HAMER: It's changed a whole lot!

McMILLEN: What about the highway patrol, do they mistreat blacks nowadays? They did at Jackson State a couple of years ago, I think.

HAMER: Well, not to my knowing in this Delta area. Somebody else might know it and I not know about it. But they haven't, you know, hit nobody or nothing like that.

McMILLEN: Yes. What about county supervisors? Are there county supervisors in Sunflower County who are black?

HAMER: No, we don't have no black supervisors, but we did have people in that last election to run against the supervisors. One white guy that ran for supervisor in the county, he wasn't in this district, but he is like we've never had before as a supervisor, especially white. He moved the real machine. Now, this is what I'm talking about, working together with clean politics, how you can change. I worked under the cover with this guy and talked to local blacks because I couldn't vote for him. But I knew he was a decent guy, and he's done more than has been done in this county with all the other supervisors. He's got black people in the shop, on the road, and some in every place where you've never seen blacks. So that's the change.

McMILLEN: What's making the change? Is it the fact that now there are black voters?

HAMER: Yes, I think that's part, is black voters. Then sometimes a person who is decent will come out and want to run. That's what happened in that case. He was decent and he still is decent. But that's the kind of politics I'm talking about that we need—clean politics. Because most of these people have been exposed to the machine that had never done nothing but be crooked to keep you going. That's just what I call dirty politics.

McMILLEN: Did you support Charles Evers when he ran for the governorship?

HAMER: Yes.

McMILLEN: You think he would have been a good governor?

HAMER: I believe—I hope he would. I hope Charles Evers would have been.

McMILLEN: You can't ever tell because he didn't win.

HAMER: No, you can't ever tell. No, you can't ever tell.

McMILLEN: Do you know anything about his mayorship in Fayette, has he been a good mayor? Or don't you know?

HAMER: I don't really know too much about it. Now, some people have come to me and said he's done extremely well. Some people have come to me and said he was a rat. I'm too far really to know the day-to-day, daily basis of how he operates as a mayor. Now, I can say one thing, I don't think there's no other mayor has brought any more industry into a place like that as

Charles Evers has brought. So, you couldn't say he was 100 percent bad. Because he has provided jobs for the amount of people there that no other mayor has provided. So, you couldn't say that's bad.

McMILLEN: What are you doing today in the civil rights movement? Are you still active in the civil rights movement in a formal sense?

HAMER: Well, I guess so because I still—well, I move around speaking and working with the little co-op here.

McMILLEN: Tell me about the co-op, how did that get started, and what are its goals, and what does it really do?

HAMER: Well, the co-op, really—I was the founder of that co-op in 1969 about—

McMILLEN: What is it called?

HAMER: Freedom Farms.

McMILLEN: Freedom Farms.

HAMER: So, I went to—well, I had been going around a lot of areas and folks just not having enough to get food stamps and all of this kind of stuff. We just thought if we had land to grow some stuff on, then it would be a help to us. Because living on the farm, on some plantation, they still don't give you a place to grow stuff. So we founded Freedom Farms in 1969. We go, in February, we got some money, just donations, to put an option on forty acres of land.

McMILLEN: Was this from northern people?

HAMER: The northern people, that's right. Well, Madison Measure for Measure, a small organization out of Madison, Wisconsin, raised enough money for us to put the option on the land. And then another guy who works in Nashville now, at Vanderbilt, a young guy named Lester Salamon, I called him and told him about the tight and the jam that we were in, and he ran an ad in a paper at Harvard in Cambridge, Massachusetts. So, he ran that article and in about a week they had raised about nineteen hundred dollars. So, we got the option on the land, and we started, and we saw that it was going to be a success. Then in 1970 or 1971, we put another down payment, eighty-five thousand dollars, on 640 acres, so we grow vegetables.

McMILLEN: How many acres do you have all together now?

HAMER: Well, it's 640 and 40—680 acres. It's in the 700s I imagine because we bought some [for] cash and didn't have no payments on it. So, that's our cost [inaudible]. But that's not ours, now, but we bought it, you know, Freedom Farms did buy it. So, what we've done is—a lot of this neighborhood, we just—there was a man, before he died, told his wife that he wanted black folks to have his land. She followed through with it. We put options all out there for real nitty-gritty folks, and that's this housing part, 95 percent of the houses. Freedom Farms put the option there and then the people got the loan.

McMILLEN: What do you mean put the option, how does that work?

HAMER: All right, like they was going to sell a lot, and this lot was going to be 65 by 120. Well, to hold that lot in your name to keep somebody else from buying it, you put a hundred dollars on it and then you protected your lot until you could go through a loan and see could you get it. We done that, and as a result, we got a lot of people out of these shacks in the rural areas before they cut off this housing money for lower income families here the other week. This whole thing, we got in this area here and then back behind the schoolhouse, I think we put about twenty-nine hundred dollars over there for options. Then we instated this pig bank program, and we grow our own pork and we grow our own vegetables, you know, like butter beans, peas, okra, potatoes, peanuts, and then cash crops.

McMILLEN: How many families are involved in Freedom Farms?

HAMER: Well, I would believe it's over a couple of thousand people that's involved here. Because the people up there on the other end benefit more than them in Ruleville do because it's really worse up there. It's a funny thing that if you don't speak out ain't nobody going to speak out for you. We've been able to save, we've been able to help a lot of people, and they hadn't all been black.

McMILLEN: You mean, too, a couple of thousand people earn their livelihood off of this?

HAMER: Well, they don't get everything, you know, but it helps them a whole lot.

McMILLEN: I see.

HAMER: And we don't sell the vegetables.

McMILLEN: They're just consumed by [the people]?

HAMER: That's right.

McMILLEN: And you said some of these people are not black?

HAMER: That's right. So, the plan of the thing is that it can grow to produce enough that people just won't know what hunger is, you know. See, because I hope—well, we didn't get to gather all the crops, you know, so we were in a great strain with the note thing, and we still need some money. But if we can kind of come out of this, people will be able to have his own vegetables, and if you've got your vegetables, you got your—if we can get some cows, some cattle, so they can have their meat. If people didn't have to have food now, buy food, you could get off a lot cheaper.

McMILLEN: Oh, yes.

HAMER: But you see if we don't do this, people can go back right back into this thing that we've been trying to fight, hunger, you know, and all that. So the main purpose is to feed and build the economic standard up.

McMILLEN: But so far, the cash that you've gotten from the cotton, and soybeans, and other things, has been about enough to pay for the annual note on the land.

HAMER: Yes, but we didn't even get out enough out to pay that annual note this time because it was raining so. So there are some people are coming in from New York Sunday, and they've got a marketing place in New York, and I guess we will talk about how much vegetables that we can grow. They've got refrigerated trucks and, see, that can make really a good thing.

McMILLEN: One thing I've never understood about Mississippi is why it didn't grow more vegetables. This cotton, this Delta country, is perfect vegetable-growing country.

HAMER: Yes. It grows them, oh, I've seen. I've seen thousand bushels of peas up there where we've got that Freedom Farm. Folks just go up there like they're going to a meeting, you know, and gathering their stuff. Some of them is white. Corn and all of that.

McMILLEN: You helped found Freedom Farms; who else was involved in the founding of this, Mrs. Hamer?

HAMER: Joe just stood by me like a son, and it was mostly two of us for a while. Then as it got bigger—it got bigger than we could do—then it was organized. Our board was elected from across the country with eleven people.

McMILLEN: Who was Joe?

HAMER: Joe Harris, that's my business manager.

McMILLEN: Joe Harris.

HAMER: And he is the director—no, he is executive director of Freedom Farms, business manager for the whole farm.

McMILLEN: What other cooperatives are there in the state that you know of?

HAMER: North Bolivar has a co-op, and then they have a co-op at Batesville. But I think this is one of the most helpful things.

McMILLEN: I do, too.

HAMER: It's one of the most helpful things, you know. People are working together. I don't be ashamed when someone comes here, and I can go in the kitchen and fry some ham, and open some soup, and have some vegetables, because we put it up. It's not only essential that you have food, but it's healthy food.

McMILLEN: Did Mr. Hamer work on the farm?

HAMER: Yes. He worked on the farm some. See, when [he] get out of the school and Head Start, then he had a chance to work some in the summer. We had some tractors and things donated, by the kids called the Young World Development.

McMILLEN: Young World Development?

HAMER: Young World Development, they walked in different areas like at Madison, Wisconsin, and Milwaukee, Wisconsin, they walked and bought like fifty-four hundred dollars' worth of farm equipment. One about eighty-some-thousand. And paid for it on the spot. And it was called the Young World Development. They was walking against hunger. So, they have—

McMILLEN: People were donating to them for their walk?

HAMER: Yes. Everybody that walked got somebody to sponsor him, you know, and they would walk for less than three cents a mile. But they brought in a lot of money. They didn't do it last year because I think they got [inaudible]. The structure of the whole thing, where the money had to go through the American Freedom from Hunger Foundation. They got so hung up in salaries, you know, a lot of kids dropped off. A guy called me yesterday from the American Freedom from Hunger Foundation and told me that they wanted me back in the thing. Let's try to build them up again because the kids thought there was some dishonesty going on and they kind of stopped it. But they're going to have some rock 'n' roll—I'll have to give about ten days; I'm leaving in March. This ten days will be going to where these kids are doing these rock 'n' roll concerts, and we'll be speaking about how important it is for them to walk.

McMILLEN: Yes. What about this biography Joyce Ladner is writing? How far along is it—isn't she writing a biography?

HAMER: She's supposed to be writing; I don't know how far she is about this time. Several people have called me and I don't know exactly how far she is. She told me that she's coming down here. There was another young woman down here last year, I think it was. She done a short one for kids. It's being put in the libraries in all the schools for little kids.

McMILLEN: It's a biography of you?

HAMER: Yes. A book called *Fannie Lou Hamer*. [It] just gives my life from a child up to not too long ago.

McMILLEN: What was her name, Mrs. Hamer, do you know?

HAMER: Her name, June Jordan.

McMILLEN: June Jordan. I haven't seen that book, I'll have to look into it.

HAMER: Well, the teacher, the principal's wife—I hadn't seen it either, till she brought it to me. I knew she was going to do it, but she brought it to me the other week for me to autograph it for her.

McMILLEN: Did you get a chance to look at it? Is it accurate?

HAMER: It's almost—not really. It's very seldom that you can do an interview on a paper or unless you do it on tape and they pull it word for word, it's very seldom that you can get 100 percent accuracy.

McMILLEN: Yes, I know.

HAMER: There's just something going to be messed up that you didn't say. You go and say, "I didn't say that!"

McMILLEN: But it's pretty good, though?

HAMER: It's pretty good for kids; it is pretty good for kids. I think what it is doing is teaching little kids that don't think nothing of themselves to know that they are human beings like anybody else.

McMILLEN: To take pride?

HAMER: Yes, I think that's what it mostly is.

McMILLEN: I noticed the other day that there was a new book on the MFDP by a man named Hayden, I think, did he interview you?

HAMER: Hayden?

McMILLEN: It's on black politics and most of it, I think, deals with the MFDP. I'm going to review it for the *Journal of Negro History*. I can't remember for sure what his name is, maybe it's Harris, but I just wondered if you had been interviewed by this man.

HAMER: No, I've been interviewed by a lot of people. I don't know who he is.

McMILLEN: So, you don't remember.

HAMER: So, I don't know who that could be. I know one guy in particular, Tom Hayden, who stayed here a long time and I'm wondering [if] he'd done it.

McMILLEN: It was not Tom Hayden.

HAMER: Oh.

McMILLEN: I think this was somebody who I think was probably a teacher of some sort.

HAMER: Yes.

McMILLEN: Well, what's happened to the civil rights movement? I hear it's dead, is that right?

HAMER: I don't think that you would say it is dead, but every so many years things change and go into something else. Now, you might never see demonstrations. I'm tired of that. I won't demonstrate no more. But I try to put that same energy, what I wish I had, I try to put that into politics, too. You see, if you notice, a lot of these people that was out there marching is congressmen now: Andrew J. Young, Ivanhoe Donaldson is not a politician, and he was one of the—oh, he was a great civil rights person. But, if Ivanhoe Donaldson moved into a place and stayed right there on the job, they don't lose that election. So, it means that even though it's not just called civil rights, it's still on the move to change. And it's just this phase of it has faded out and now we're pushing for something else.

McMILLEN: So, direct action has given way to political action?

HAMER: Yes! That's right, that's what it is.

McMILLEN: Are a number of black young people—someone told me this the other day—are they disillusioned, do they think, "What does it matter if I register to vote, the whites are going to run it anyway." Is that a widespread feeling in Mississippi?

HAMER: Not really with the young folk. I've seen old folk my age that just have got disgusted. I've been about as disgusted as anything after that election when we lost where we know we should have been winning. We know, we know, they have taken it away from us. For a long time, I was very angry.

McMILLEN: What election is this now?

HAMER: This was in 1971, 1971. We had a beautiful thing. We had a political thing here in this county with blacks and whites. I've had whites to come to me—you know, that hadn't been long at that. This white guy came here and he said, "You know we got so damn mad because we went to the polls and we voted for you." But as I was saying, when these elections are taken they ain't ready for that kind of politics.

McMILLEN: This was when you ran for congressman?

HAMER: Senator.

McMILLEN: Senator.

HAMER: Yes, I ran against [Robert Lacey] Crook. We saw some of the same tricky things.

McMILLEN: You think that you were robbed, that they took the election away from you?

HAMER: Yes. Well, in fact, one of the kids, one of the writers from a newspaper in Madison, Wisconsin, the student newspaper, said if the Justice Department didn't do anything about that then they were bank robbers. We watched it taken from us. So, this made people angry, this makes them disillusioned, but I tell people that somehow we have to keep on, and we can't quit. We have to go back and try it over.

McMILLEN: Do you have faith that the system will ever work properly?

HAMER: We have to make it work. Ain't nothing going to be handed to you on a silver platter, nothing. That's not just black people, that's people in general, masses. See, I'm with the masses. So, you don't ever get nothing, just walk up and say, "Here it is." You've got to fight. Every step of the way, you've got to fight.

McMILLEN: At this stage the fighting is in politics, through politics?

HAMER: At this stage. Now I don't know when, or at what time, it might change to something else, but right now it is important to fight in this field.

McMILLEN: What about violence, do the young people believe that violence gets them something?

HAMER: Well, some of them do and some of them don't. It's people feel different ways, but I know, I would say, the kids today will never take the things that we've gone through, my husband, and all of them. They ain't going to, they ain't going through it. And they're not bad either.

UNIDENTIFIED SPEAKER: But they ain't going through it, they just ain't going to take it.

HAMER: They ain't going to take it. Now, the world can forget about that. So, you push where you have to push, and these kids are going to be some really political forces in this country, too, especially in this state where—well, you never know exactly what percentage blacks are in this state. I guess 49 percent, and you might guess 45 percent. And then you ride through Mississippi and you just check things out and everywhere you look, you see us. Well, I believe there's more than 45 percent in the state of Mississippi. Well, the kids are going to school now, they're going to look for that percentage, they're going to find it out. I talked to some young people in Washington, and they said, "You know we're going to find out one day just how many blacks there are in Mississippi because we're going to travel that state over."

McMILLEN: But you think there's more than 46 percent?

HAMER: Yes, I think there's more, I really do.

McMILLEN: Certainly there are more in the Delta.

HAMER: Yes, it's so many more in the Delta. Anyway, I think we're something like 60-something percent here in Sunflower County, but they always come out a winner, you know.

McMILLEN: Yes, well, it wouldn't be fair to say that you're optimistic, but it's fair to say that you're going to continue to struggle as long as you can.

HAMER: Sure, I just couldn't afford to sit down and not do nothing. I know something out there is happening and I know I can say something, say, you know, "This is not right, and I'm going to get out here and we're going to do something about it." Because if you get yourself in that shape, you know, we can drift right on back to the plantation. Drift right back to there. But, I think it's a person seeing and feeling dignity and all of this, you know, that they decide in their mind they just ain't going back to that no more and be willing to fight for something different. A white woman called me this evening—you were here when Mrs. Baggett called me, and she talked a long time. Now, that's the reason we know if—this song that says, "Give peace a chance," if they would give us a chance we could make things better for everybody. Sure, I don't want no politics if it's just going to involve us.

McMILLEN: They'll get better.

HAMER: Yes, if things are better for me and things is better for Nook and Cookie, them two little girls in there, then they're going to be better for your two kids.

McMILLEN: I think that's right. Well, thank you very much for a very interesting interview.

HAMER: Okay.

McMILLEN: Thank you, very much.

HAMER: In 1962 nobody—and I hadn't heard of them either—in 1962 nobody knew that I exist. Then one day, the thirty-first of August, I walked off the plantation. From that time up until now I met a lot of people. I met a lot of great people, both blacks and whites. People that we have walked together, we have talked together, we've cried together, but it's been very interesting to me. The Schwerners, Andy Goodman's mother, Harry Belafonte, Al Lowenstein, it's just a whole lot of blacks and whites that I'm really happy that I've had a chance to meet in my lifetime.

McMILLEN: Did it change you at all to become famous almost overnight?

HAMER: No, you know, I never felt different. I don't think I ever felt any different because, I feel, now, very humble just to thank God I can be me.

McMILLEN: Yes. Has Mr. Hamer ever regretted that you've become so busy and involved in—

HAMER: I don't think he ever really regretted that. Sometimes I would be really tired and wouldn't want to go out. And I think that's been part of my strength that he would say, "Now, look, this is your job and this is what you have to do. You have to go to people and not disappoint people." Sometime you know, I felt like he must be sick of this by now, you know, and then he would tell me.

McMILLEN: He supported you all the way through?

HAMER: Yes, he supported me.

McMILLEN: How about your health? Are you in good health now? You look better than when I saw you last.

HAMER: I'm not in really good health, though.

McMILLEN: Is it serious?

HAMER: Yes. I think it's serious because when you've got high blood pressure, hypertension, it affects the heart and all, so—

McMILLEN: So, you've got heart trouble?

HAMER: Yes. I'm thankful that I made it this far. I don't know how many more steps I'll have to make, but I'll keep going.

McMILLEN: Maybe you ought to slow down.

HAMER: Okay. Well, I'm not going as much as I've been, but wherever I can go—you know, folks keep calling me, like for that article that was in that *Mid-South* [magazine], in that *Commercial Appeal*, you know, people write me, like Owen College in Memphis. I've just had calls, you know. If I felt it, I suspect that I'd be in there more.

McMILLEN: It would be great to have you speaking more, but speaking is a very taxing thing, isn't it?

HAMER: It is, it is. I have been just totally exhausted from speaking. And when I do maybe six or five in a run of a day by that night, why, people wouldn't have no idea how tired I would be.

McMILLEN: Yes. Where have you spoken, all over the country?

HAMER: All over the country. I've been to just about every major college campus in this country.

McMILLEN: Who's the most important black leader in the United States today? Can you think of one who really is important, makes a difference?

HAMER: Well, it would be so many people. A woman that I really respect more than I do any other living woman at this time for her role in civil rights and activity is a woman in New York City named Miss Ella Baker.

McMILLEN: Miss Baker?

HAMER: She's a beautiful human being that I respect for the role she has played. If it's men, I wouldn't be able to name them.

McMILLEN: Too many?

HAMER: Just a lot people, just guys round here, everyday guys, that have worked with me like Charles McLaurin that works with a poverty program now. He was just so forceful that he just made me believe that, "You're somebody, you're important." It's people like that that you can never sweep under the rug. Well, Joseph Harris, this guy I was talking to, I could just go on a long time and name people, but it would be impossible to name.

McMILLEN: Thank you, Mrs. Hamer.

HAMER: You're welcome.

"We Haven't Arrived Yet,"

Presentation and Responses to Questions at the University of Wisconsin,
Madison, Wisconsin, January 29, 1976

On a cold January afternoon in a packed third-floor lecture hall at the University of Wisconsin–Madison campus, Fannie Lou Hamer described the challenge that remained before both Mississippi and the nation. The year was 1976. Four years had passed since Hamer limped her way to the podium at the Democratic National Convention to offer words of support for Frances "Sissy" Farenthold. She had been in and out of the hospital since 1972, when she was first admitted for nervous exhaustion. Her list of illnesses multiplied—she was suffering from exhaustion, hypertension, diabetes, bouts of grave depression, and breast cancer. Her poor health precluded her from honoring the steady stream of speaking requests that poured into her home.

In January of 1976, though, a noticeably weakened Hamer managed to travel one last time to Madison to celebrate the eleventh anniversary of the Measure for Measure organization. Flanked by a travel companion who enabled her mobility, Hamer made the most of this now rare out-of-state trip. Speaking in at least three locations in just two days, she received countless standing ovations, a key to the city of Madison, and keenly focused local media attention. A handwritten poster with the small illustration of a farmer hoeing a row plastered the University of Wisconsin campus and hailed Hamer not only as a "Renowned Black Civil Rights Leader," but also as a "Dynamic Lecturer and Warm, Loving Human Being." The poster implored members of the campus community to "Hear and Meet Fannie Lou Hamer. You owe it to Yourself."

At noon on Thursday, January 29, flashing cameras and rolling tape recorders captured Hamer speaking at a slower pace, but in a no less impassioned tone, about the problems that persist, the progress that has been made, and the power of interracial cooperation. This address carries forth the confrontational candor of Hamer's speech, as she chastises political figures ranging from the mayor of Ruleville to President Gerald R. Ford, challenges northern black members of the audience who "think they have arrived," and exposes the hypocrisy of the nation's bicentennial celebrations. Hamer pairs her harsh criticism of the country's ills with a rather surprising cure: she holds the South up as an exemplar of interaction between the races, featuring her more recent experiences there and the larger political advances that the region has made as evidence both of love's unconditional power and the promise of forgiveness. In this address, one of her final speeches on record, Hamer provides a fresh perspective on race relations, even as she brushes her confrontational candor with a new subtle softness.

Little more than a year after Hamer delivered this address, she was admitted to a hospital in Mound Bayou—just twenty miles from her Ruleville home— where she stayed until the cancer, hypertension, and diabetes caught up with her. Fannie Lou Hamer's heart failed on March 14, 1977; she was fifty-nine years old.

✳ ✳ ✳

Thank you very much. I am glad to be here. As I look out into the audience and look at Sarah and Jeff and I saw Debra's mother—Mrs. Sweet—a lot of people, yeah, I see you all now again. A lot of my friends here that's done a tremendous job in helping us in the state of Mississippi.

I want you to become aware—even though we've received, you know, quite a bit of assistance from the organization Measure for Measure and this concerned people from Madison, Wisconsin—we haven't arrived. You know, you here and we there haven't arrived yet, because this morning before leaving Martha Smith's house, you know . . . I thought that we, at one time we were really moving forward, but as I looked at George Wallace making his pitch in Boston, Massachusetts, you know, what is really a place they call "Freedom" and a place of democracy—when I looked at him making his pitch this morning and how the people was standing up applauding . . . you know I'm still saying, *Jeff*, "this up South and down South because it ain't no different." And these white folks with this power. And I want you to understand that because 1976 we are really living in a crucial time. We were just at the peak of being in dictatorship under Nixon's administration with his roguish self.

See, some of you all ain't going to like it because you know, and I am just telling the truth and so you can, you know, you can respect the truth because if changes is not made in this sick country, it's not going to be *me* crumbling, *we* are going to crumble, because a house divided against itself cannot stand. A nation that's divided against itself is on its way out and when you see a place that's so prejudiced that anything is divided, you know anything is divided, not only for kids is for grown-ups. To brainwash and to give you what America is really, what is all about, you know like everybody is running around talking about the "*bicentennial* year of the two hundred years of American progress." Now I just want to ask one question: how do you think black people, Indian people, and any other oppressed folk feel celebrating something that, years ago, that destroyed over twenty-five million of my people that was being brought here on the slave ships of Africa? Wiped out our heritage; raised families by our grandmothers; and taking our name and today saying that it's wrong to bus a child for equal education! See, this kind of crap is nothing but an excuse. See, this is an excuse when they talking about you know, "we don't want the kids bused," and folks is buying it! And we saying that we are for democracy and justice and placing mercenaries and Central Intelligence Agents to kill my people in Angola.

And it's something wrong when any place . . . you know we have supposed to been an example for the rest of the world, but how you think it feel when a man as nonviolent as Dr. Martin Luther King, that preached nothing but love and says it's wrong to kill, he was assassinated in Memphis, Tennessee? But it was people involved in that from the top to the bottom and they didn't all live in the South.

You see, we are sick. America is sick and man is on the critical list. You know I have watched in the South, I have watched politics, and it got a beautiful name, because it's becoming "politic" and, you know, saw what they are doing and you know I wonders, will there ever come a time that we will actually have free elections and freedom of speech? It's people right in this room that's been fired because of what they said and believed, so that's not too much of freedom of speech. There were people in this room with twelve and thirteen kids that live on less than a hundred dollars per month and the excuses that they are giving in the institutions and throughout the country "of people on ADC are shiftless and lazy." And if people had a chance, they would be glad to work. But it's people, minority people in this country—not only Indians, Puerto Ricans, blacks, and poor whites—that can't get jobs. And you see, I just can't see how people can say that we will support people in other countries and give millions of dollars and not doing nothing for their own people. See, I can't see that. And you can't see it; you might not want to admit it.

You know, I used to just *love* to go north because I figured that people was, you know, kind of free, but you isn't—but blacks in the North is in the worse condition, most of them, than we are in the South because we know where we stand! And a lot of you don't. You know, some of you get a few degrees, a pretty good house, and a bill you can't hardly pay—trying to live like somebody else and think you have *arrived*. But, honey, regardless of how you feel, we are in this bag together. And there's nobody at the University of Wisconsin and no other place in this country is free until I am free in the South. And, to be perfectly honest, we got more contact with each other than is here in the cities throughout this country. We can talk and we got more communication than you have in most of the places in the North.

In 1964, I was one of the founders of the Mississippi Freedom Democratic Party that was organized to challenge the injustices and the different kind of inhumane things that was happening to us in the South. Today across the country other splinter groups have come up and made challenges—challenging not only Mississippi, but challenging America's democracy because it's pretty hard to stand up and pledge allegiance to something we've never had. You know the words really mean something if it was enforced. But the shame that we have before us today is whatever happened to us can have to be legislated. But you can't legislate love. That's one thing that you can't do. And what America and the rest of the world need today—some kids put out a song some time ago is what the world need now is love—but today people is not seeking and trying to find *love*, one of the greatest things of survival on earth, but seeking for more power and power corrupt. And you know what, maybe some of you say, "Well, I'm an atheist, I don't believe in God." But He's there.

And the sixth chapter of Ephesians and the eleventh and the twelfth verse said: "Put on the whole armor of God that He may be able to stand against the wiles of the devil." And the twelfth verse say: "For we wrestle not against flesh and blood, but against power. Against principalities. Against the rulers of darkness of this world. Against spiritual wickedness in high places."

And people will go to any limit just for personal power. It doesn't really matter how the masses suffer, but just the few people, you know, controlling. I was really sickened when I watched one day I turned on television and they was saying how much had been put in Angola to help a *handful* of white folk over there exploit *millions* of black people over there. So, what I'm saying, if there's going to be any survival for this country, there must be, we have to make democracy a reality for all people and not just a few.

Because there's no way in the world you can tell me how it feels to be hungry, if you've never been hungry yourself. And you cannot say that you represent me when you don't know how I feel. People is going to have to have a chance to work and work together to bring about a change.

You know today I feel, I feel, very humbled and being in your midst going through some of the problems that we going through, I was almost ready to—I don't know really how to put it in words—but when we had a woman mayor elected which is a doctor, and a mayor, and a judge, and a justice of the peace and a real goof-off that have goofed up the town of Ruleville, the little town where I'm from. And then you know, I started reading and I read about Eve and about Adam and how when Eve and Adam was in this beautiful garden and all of this temptation was put out there. And finally they were told of the fruit not to eat—now, you know a lot of people say you know well that's *sex*, but it was actually a tree—and it was called the tree of knowledge and out of all of those trees it was just that one tree, the tree of knowledge, were they forbidden not to eat that fruit. And that woman, Eve, was just exactly like the mayor we've got. And you know she, she ate the fruit and then persuaded Adam to eat him a mess of it. Do you all get what I'm saying?

You know I want the women—you know I'm talking to everybody—but I really want the women to think. Because we are living in real perilous times; we are living in the time when people can legislate to you whether you should kill your baby or go on and have your children. And you know somebody put it, said well: "You know they might not be married and what about this kid that come out of wedlock?" I said, "Well, you know they wasn't married before they conceived it, right?" They know they wasn't married. So, you can't legislate how you murder a person.

Take it from me, we are sick. And we've done so many things. A man was driving us, my cousin Sufronia Conway and me, a couple of weeks ago from the National Airport to Bethesda, Maryland, and he was telling us that in the '40s when he was in the service, a black man, when he was in service, they had captured so many Germans, and he said, "You wouldn't believe this Mrs. Hamer," he said, "even though they was prisoners they were given more rights than we were." Said, "They was allowed to go in places and theatres that we were barred out, but we had to stand on the outside to protect them." This is ridiculous!

Where millions of my folks have been destroyed, stripped black men of their heritage—and Indians and any other minority group—but stripped us of our heritage, taken our names, integrated our families—from the beginnings . . . my grandmother was a slave and I just had plenty white blue-eyed uncles . . . and today telling me, George Wallace, in Boston, Massachusetts, that "let the states handle it, and don't bus the kids." Do you realize how sick we are? Because the political science that you are reading and that you are teaching here at the university is not the political situation that we are faced with out there day after day. But I want you to know something: we are not only fighting to free ourselves in the state of Mississippi, but we are fighting to save you here in Madison, Wisconsin, and all over the country!

And our struggle has been very hard from the jailhouses to the graveyard, but we still have put 215 blacks in office in the state of Mississippi. We are going to fight for the kind of education that not only black folks should be aware of, but whites as well. Because you have been conditioned into the system too. I know you don't agree, maybe, with what I'm saying, but there is one thing for sure: you got a feeling it's the truth.

When I watch sometime, I don't allow my kids to watch it, but when I sat down and look at television and this guy playing the role of Tarzan, and the navy—the kind of things that you have distorted and said about my people in Africa and going to Africa, meeting people, and having a chance year after year to meet my people from Africa, it's nothing for us to be ashamed of is being black. And I am not fighting to be equal with you, but I'm fighting for human dignity.

Because we are really *sick* when the kind of stuff that's coming out now, they try to cover it up and they cover it from one side and it leak out over here and they wonder who done the leaking and who is telling on who? And then about all of them is confused as Richard Nixon. I will never forget the time that I went to a conference on nutrition and Nixon spoke to us that night and after that I told him, when the conference was over, I said, "Well, you don't worry about me coming back to a conference on hunger to Washington because they don't even know what they're talking about."

But we are sick, you know when we have a man like President Nixon that finally resigned for stealing, but was powerful enough to dictate who the next president would be, which is your president now, Gerald R. Ford. I was on television in Washington on the panorama and the man said, "Well, President Ford is a good man." Well, we was on television, I didn't want to hit that black man, because that man is powerful. I didn't want to hit him. Not going to see us on television. If he would've been around the corner, we would have been running till now!

But to do just some selected few, a few people out of millions with jobs and people throughout this country suffering from hunger, malnutrition, and this kind of thing. We better straighten up America, because everybody is not going to be as nice as the Indians when they welcomed Columbus and his group here that he said he discovered and it was already fourteen. Just like you know we walked out there and get in a car and said we discovered it, how did we discover it if it was already made?

It's later than you think and it's time for us to work together to make this a better country because together we stand, but divided we all cave. Thank you.

Question and Answer Period

(Questions are represented verbatim when audio quality permits; otherwise, the essence of the query is captured.)

Q: Question about changes in Mississippi since the passage of the Voting Rights Act in 1965.

FLH: There have been changes, but there are still a literacy test—not the kind that it was in the '60s, but people have to still take a literacy test. But we do have 215 elected black officials. And, you know, to say that we have moved some would be really not telling the truth. Because, if I would have to take the chance I would take it in the South because if you convince one that he is wrong you don't have a hypocrite; he's real. And we have made some changes. There haven't been enough changes. But we have made some strides in the state of Mississippi. In fact, what they're going through in Boston we done it ten years ago.

Martha Smith interjects, "Tell them about Senator Eastland's son-in-law, the other day—"

FLH: Well, it was, I been in court against Senator Eastland's son-in-law. We always go in nose to nose. Because if he for it, I was always against it. Even if I hadn't heard what it was. Just knowing who he was, I was against it.

So, it was the fifteenth of January, we were on our way back leaving Rockville, Maryland, where we had gone up to HEW and we was at the National Airport and who walks in but the son-in-law of Senator Eastland, his name is Attorney Terney. And when he walked in—now this is one thing that we have in the South that you don't have in the North that it was hard for me to get used to: nobody speak in the North. But, you know you can be fixing to fight a person in the South and before you hit him you'll say, "Good morning!" You know you got that kind of respect for each other—so, when I saw him in the airport I said, "Good evening, Attorney Terney," and he said, "Well, yes, Mrs. Hamer." So, he shook hands with me and he had another, older guy with him, and he said, "You meet Mrs. Hamer," said, "This is Mrs. Fannie Lou Hamer from Mississippi." So the guy looked at me real funny and he said, "Howdy, Fannie Lou," and I said, "Howdy." So we didn't talk anymore.

But anyway after we got to Memphis we met up again, I was getting on the plane with a huge picture of Dr. King, that I was carrying back from Rockville, Maryland. And I got all kinds of reactions from white folks.

Some of them, you know, would look at it. One stewardess told me, said, "You know you can't carry it on that plane."

And I said, "I brought it from Washington," I said, "I'm carrying it on home." I said, "If I made it from Washington to Memphis, I certainly can go to Greenville with it." So, she know there wasn't going to be no argument.

But anyway when I got on the plane in Memphis, there was Senator Eastland's son-in-law again. So, at this point you know I just felt good going by. And he said, "Hold it, Mrs. Hamer." He said, "You done fought to ride in the front. You ain't going back to the back now; you going to set down here with me." I sat right down. And we talked, you know, from Memphis to Greenville.

And I was telling him about the rotten things they done in the court. You know like they had some girls fired—women—fired at the public school because they said they'd had a baby out of wedlock. So we went in the court and I said, well, "Judge Keady," I said, "you know, if that's who you going to fire then ain't nobody going to be teaching because the white folk been doing the same thing." I said, "And the beautiful thing," I said, "it's a good thing that Mary wasn't here when she was carrying Christ because she'd be going through the same thing." And then one white man screamed and told me to hush.

But what I am saying—what I am saying—I had a chance to talk to Senator Eastland's son-in-law and he told us when we got to the airport, said, "There's nobody there to take you home," said, "I'll carry you on home." So, that's come a long way. Because I known the time that he would have got off the plane and kept from riding with me. As we got to live with each other, he going to see me there a lot of time.

Q: "I am just wondering whatever happened to the feeding co-op, the one in Greenville, I mean, Mound Bayou—"

FLH: One in Mound Bayou and we have one in Sunflower County too—

Q: "You did?"

FLH: *Yeah!* We had the first fifty pigs. You know five males, it was hard on them, but five males and fifty females. And each family had to sign a pig agreement—you know this sound funny to you, but you know you don't believe, we really lived it—each family that signed a pig agreement he couldn't kill the pig or trade him off. If the pig got sick he'd have to report it to the pig chairman. And the pig chairman, you know, would get a doctor for the pig. But as a result, with the pig bank program, we have distributed over four thousand pigs.

Q: "Why don't you tell us a little bit about the jails they have there?"

FLH: Oh, the jails is something else. I went to jail in 1963, the ninth of June. And from the orders of a state highway patrolman, I was beaten by two black prisoners until my body was hard as metal. And the day I was leaving jail, which was the twelfth of June and I was, you know, less than fifty feet from the jail, that's when I was told that Medgar Evers had been shot in the back.

But I want you to know something, that Charles Evers, a lot of people might not understand, but Charles Evers has done a tremendous job in helping his people and helping really people in the state of Mississippi. He is a beautiful human being once you get to know him because he is one human being that got houses out of Nixon's proposal. And I still don't understand it, but he did, you know.

But the jailhouses in Mississippi—not really unbelievable because prisoners, especially black, catch hell in nearly any jail in this country, in the minority.

Q: Question about the police in Mississippi trying to suppress the movement.

FLH: Oh, they tried. They tried. You know I remember once, I know people have read the *Jet* magazine, Larry Steele. Larry Steele was leaving my house one day and he was arrested for being drunk and the reason they said he was drunk, he was driving too careful.

But you see I just kept staying there in Ruleville and I let them know that nobody would determine who come to my house and who don't come to my house. I couldn't boss theirs, and they wasn't going to boss ours. And some of those same people today call me Mrs. Hamer. If you respect yourself, they might not want to do it, but just keep standing there, as long as you right, *somebody's going respect you.*

Q: Question about upcoming Democratic National Convention.

FLH: Well, right now I'm an uncommitted delegate. This is a funny thing that happened, last Saturday was the caucus for who go to the precinct meeting. So I ran in there four minutes before the thing closed and got to be a delegate uncommitted to the county caucus which will be the fourteenth of February. But I ain't got nobody out there. Most of the politicians—ain't too many of them saying nothing. Not too many.

Q: Question about the activity of the Klan in Mississippi.

FLH: Well, I tell you, now we have heard, that the Klans are organizing again. But when they had the last demonstration was in south Mississippi and the little kid was just splitting up laughing at them, you know, with the sheets and that kind of make a person feel a little bad.

Q: "Mrs. Hamer, I was wondering—you're talking about Mississippi being, perhaps, better than the way we have it up here—"

FLH: I didn't say we had arrived—

Q: "If you were talking to young people from Ruleville, would you say to them 'stay here and make your life here.' Or would you pat them on the back and put them on the bus to Chicago?"

FLH: I would tell them to stay in Ruleville—

Q: "What kind of life would they make?"

FLH: You know a little black child would have just as good a chance in Ruleville, poor and black, as he would have in Madison, Wisconsin, or Chicago, Illinois. So I say stay at home, let's make that better.

Q: "Can you explain a little of what went on behind the scenes with the Mississippi Freedom—why you refused the two seats at the Democratic National Convention?"

FLH: Oh, that was when we found out a little about how sick politics are. You know people was pressured. You know like I could meet a group today and conference with a delegation and they would almost be afraid of us tomorrow. And the real leaders was threatened. And they told them what they wasn't going to do. I never will forget like Walter Reuther threatened Dr. King. And President Johnson, you know, told the cameras to "take the cameras off them niggers from Mississippi" when I was testifying before the Credentials Committee. That was a real situation, you know, where I couldn't fight a man, because if God said he was over every creature on earth than [inaudible]. But anyway, I threatened a guy who wanted to accept the two votes, you know.

Q: "Dr. King and some of the other more moderate civil rights leaders tried to talk you people into taking just the two seats, is that right?"

FLH: Well, he actually did, but in the end, at that convention at first he didn't, but then when they say, "A compromise [could] be nice for us and we were just local Mississippians who didn't know nothing about politic and we should go on back to Mississippi because two votes at-large would be a moral victory." Dr. King did tell us that that would be best and a lot of other people did too. But we refused to accept it whoever told us because that's all we been doing, you know, compromising our lives in Mississippi.

Q: "Did Senator Humphrey try to work a deal with LBJ?"

FLH: Senator Humphrey, I saw him shed crocodile tears because he told us if we didn't compromise that President Johnson wasn't going to be nominated. You see, that ain't had nothing to do with me because I still wasn't going to compromise! Finally they stopped making me go to the meetings.

But, you know, they had some men to go and the men had decided to really accept the compromise and coming out of the church building that day is when I heard the man. I am sorry I done that, but I can't accept the compromise and was going to put his throat in the guillotine.

Q: "I used to work with YWD in Washington State and used to hear a lot about Freedom Farm, can you tell us a little more about that?"

FLH: Well, that was organized and founded in 1969 and the purpose of that program was to get some land that we could grow vegetables that people wouldn't have to leave Mississippi because our whole thing was, you give a man food he can eat for a few days, but if you give us the tools we can produce for ourselves. And that was the kind of thing we tried to get set up. And it's played a tremendous role—it hadn't alleviated all of the problem that we have in Sunflower County, but it's been one of the things that we've been working with since the organization Measure for Measure and other concerned people have given money not only to help us grow vegetables, but we got our own machinery and all of that to work it with. But also people are in decent houses for the first time. You know like, what is your loan, Mrs. [inaudible]? Thirty-nine dollars, you know, paying thirty-nine dollars a month and she's getting a house to stack four or five kids in. It's been a tremendous thing in helping people and it hadn't only benefited black people, but white people have been helped by the Freedom Farm.

Q: "Are you helpers helping people, other people in the South? In the state of Georgia—I can't remember any kind of programs like that. They had the 235 come in once that the government paid half of your house bill, but it wasn't as—"

FLH: Well, I'll tell you I know the program is in Mississippi some of the same kind of the program is in Alabama. I don't know what they be wanting to talk about, but I have been invited to come to Georgia in April. And I don't know what kind of thing . . . They might be talking about setting up that kind of a program. But they do have a cooperative in Alabama and not only with Freedom Farms co-op that's in Sunflower County, but Mr. Ronald Thornton—a great human being—is over there in North Bolivar County Co-op—would you stand up, Ron? That's doing a fantastic job. You can fry ham when a lot of you can't even afford to grow it out here.

Q: "What do you see as the benefit of unifying all of the different factions in this country?"

FLH: Well, that would have to be something that happened in the communities not only with the white folk, but I would really like to see the black folk unified and know that there are no difference in us regardless of your

ability and your degree. If you black like me it's no different. And we have to
work together and that's one of the reasons I am grateful for being here this
evening that I can talk to all of the people and my sisters and brothers.

Q: "How do you feel about black people supporting George Wallace?"

FLH: Well, you see, in 1965, when the voting rights bill was being passed in
Washington, D. C., John Lewis from VEP was having his skull fractured on
that Selma march. Now, I can't help what nobody else do, but George Wallace will not be getting no vote from Fannie Lou Hamer and people like
[inaudible] and folks know what it is to be beat and all of this kind of stuff
in jail. Not from the South. You know a lot of folk that hadn't suffered get a
little money will do some funny little things, but not to us.

Q: "What are the schools like in Mississippi? How come they don't have man-
datory grade school laws requiring your children to go to school?"

FLH: You mean something like a compulsory law?

Q: "Yeah."

FLH: For the first time, the new governor, Cliff Finch, called in the black principal and other people to talk about a compulsory school law. This has
never happened you know until, Finch was just inaugurated last week.

*An audience member interjects to explain to the group about why Mississippi—
a historically agricultural state—wouldn't have compulsory school laws.*

FLH: Yeah, because kids, you know, from six years old on work. I was working
at six years old.

Q: "Yes, Mrs. Hamer, I wonder if you would tell us about black voting in Mississippi now. How many blacks out of total possible black votes are being
cast? And once cast, are they being counted?"

FLH: In some areas they are. And in some areas they are not. You know we
still have a problem of dead folks voting and unborn babies—we still have
that problem. But, you know, in some areas where they are just almost 70
percent black they is more people that is elected from that. We still have a
problem.

Q: "Do the ballots sometimes get cast and not counted—lost on the way or
something?"

FLH: That happened, you know, until I remember in the primary we demanded people to be in there and be there on time and it was the first time that
we got a lot of people in office because we had people in there to watch—
they're called watchers. Because now, Judge Keady in Mississippi ruled
that a person not knowing how to read and write could ask anybody they
wanted to go in with him and show.

Q: "What is the approximate percentage of black people in Mississippi?"

FLH: They say, you know white folks counted it, we're 45 percent, that lets you know we're 54.

Q: "It's not a question, sir. I'd like to tell you Fannie Lou is featured in two books: *Black Women in White America* and there's a children's book out about her, but we found out on the way in that she's receiving absolutely nothing for the sale of these books. And so we're going to investigate it and see what's going on. And from then on in we will advocate the sale of her book, but as of now she's not receiving anything, but they're beautiful books."

FLH: [To the audience] Thank you.

Interview with Vergie Hamer Faulkner

by Maegan Parker Brooks, July 14 and July 17, 2009

Vergie Hamer Faulkner is the second-oldest adopted daughter of Fannie Lou and Perry Hamer, who had no biological children of their own. In 1954, the couple began caring for five-month-old Vergie, who had been badly burned by a tub of boiling water and whose large biological family was unable to provide her with the attention and care she required. Throughout the 1950s and 1960s, Vergie was raised by the Hamers in Ruleville. She moved to Memphis in 1975, where she still lives today working as a cook for a local church.

This interview is a transcript of two phone conversations recorded with Mrs. Vergie Hamer Faulkner, covering a variety of topics including heretofore un-published information about her father, Perry Hamer, her older sister, Dorothy Jean, and her grandmother, Lou Ella Townsend. Aside from providing insight about the persons who comprised Fannie Lou Hamer's intimate family circle, Mrs. Faulkner also offers an in-depth account of her mother's influences, her personality, and an assessment of her lasting legacy.

* * *

Part I

BROOKS: Well, I just wanted to start to learn a little bit about you. So, would you mind telling me a bit about what you do in Memphis and about what life is like there for you?

FAULKNER: Well, I work every day. I cook.

BROOKS: Where do you work?

FAULKNER: I work at this church, it's called Israel of God.

BROOKS: Do you cook for them?

FAULKNER: Yes, part of it is like a little restaurant.

BROOKS: Do you have family there in Memphis?

FAULKNER: Yes, all my children are up there but one. I am the mother of four children—two girls and two boys. Everybody's up there, except for my baby—he's in Mississippi; he's in Ruleville.

BROOKS: So, when did you decide to move from Ruleville to Memphis?

FAULKNER: In 1975.

BROOKS: And what made you want to leave Ruleville?

FAULKNER: Well, it's a long story. And I really don't want to go into that. It's a long story. My first husband and I—we wasn't getting along too good. So, I decided to leave.

BROOKS: Okay, and do you go back to visit that area much anymore, or do you pretty much stay around Memphis?

FAULKNER: I go back, you know, because, I'm going to put it like this: it's water under the bridge now. So, that being, it was just, it was a lot of heartache and I just told Mamma I had to get away. So, I moved to Memphis.

BROOKS: And how did your mom take that? Was it hard for her to have you leave?

FAULKNER: Nah, it really wasn't hard for her, you know, because she knew the situation and a change did me all good.

BROOKS: Did you still see her quite a bit after you moved to Memphis?

FAULKNER: Well, no, I'm not going to say I did because, during the time, I didn't have a job and I didn't have transportation. So, I came up here and I stayed with my auntie. And then, you know, later on—well, it really; it was kind of, it was hectic. It wasn't just peaches and cream; I'll put it like that. I had good times and bad times, you know, but God knew that. Things worked out and eventually I did get a chance and I'd go back down there, but I didn't go often because I was just ready to leave.

And then something about—I moved back home after Mom died. I moved back in '80 because Daddy had started getting sick and my auntie had called me and said I need to come home, you know. So, he wouldn't listen to anybody. She said, "Bebe, you got to come back to get him to go back and forth to the doctor." So, I came home; I moved home in '80. I tried to stay there—day three, I decided I wanted to go back to Memphis; well, come back to Memphis and I stayed up here two weeks and went back and I stayed there till Daddy died.

BROOKS: And what year did he pass in, was it ninety—

FAULKNER: He passed away in May of '92.

BROOKS: So, you did move back there for quite a while. What did your father pass away from? What was his ailment? What was he suffering from?

FAULKNER: Nothing, he just had a massive heart attack.

BROOKS: What was your father like? There aren't many accounts of your father—we hear a lot about your mother, but can you tell me a bit about what he was like?

FAULKNER: Well, I had a great daddy. He was real nice. One thing about it—I would tell anybody: I'm a daddy's child. I love my mom; don't get me wrong, but I'm a daddy's child. One thing I can tell you about him, and people don't realize, when Mom—on August 31, 1962—when Mamma went to this mass meeting in Ruleville, Mississippi, for the Williams Chapel church, and if Daddy didn't want Mamma to go, she wouldn't have went. But he told her—because she wanted to go—so he told her, said, "Baby, if it's what you want to do, go right ahead." That's what she did and when she came back—because, I went with her to the mass meeting—and when we came back she told him that she was going to go to Indianola.

Now, it wasn't the thirty-first of August because the thirty-first is when she went to *try* to register to vote. And he told her, "If you want to, if that's what you want to do"—everything she told him, he said, "If that's what you want to do," he was going to be behind her 100 percent and he was.

And I feel like, one thing about it, you have to give it to him because he was a man. And he didn't back down from nothing or nobody. He would treat you with the utmost respect. Even though my father couldn't read or write, but he had that mother wit. He knew how to treat people; he knew how to talk to people.

You know, Mom taught him how to write his name. And she showed him how he could recognize his name and anything else. And he learned that, he learned that. So, you know, that was a blessing.

BROOKS: Absolutely. Did he care for you girls while she was on the road traveling?

FAULKNER: At the time, wasn't nobody home but me, because Dorothy, she had left home. There wasn't nobody home but me. And, yes, he took care of me. I know one thing, he learned how to cook. Because my daddy used to be [inaudible]. He learned how to cook or we were going to starve to death, one of us, because I got tired of bologna and eggs, smoked sausage and eggs, hot dog and eggs—honey, I thought I was going to be a hot dog and bologna egg creature!

He did what he had to do, you know, but he learned how to cook. And I'll tell you one thing—I knew my mom could cook, she was, *whew*, she was an excellent cook, but Daddy got so hungry he could just about beat

Mom in that kitchen. One thing he couldn't do—he couldn't do cake and he couldn't bake pies, and homemade biscuits, but anything else like frying food or boiling food, he had her beaten.

BROOKS: How did he feel about your mother traveling so much? Was your father supportive of her traveling so much?

FAULKNER: Oh yeah! He supported her; he supported her in *every* way. Nah, not one time did he tell her, "You don't need to be doing this"—he wasn't that type of a person. That was a good man.

BROOKS: Was he a really friendly person by nature? It sounds like you had a lot of people coming in and out of your house during Freedom Summer and everything—

FAULKNER: We did.

BROOKS: What was that like for your father?

FAULKNER: He wasn't at home. He'd leave the house [laughter, inaudible]. I'm being serious with you, Maegan. Most of the time, people would come and they would just come to see what they could get out of my mom.

BROOKS: Really?

FAULKNER: Their common excuse, some of them be in terms of their children there, and there you have a lot on the line—"I need some money," "They going to turn my lights off," "They going to cut my gas off," or "My rent got to be paid." It was just chaos; it was just conflict, you know. But she was the type of person, she didn't turn them down. She would give her *last*. And for every one that she was helping, when my mom got down and couldn't do for herself, you could count on one hand and half a finger on the left, how many were there to help out.

BROOKS: Was that pretty hard for your father to watch?

FAULKNER: Yeah, it was because it upsetted him. It really did. He was the type of person who would just tell you where it was, how he felt—he didn't hold back. He just let it go. And I just thank God, I am so blessed in a way—I'm just like that. I'll just tell you where to get off at. But if you mean well, I'll treat you—but if you out to harm, then I'll let you know where to go from there.

BROOKS: Who do you remember being around your mom toward the end, do you remember who was there to help her?

FAULKNER: Yes, my auntie Dora. She had a niece named Hazel—Hazel was living, I'm thinking she was living in Detroit; it's been so long ago. It's been over thirty-two years. She's been dead over thirty-two years this past March. And that's a long time. And, you know, to try to keep this all in your mind. But you know, one thing about it, I thank God for blessing and keeping my mind. You know, it's just like He reevaluate me. And I thank Him for that.

BROOKS: How do you tell people about your mother, do you talk about her much?

FAULKNER: Not really. You know, only when I'm called to speak. I go to like different engagements or something. They call me and ask me can I come and I speak on her then. But other than that, I just leave her alone. Sometimes, Maegan, you might not believe this, sometimes it hits me just like it just happened.

BROOKS: I do believe that, it's not something easy to get over. I understand that.

FAULKNER: And then I think about the times before she even got involved in civil rights. And she was working on this white man's plantation and she and my dad and Dorothy, they would be in the field. I would be at home with my grandma, because Grandmamma was blind and she was confined to a wheelchair, and me being the baby in the house—five and six years old—I was taking care of her.

BROOKS: What was your grandmother like, do you remember much about her?

FAULKNER: Grandmamma was sweet. Yeah, she was a sweet person, you know. She was sweet and I was a terrible little girl—*oh*. I remember one time, she told me she wanted to go to the bathroom and I wanted to play. And she kept telling me, she'd say, "Baby, Grandmamma got to use the bathroom." And I was being just mean, that particular day, and I said, "Use it on yourself." And she did. And I cleaned her up and I got me a switch and I caught myself whooping her. And my daddy seen me, but I didn't see him. And he went to the field and told my mamma. And she got home and tore my butt up. And even though I was *wrong*, you know my grandma was still trying to stick up for me? She told her, she said, "Don't whoop her, she just a baby—she don't know, she don't know no better." Mamma said, "Yes, she do." I knew better, my grandma was just trying to keep me from getting a whooping. That was sweet.

BROOKS: What was the relationship like between your grandmother and your mom? Do you remember how they interacted?

FAULKNER: Oh baby! Mamma was Grandmamma's *heart*, because Mamma was the baby. And she didn't want to stay with nobody but my mamma and my dad. She didn't want to stay with Aunt Laura, she didn't want to stay with nobody but Fannie. And I remember when my grandmother—she died of old age—and Mamma didn't want me to know that she had passed away that night, and she passed away in my bed. A white lady had given me a baby bed, but it was like a bunk bed, you know. It was kind of like half rails and the rest of it—but it was a pretty bed. But anyway, when Grandmamma got sick she was sleeping in my bed. And she passed away. And sometimes it just seem like yesterday, because she was sweet. She had long pretty hair—and even though she was blind, she had her glasses on. There was something—you know that was amazing to me: being a little girl and everything, you know, she could tell a nickel from a quarter, a dollar from a five. So, Mamma had given me some money and she told me to give it to her. She said, "Baby, take this money in there and give it to Mamma."

So, it was like a five and a dollar. So, I gave her a dollar and said, "Here, Grandmamma, here's five dollars."

She felt that money and she said, "No, that's not." She said, "No, it ain't. That's not a five, that's a dollar."

I said, "How'd you know? When you can't see."

She said, "Baby, it's just something that happens when you lose your sense of sight, it goes into your hands." At the time I didn't understand that. When you lose your sense of hearing, it goes to your feet. I knew a girl though she couldn't hear or talk, but when she hear music, you know, the vibrations, she could feel it in her feet. That's how I learned how to deal with people like that.

BROOKS: So, it wasn't long after your grandmother died that your mom went to that mass meeting, what changed after your mother became active—

FAULKNER: Grandmamma died in '61, [we] attended the mass meeting in '62.

BROOKS: So, a lot of life changes for your family right away. Did you move out of Ruleville with your mother when she left, after being kicked off the plantation, what was that like?

FAULKNER: We went to my mamma's niece's house—first Mamma went to Mrs. Mary Tucker's house—that's in Ruleville, on Byron Street. My daddy didn't feel comfortable back when he had taken her there. He just didn't feel comfortable. He went and got her and took her to Sumner, Mississippi— and we stayed there, we stayed with Jeanette until December. You know the thing that was so hard for me, at the time, the house that they was living in—winter had came and it would be so cold there. Around midnight I would cry and want to go home, but we didn't have no home to go to. And Mamma would tell me, she said, "Baby, it's going to be all right."

And I told her, I said, "I'm ready to go," I said, "I miss my dad."

And, so in December of '62 we finally moved to the *town* of Ruleville. We going down into the Ruleville area; we had moved to town. It was a three-room house, had a bathroom, but no bathtub, no face bowl, no running water—only the water that was running [was] in the toilet, you know, when you flushed it, it would flush. Outdoor hydrant—had to carry water, heat water on the stove to take a bath, but you know through it all we made it. We've had good and bad times there, and then finally my mom bought this house. It was a two-room house and she had that house moved to 721 James Street, which—after she passed away—years later they finally named the street Fannie Lou Hamer Drive.

BROOKS: Yeah, I noticed that when I was out—a couple of summers ago there, in Ruleville. Does Lenora live in that house?

FAULKNER: Yeah, but the original house burnt down, New Year's Day of this year—

BROOKS: Oh, I think I heard that from a cousin—

FAULKNER: —burnt to the ground. So, Lenora had it built back. So, now it's *Lenora's* house. The house that we had, it was the family's house. You know, with her and her family—I thank God because they went through a lot, living in hotels. I wished for a moment that she would have just—before the house burned, I wanted to turn it into a museum.

BROOKS: Oh, that's a great idea.

FAULKNER: But, unfortunately, she didn't want it like that. So, I guess the Lord saw this—to keep from disputing over property, do it like that. It just burnt to the ground.

BROOKS: Do you keep in good touch with Lenora and Jacqueline? Do you hear from them regularly?

FAULKNER: Yes, I talk to Jackie. She's in Missouri; she moved closer to home. She was in Grand Rapids, Michigan, and I told her, "You need to move closer to home, you're too far away." So, she moved to Missouri. She's doing good; she got married—she's doing good.

BROOKS: Can you tell me a little bit about what life was like growing up after your mom became active in civil rights? Can you tell me what you remember about that period?

FAULKNER: It wasn't easy, always getting threats, you know, phone calls—threats on her life. Phone calls all time of the night, sometime they call and hang up, wouldn't say nothing—either they call and say, "I'm going to kill you, nigger," or "I'm going to do this, I'm going to do that." It wasn't easy. But, through it all—you know, one thing about it: what God has for you, it is for you. Can't nobody take that away.

And long before she even got involved in civil rights, she always have been an outspoken person. She was a Christian; she was a Christian and that was the best part of it. Back then, I didn't understand it, she would always say, "The Lord is going to do this, the Lord is going to do that."

And I'm like, "Where is He now," you know?

But then when you get older, you learn. [Inaudible] Train up a child and the way that they should grow and when they get older they won't depart from it. That's one thing I can say that Mom did, a lot of times she would send us to church even if she couldn't go, she would make sure we go. And she taught us right from wrong, she taught us the Bible. You know, how to live a Christian life.

And I thank God for her because, you know, I'm not going to say that I've been doing it all my life, because I haven't. Like I told you earlier, I got a lot of my dad in me. I thank God that he's working with me to get that dad stuff out because I used to tell people some things, honey, it wasn't nice; it wasn't nice at all. Daddy would step up and call you an "s.o.b." in a minute. If it wasn't "s.o.b," you was a hail Mary. And like I say, a lot of that rubbed off on me. I was the type of person, I would cuss you out—tell you where to get off at and then if that didn't work, I would pull a gun on you, either pull a knife on you—one of the two, I was going to do something to you.

I thank God; he changed me. I always had said I would never join a sanctified church, but never say never. That's how I got changed. My baby daughter started going to this church, and my baby got saved. She got filled with the Holy Ghost. She was staying with me—her and her husband were all in the same place. And I was watching her. It would so amaze me. My baby got saved, she was filled with the Holy Ghost and she was shouting up in the house and I was looking at her and I said, "Lord, I want me some of that." And I started going to the church. And you know they was so—they was like they had been knowing me all my life. They didn't look at you strange. They didn't treat you a different way. They treated you like you was family; they welcomed you with open arms, you know?

So when I started going, I started getting a little closer to God. That's when I really learned how to pray because I really didn't know how to pray. I had to ask the Lord to teach me and help me and know what I was praying for. Don't just be saying words because they can come out your mouth. You say things, when you pray, when you say a sincere prayer, God's going to answer. And He knows that you are sincere because He is nothing to play with—and I thank God for that. So, I'm saved. I don't curse no more, no fighting. I just hold my peace and let the Lord fight my battles.

BROOKS: How long ago was this? How long ago did you get saved?

FAULKNER: Believe it or not, well, 2000 and let's see—my uncle died in 2005; I got married in 2000. He started working on me in 2003, when he started working on me; 2005 and 2006 really was the countdown.

BROOKS: Does this experience of being at church and close to God remind you of your mother? She was so deeply religious—

FAULKNER: Yes, ma'am. You see, I never knew her daddy. Her father was a minister.

BROOKS: That's what I read, yeah—

FAULKNER: But he died before we was born, but he was a minister. And Mamma could quote from scriptures. From that Bible, it's just like she was sitting right there reading it to you. And I used to hear her recite some of those scriptures. She would go, like, the seventeenth chapter of Acts and the twenty-sixth verse said: "Hath made of one blood all nations," and she would just go on and on and on—

BROOKS: Oh, I remember, yeah, I've heard her say that—we've got that in a lot of the speeches in this collection. She seemed to return to that verse a lot. What else do you remember about her speaking? Did you ever get to hear her speak at some of these meetings?

FAULKNER: Oh man, me and my mom went on a seven-state tour! She wasn't doing nothing but speaking.

BROOKS: When was this?

FAULKNER: It started in 1965 and every state I went to I had a birthday party because it was my birthday; it was in August. My birthday is the ninth of August and we went to Newport, Rhode Island, to a folk festival. They paid us fifty dollars a day, you know, we was singing. And she said, "This is my baby and she's going to sing with me." And we would get up there on stage—that's the first time I met the Staple Singers, come to find out they was our cousins. Then, I met Howlin' Wolf—oh, I had met so many people. Do you remember Peter, Paul, and Mary?

BROOKS: Yeah!

FAULKNER: I met them; they was at the festival. Pete Seeger, so *many* people! We got our little ticket all—we was there three days and it was $150. And I got $150 as well.

BROOKS: What songs would you sing there?

FAULKNER: Oh honey, I don't even remember—know what songs we sang back then. It's been—honey, that was in 1965! Nah, that was in '66; that was in 1966. Because Lenora was born and Dorothy was pregnant with Jackie. That was in '66, in August because we made it back home just in time.

Because Dorothy gave birth to Jacqueline September the twenty-second, 1966.

BROOKS: Did she fall ill after her pregnancy, or can you tell me a bit about what happened to Dorothy?

FAULKNER: Dorothy had been ill all her life—she was a sick baby. She always have been sickly, but she, in 1967, she start with a nosebleed. Because her nose used to bleed all the time, but this particular time her nose started bleeding, we couldn't get it to stop . . . She taken sick, had this nosebleed started on the first of May in 1967. And like I say she always have had nose-bleeds, but we could get them to stop. But this particular time we had to take her to the doctor. We took her to this doctor over there to this little place called Minter City to this doctor, his name was Doctor Creek and he worked with her, he worked with her. Finally he got her nose to stop bleeding. So, we brought her back home, Mamma laid her down. And quite naturally, with bleeding like she did, she was weak. So later on, that Saturday, it was a Saturday, Saturday evening it started back again. So, Mamma took her to Mound Bayou hospital in Mound Bayou, Mississippi.

And my sister stayed in that hospital from the first of May to the twenty-third of May. When she—Mamma was transporting her from Mound Bayou to Memphis, what used to be John Gasden now it's a Med now—and they brought her by the school because she wanted to see me. And that was the last day of school because school was—we got out of school on the twenty-third. But my sister looked like she was nine months pregnant. She had a growth and they was taking her to Memphis.

And she was so—she was oh, honey she was so much fun! She would keep you laughing. And she told me, she said, "Girl," said, "Mamma said she was going to take me up there to Memphis and leave me." And some time this transfer, this eighteen-wheeler, this truck was going by and it had this camel on there and the thing said, "Humping to please." And she said, "You see that there, see how that camel has a hump on his back?" She said, "That's probably going to be me. I'm going to be straightened out like that humpback camel." She said, "I ain't got no hump in my back, I got a hump in my stomach!"

I said, "Girl, please!"

And sure enough, when they got her up there, Mamma said the doctor had told her if she had brought Dorothy when it first happened, they could have saved her because there was a growth. And I never will forget what Mamma said they told her that growth was a *molecule moles*. It's growing and it was eating up her blood. And she lost her on the twenty-third, but

Mamma prayed and the Lord brought her back and she died on the twenty-fourth. She was only twenty-two years old, had two children. Lenora was born October the twenty-ninth, 1965, and Jacqueline born September the twenty-second, 1966.

And Dorothy's death, it took a toll on Mamma. With the beating Mamma went through in 1963, and with the cancer and then Dorothy's death, Mamma never did get over Dorothy's death. Dorothy's death took tolls on Mamma's little heart. Mamma didn't even go that way, you know, she didn't go like that when Grandmamma died—and that was her mamma. But Dorothy's death just took a toll on her. A lot of times she would be looking at me and she would say, "Dorothy, go bring me some water."

And I'm like, "Mamma, I'm Bebe."

She said, "Baby, I'm sorry." She said, "Forgive me." She said, "I just can't get over it." It took a long time for me to get over that too because we was close, very close. Even though she was a lot older than me, like nine years older than me, she was sweet.

BROOKS: You mentioned your mother's beating in Winona, what do you remember about her after that? Did she talk to you much about that? Did she try and keep it from you children?

FAULKNER: No, in '63 I was ten years old. When the beating taken place, it was taking place in June. She was in jail when Medgar Evers got killed. Medgar got killed on the twelfth of June; she was in Winona jail. But the thing about it, we didn't know, I didn't know that she had gotten beaten like that because we was with Aunt Laura, Mamma's sister. We was staying with her. And it was a long time before we seen our mamma. You know, we were all asking Aunt Laura, "When's Mamma coming home, when she going to come get us?"

When you go without seeing your mamma that long, you really wonder what's been happening. You thinking something had happened—well, something did happen—but we didn't know, we wasn't aware of it. But my auntie knew—she kept it from us. So, it was a while before we seen our mamma; she had healed up when we seen her. But, you know, she told us about it and while she was telling us about it, you couldn't do nothing *but* cry.

BROOKS: Yeah, oh yeah. How did your dad respond when he heard about it?

FAULKNER: Well, see, the thing about it, that's what I'm saying, we was with Aunt Laura—with my auntie—and he was staying at the house. I didn't know what my daddy—

BROOKS: Yeah, oh, ok.

FAULKNER: —because, you know, we was with her [Aunt Laura].

Part II

BROOKS: Well, I was listening to the interview that we did earlier this week and I wanted to see if we could focus for a couple minutes on talking a little bit more about your experience hearing your mother speak, you know, because our collection is about her speeches. And it sounds like you had an opportunity to hear her deliver some of these speeches, so I really wanted to ask you about what it was like to see her up there on stage and to hear her—

FAULKNER: [Breaks into laughter.]

BROOKS: —what did you think about that?

FAULKNER: Oh, honey, it was awesome; it was awesome. But I always—whether she was in front of a crowd or just at home—I always loved to hear her talk, you know. She was my pride and joy. To me, she couldn't do no wrong.

BROOKS: I understand that. What stands out in your memory about listening to her speak?

FAULKNER: Well, most of the times, Maegan, when Mom would speak, she was concerned about children going to school and getting an education and making something of themselves. And her addressing to the people—adults—to get out and register to vote because your vote count. She said, "Don't never say 'my vote don't count.'" She say, "Because every vote count."

Let me tell you something: after she passed away, I stopped going to vote and then it just dawned on me—why you being like that? Because that's what she stood for. So, I started back and I've been doing it ever since.

BROOKS: Oh, good. What do you think your mom would think about this election we just had? What would she think about Barack Obama becoming the first African American President?

FAULKNER: About like me—jumping and hooting and hollering!

BROOKS: Do you think she would see this as a culmination of what she stood for and what she was working for?

FAULKNER: Mmhmm, because that's what every pioneer believed in. That was every American's dream that one day we going to have a black president. Like I said, when I was in Jackson—I went to Jackson for the unveiling of the postage stamp—and my thing was: never in a million years did I dream that we would have a black president. I said, "Never in a million years did I thought that I could see my mamma on a United States postage stamp." Now tell me, haven't we come a long way? And we still got a long way to go.

BROOKS: What did your mother think about her fame? Did she see herself as a famous person? An able speaker? How did she understand—

FAULKNER:—No, Mamma saw herself just plain Fannie Lou. She didn't think of herself as—I'll put it like this: a "big shot," you know, she wasn't like that. She was just a common down-to-earth person. She just tried to tell you what's right, and tell you what's right and don't do no wrong.

BROOKS: Vergie, do you remember her going to Africa and coming back? What did she tell you about that trip to Africa?

FAULKNER: It was beautiful because she brought me an African outfit and some kind of little instrument. I don't know what the heck it was—made out of like a turtle skin, I mean not a turtle skin—made out of some sheepskin or cow skin or something. But it was an instrument and I didn't like that thing! But I loved my outfit, but that's all we talked about. And I thank God that she went to Africa. And believe you me, 1987, I was ready to go!

BROOKS: Yeah, did you get to—have you ever got the chance to go to Africa?

FAULKNER: Yeah, I went.

BROOKS: Oh, well, tell me about that—where did you go?

FAULKNER: I went to, what's it called—over there in Tripoli. Yeah, it was real nice. I left on the eighth of April and made it back to the United States on the nineteenth of April.

BROOKS: Did you have some of the same impressions as your mom? I've heard her talk about being really impressed by the positions of power that Africans held there and their beauty, connection to their family. Did you feel some of those same emotions when you were there?

FAULKNER: Well, from where we were, it was beautiful and [inaudible] too. If I didn't have kids back home, I sure wouldn't want to come back.

BROOKS: Really?

FAULKNER: I *loved* it over there!

BROOKS: Just a couple more questions about her speeches . . . was your mother ever nervous before she spoke? Was she an anxious speaker or was she pretty comfortable up there?

FAULKNER: She was *always* comfortable. She wasn't nervous; she wasn't a nervous type of person. She spoke from the heart. That's another thing she didn't do—she didn't read from no paper; she didn't read no paper. She just spoke from the heart.

BROOKS: How do you remember audiences reacting to her when you saw her speak? Did people feel like they agreed with her? Were they supportive of her; how did they respond?

FAULKNER: Yes, they did. It's going to be some that there's going to be disagreement with, but then that's with anybody. That's with any and everybody, you going to have some that agree and some disagree. That's one thing about it: you cannot please everybody. So, that's one thing I don't do; I don't even try. You either love me or leave me. So, you chose.

BROOKS: Did your mom feel that way too—did she have that opinion, that she wasn't going to convince everybody?

FAULKNER: Well, the other thing she say: if you don't, then it's not my fault. Then, if you do: may God bless you. It was just like, if I should die my soul be lost—ain't nobody's fault but mine. You know, she put it out there, either you accept it or you don't accept it. A majority of them was accepting it. There were very few that wasn't, but we don't count that.

BROOKS: What did people in your community think about her? Was she supported or were there some people that held some resentment about her popularity? How did people in Ruleville act after she became such a national figure?

FAULKNER: Baby, they was moved. Like I say, the majority of them was showing appreciation and then you had a lot of them that come there to get what they could get. If there was free food given out, they come get the free food. Clothes, they come get the clothes. And she would have established a pig bank—

BROOKS: Yeah, Freedom Farm, tell me about that.

FAULKNER: She had this little co-op where you plant greens, peas, butter beans, okra and stuff. Had a little garden, called a truck patch—old people call it a truck patch. And if you didn't go out there and pick some peas, you didn't have no excuse to be hungry. If you didn't go out and pick some peas, butter beans, and stuff like that, process that stuff and put it in Ziploc bags, them freezing bags, put it in your freezer for the winter, because you know the winter is coming—if you didn't do that, if you was too lazy to do that, then you deserve to be hungry.

BROOKS: Why do you think that Freedom Farm ended up failing in the long run? Why didn't that work out?

FAULKNER: Every dime she got she given it away instead of paying the payments on it. Trying to help folks pay their bills and stuff like that and just lost it.

BROOKS: The last couple questions I want to ask are just about what you see as your mother's greatest accomplishment. If you could tell someone, you know, what you see as her greatest accomplishment or legacy, what would that be?

FAULKNER: My mom's greatest accomplishment in life is that she wanted all men to be created equal. And that young people get out there and register to vote. Older people help teach your children; teach them because your children are the future. And the best thing I could say about my mom—everything I say about her is good—but the best thing that I loved of all about my mom is that she was a Christian; she stood for what's right; she tried to help anybody—she didn't pick, she didn't discriminate.

And she showed love. She showed love in everything she did. She showed love in her cooking, raising her children, being a wife to her husband. She showed love most of all when she get up there and she'd speak. She either sing before she speak or she'd sing after she speak—but that's one thing I can say, I was proud of her and I'm still proud of her. Even though she's deceased, but her spirit still lives on.

BROOKS: Absolutely. Well, thank you so much, Vergie. I really appreciate you taking this time again to talk more with me.

Acknowledgments

Researching the oratorical contributions of black female freedom movement activists—women whose words were not commonly recorded or preserved with any great care—is no easy task. Recovering Fannie Lou Hamer's texts was made much easier by fellow researchers and devoted archivists, as well as friends and family members of Mrs. Hamer who generously shared their resources with us. In particular, we would like to thank two of the Mississippi Department of Archives and History's finest: Clarence Hunter, curator of the Tougaloo collection, and Celia Tisdale, audiovisual curator. Kenneth Chandler, archivist at the Mary McLeod Bethune Council House was instrumental in locating, repairing, and digitizing the Hamer speeches within their collection. Special thanks is also owed to Wendy Shay, audiovisual archivist at the Smithsonian's National Museum of American History, who allowed us to copy vital portions of the Moses Moon Audio Collection. For scholars and students of the black freedom movement seeking a compelling account of what the movement sounded like, the Moon archive is without peer—our sincerest gratitude goes out to Dr. Bernice Johnson Reagon for her diligent work in establishing and securing the collection. Peter Filardo, of New York University, graciously provided us with a very rare civil rights audio moment: an interorganizational meeting headlined by Fannie Lou Hamer and Malcolm X. That meeting provides compelling evidence that Malcolm X was moving toward a rapprochement with the major civil rights organizations before his tragic murder. Dr. Louis Kyriakoudes of the University of Southern Mississippi went far above the call of archival duty by granting us early access to the papers of Sue Sojourner Lorenzi, an activist who worked for several years in Holmes County, Mississippi, and who personally recorded one of the real treasures of this collection. Jean and Charlie Sweet, Measure for Measure activists from Madison, Wisconsin—with whom Hamer would often stay while speaking there—also personally recorded several of Hamer's speeches and willingly shared these recordings with us; our sincerest thanks to Kay Mills for putting us in touch with the Sweets and for sharing all of the Hamer speeches in her possession.

Lucy Patrick and Burt Altman, of Florida State University's Department of Special Collections, very kindly scoured the university's archives for traces of Mrs. Hamer's on-campus appearance in 1972. Stephen E. Lucas, of the University of Wisconsin, Madison, generously shared with us his archival findings from George Breitman's papers at New York University. Leigh McWhite, from Ole Miss's Department of Special Collections, has been a great help in locating Fannie Lou Hamer materials and in doing us favors large and small for several years. The staff at the Avery Research Center for African American History and Culture in Charleston, South Carolina, kindly provided us with an audio copy of a speech that Mrs. Hamer delivered in Chicago. We also greatly appreciate the staff at the Wisconsin Historical Society for helping us locate everything from Hamer recordings to photographs and an old flyer advertising one of her frequent on-campus visits. The Fannie Lou Hamer National Institute on Citizenship and Democracy deserves recognition—especially Dr. Leslie McLemore and David Deardorff, who shared invaluable contact information and a comfortable space to conduct oral history interviews. Thanks, too, to the staff of the Amistad Research Center at Tulane University, who, just months after Hurricane Katrina devastated the city, provided a very hospitable research environment.

Several students have been indispensable to our project. A special thank you goes to Beth Walker Frady for her long-suffering work in tracking down the federal trial transcript involving the Winona, Mississippi, beatings. That document serves as a sad testament to Jim Crow justice—even with the federal government's involvement. Steve Andon put the unwieldy one thousand-plus pages of the transcript into PDF format. Matt Hittel expertly moved audio duplicated recordings on cassette tapes to a digital format, thereby facilitating a wide distribution of the Moon archive. Jenna Stolfi did ace transcription work on a particularly long and difficult address. Sean O'Rourke's undergraduate students at Furman University also logged many hours on transcriptions from the Moon archive, notably Emily Paige Pusser and Margaret Holmes.

Colleagues and mentors alike have also pitched in to make this project possible. We would like to thank the anonymous reviewer both for his or her careful editing suggestions and for bringing an additional Hamer text to our attention. Jeff Drury familiarized us with Mrs. Hamer's speech on the University of California's Berkeley campus, while Paul Stob came through in the eleventh hour with a vital transcription-to-recording check. Susan Zaeske,

Erik Doxtader, Robert Asen, Robert Howard, and Christine Garlough, furthermore, provided support and encouragement during the early stages of the research process. Christina Greene was both supportive and inventive—we clearly appreciate her suggestion of using Hamer's famous refrain—"to tell it like it is"—in the collection's title.

We would also like to single out several activists who worked very closely with Mrs. Hamer and whose contributions to this project are profound. Reverend Edwin King of Jackson, Mississippi, remains one of the truly outstanding educators of the movement and a great friend to students of all stripes. Charles McLaurin of Indianola, Mississippi, has kept Mrs. Hamer's legacy alive and vibrant in Sunflower County—and well beyond. For helping us contact Mrs. Hamer's daughter—Vergie Hamer Faulkner, a constant and supportive influence for this project—we will be forever grateful. Dr. L. C. Dorsey, Owen Brooks, Dr. Leslie McLemore, and Jeff and Sarah Goldstein deserve great thanks as well for sharing their perceptions of Hamer's life and legacy with us. Lawrence Guyot has also been a dear friend, a sage counselor, and an enthusiastic supporter. As a survivor of the awful beatings administered in the Winona jail in June 1963, Mr. Guyot bled and cried with Mrs. Hamer in one of the defining moments of her life. We thank him for sharing these memories with our students and with us.

Finally, and perhaps most importantly, we'd like to thank our friends and families for not just putting up with our all-too-frequent isolation but for sharing in our passion—even encouraging it. From Maegan, thank you to my husband, Dave, who never tires of listening to tales of my research triumphs and travails and who supports me—as Vergie says—"in *every* way!" And from Davis, thank you to my wife, Ingrid, who not only cheerfully read every page, but who gamely navigated the Delta with me and who made this book better through her diligent research in many a dusty archive.

Suggestions for Further Reading and Research

MANUSCRIPT COLLECTIONS

Fannie Lou Hamer (FLH) Papers and Accompanying Audiotapes, Amistad Research Center, Tulane University, New Orleans, Louisiana

Oral History Collection, Civil Rights Documentation Project, Moorland-Spingarn Research Center, Howard University, Washington, D.C.

Student Nonviolent Coordinating Committee (SNCC) Papers, Martin Luther King, Jr., Center for Nonviolent Social Change, Atlanta, Georgia

Fannie Lou Hamer File, Mary McLeod Bethune Museum and Archives, Washington, D.C.

Fannie Lou Hamer, Vertical File, Funeral, and Tougaloo College Collection, Mississippi Department of Archives and History (MDAH), Jackson, Mississippi

George Breitman Papers, New York University, Tamiment Library/Robert F. Wagner Labor Archives, New York, New York

Moses Moon Collection, Smithsonian Institution, Washington, D.C., National Museum of American History Program in African American Culture

Project South Papers, Stanford University, Special Collections, Stanford, California

Civil Rights and Race Relations Collections, University of Mississippi Archives and Special Collections, Oxford, Mississippi

Civil Rights Collection, Fannie Lou Hamer Papers (microfilm), Measure for Measure Files, Mississippi Freedom Democratic Party (MFDP) Files, and Sweet Papers, Wisconsin Historical Society, Madison, Wisconsin

Bernice Robinson Papers, Avery Research Center, College of Charleston, Charleston, South Carolina

Sue Sojourner Lorenzi Papers, McCain Library, University of Southern Mississippi, Hattiesburg, Mississippi

INTERVIEWS AND ORAL HISTORIES

Interview with Fannie Lou Hamer by Jack Minnis, March 17, 1964, Winona, Mississippi, Martin Luther King, Jr., Center for Nonviolent Social Change, Archives Department, Atlanta, Georgia.

Excerpts of Interview with Fannie Lou Hamer by Colin Edwards, 1965, Collected Speeches of Fannie Lou Hamer, Pacifica Archives, North Hollywood, California.

Interview with Fannie Lou Hamer by Project South, 1965, MFDP Chapter 55, Box 6, Folder 160, Department of Special Collections, Stanford University Libraries, Stanford, California.

Interview with Fannie Lou Hamer by Anne Romaine, 1966, MFDP Papers, Wisconsin Historical Society, Madison, Wisconsin.

Interview with Fannie Lou Hamer by Robert Wright, August 9, 1968, Oral History Collection, Civil Rights Documentation Project, Moorland-Spingarn Research Center, Howard University.

Oral History Interview with Fannie Lou Hamer by Neil R. McMillen for the Mississippi Oral History Program of the University of Southern Mississippi, April 14, 1972. Part II of McMillen Interview, January 25, 1973.

TRIAL TRANSCRIPTS

United States of America v. Earle Wayne Patridge, Thomas J. Herod, Jr., William Surrell, John L. Basinger and Charles Thomas Perkins. U.S. District Court, Northern District of Mississippi, Western Division, Criminal Action No. WCR6343. National Archives and Records Administration, Southeastern Region, Morrow, Georgia.

ARTICLES AND BOOKS

Asch, Chris Meyers. *The Senator and the Sharecropper: The Freedom Struggles of James O. Eastland and Fannie Lou Hamer.* New York: Norton, 2008.

Belfrage, Sally. *Freedom Summer.* New York: Viking, 1965.

Bramlett-Solomon, Sharon. "Civil Rights Vanguard in the Deep South: Newspaper Portrayal of Fannie Lou Hamer, 1964–1977." *Journalism Quarterly* (1991): 515–21.

Breitman, George, ed. *Malcolm X Speaks.* New York: Grove Press, 1966.

Brevard, Lisa Pertillar. "'Will the Circle be Unbroken': African-American Women's Spirituality in Sacred Song Traditions." In *My Soul Is a Witness: African-American Women's Spirituality*, edited by Gloria Wade-Gayles. Boston: Beacon Press, 1995.

Campbell, Karlyn Kohrs, ed. *Women Public Speakers in the United States, 1925–1993: A Bio-Critical Sourcebook*. Westport, CT: Greenwood, 1994.

Carawan, Guy, and Candy Carawan. *We Shall Overcome!: Songs of the Southern Freedom Movement*. New York: Oak Press, 1963.

——. *Freedom Is a Constant Struggle: Songs of the Freedom Movement*. New York: Oak Press, 1968.

Carson, Clayborne. *In Struggle: SNCC and the Black Awakening of the 1960s*. Cambridge: Harvard University Press, 1981.

——. "1965: A Decisive Turning Point in the Long Struggle for Voting Rights." *The Crisis* 112 (July–August 2005): 16–20.

Collier-Thomas, Bettye, and V. P. Franklin, eds. *Sisters in the Struggle*. New York: New York University Press, 2001.

Cortez, Jayne. "Big Fine Woman from Ruleville (for Fannie Lou Hamer)." *Black Collegian* 9 (May/June 1979): 90.

DeMuth, Jerry. "Tired of Being Sick and Tired." *The Nation*, June 1, 1964, 548–51.

Dittmer, John. *Local People: The Struggle for Civil Rights in Mississippi*. Urbana, IL: University of Illinois Press, 1994.

Egerton, John. *A Mind to Stay Here: Profiles from the South*. New York: MacMillan, 1970.

"Fannie Lou 'Tell It Like It Is.'" *Harvard Crimson*, November 23, 1968, 1.

Forman, James. *The Making of Black Revolutionaries*. Seattle: Open Hand, 1985.

Gray, Lloyd. "The Glitter Is Gone, but the Fight Goes On." *Delta Democrat Times*, October 3, 1976, 1, 12.

Griffin, Farah Jasmine. "DNC Day 4: Remembering Fannie Lou Hamer," from Conventional Wisdom, National Public Radio Transcript, August 29, 2008. Available online, accessed 1/7/2009, www.npr.org/blogs/newsandviews/2008/08/dnc_day_4_remembering_fannie_l.html

Hamer, Fannie Lou. "'Sick and Tired of Being Sick and Tired.'" *Katallagete!: The Journal of the Committee of Southern Churchmen* (Fall 1968): 26.

——. "Fannie Lou Hamer Speaks Out." *Essence* 1 (October 1971): 53–75.

——. "To Praise Our Bridges." In *Mississippi Writers: Reflections of Childhood and Youth*, volume 2, edited by Dorothy Abbott. Jackson, MS: University Press of Mississippi, 1986.

"Hamer Rites: Civil Rights Leaders to Attend." *Jackson Daily News*, March 20, 1977, n.p.

Hamlet, Janice D. "Fannie Lou Hamer: The Unquenchable Spirit of the Civil Rights Movement." *Journal of Black Studies* 26 (1996): 560–576.

Harris-Lacewell, Melissa, "Obama and the Sisters." *The Nation*, August 13, 2008.

Hibbard, Tom. "Local Students Tell Why Blacks Didn't Get Vote." *Capital Times*, November 12, 1971, 9.

Houck, Davis W., and David E. Dixon, eds. *Rhetoric, Religion, and the Civil Rights Movement, 1954–1965*. Waco, TX: Baylor University Press, 2006.

Houck, Davis W., and David E. Dixon, eds. *Women and the Civil Rights Movement, 1954–1965*. Jackson, MS: University Press of Mississippi, 2009.

Johnson, Susan. "Fannie Lou Hamer: Mississippi Grassroots Organizer." *Black Law Journal* 2 (1972): 154–162.

Johnson, Thomas A. "Mississippi Poll Watchers Say Harassment Barred Fair Tally." *New York Times*, November 6, 1971.

Jordan, June. *Fannie Lou Hamer*. New York: Thomas Y. Crowell, 1972.

Kelley, Robin D. G., and Earl Lewis, eds. *To Make Our World Anew: A History of African Americans*. Oxford: Oxford University Press, 2000.

King, Edwin. "Go Tell It on the Mountain: A Prophet from the Delta." *Sojourner* (December 1982).

Kling, Susan. *Fannie Lou Hamer: A Biography*. Women for Racial and Economic Equality, 1979.

Landauer, Megan, and Jonathon Wolman. "Fannie Lou Hamer '. . . Forcing a New Political Reality.'" *The Daily Cardinal*, October 8, 1971, n.p.

Lee, Chana Kai. *For Freedom's Sake: The Life of Fannie Lou Hamer*. Urbana: University of Illinois Press, 1999.

Lerner, Gerda, ed. *Black Women in White America: A Documentary History*. New York: Vintage, 1972.

Leslie, Gay. "Rights Matriarch Pleads for Action Now." *Wisconsin State Journal*, July 19, 1969, n.p.

Ling, Peter, and Sharon Monteith, eds. *Gender in the Civil Rights Movement*. New York: Garland, 1999.

Locke, Mamie E. "The Role of African-American Women in the Civil Rights and Women's Movements in Hinds County and Sunflower County, Mississippi." *Journal of Mississippi History* 53 (1991): 229–239.

Marius, Richard C. "Ruleville: Reminiscence, Reflection." *The Christian Century*, September 23, 1964, 1169–71.

Marsh, Charles. *God's Long Summer: Stories of Faith and Civil Rights*. Princeton, NJ: Princeton University Press, 1997.

McBride, Marian. "Fannie Lou Hamer: Nobody Knows the Trouble She's Seen." *Washington Post*, July 14, 1968, H12.

Mills, Kay. *This Little Light of Mine: The Life of Fannie Lou Hamer*. New York: Penguin, 1993.

Moye, J. Todd. *Let the People Decide: Black Freedom and White Resistance Movements in Sunflower County, Mississippi, 1945–1986*. Chapel Hill, NC: University of North Carolina Press, 2004.

O'Dell, J. H. "Life in Mississippi: An Interview with Fannie Lou Hamer." *Freedomways* 5 (1965): 231–242.

Payne, Charles M. *I've Got the Light of Freedom: The Organizing Tradition and the Mississippi Freedom Struggle*. Berkeley: University of California Press, 1995.

Payne, Elizabeth Anne, Martha H. Swain, and Marjorie Julian Spruill, eds. *Mississippi Women: Their Histories, Their Lives*. Volume 2. Athens, GA: University of Georgia Press, 2010.

Peterson, Franklyn. "Sunflowers Don't Grow In Sunflower County." *Sepia* 19 (1970): 8–18.

Pfefferkorn, Robert. "From One Who Pursued Equality, a Plea for Love." *Wisconsin State Journal*, January 30, 1976, n.p.

Raines, Howell. *My Soul Is Rested: Movement Days in the Deep South Remembered*. New York: Putnam, 1977.

Ransby, Barbara. *Ella Baker and the Black Freedom Movement: A Radical Democratic Vision*. Chapel Hill, NC: The University of North Carolina Press, 2003.

Reagon, Bernice Johnson. "Let the Church Sing 'Freedom.'" *Black Music Research Journal* 7 (1987): 105–118.

————. "Women as Culture Carriers in the Civil Rights Movement: Fannie Lou Hamer." In *Women in the Civil Rights Movement: Trailblazers and Torchbearers, 1941–1965,* edited by Vicki Crawford, Jaqueline Rouse, and Barbara Woods. New York: Carlson, 1990, 203–32.

————. *Voices of the Civil Rights Movement: Black African Freedom Songs, 1960–1966.* Booklet accompanying audio-recording of the same title. Smithsonian: Folkway Records R023, 1980.

Reed, Linda. "Fannie Lou Hamer (1917–1977): A New Voice in American Democracy." In *Mississippi Women: Their Histories, Their Lives,* edited by Martha H. Swain, Elizabeth Anne Payne, Marjorie Julian Spruill, and Susan Ditto. Athens, GA: University of Georgia Press, 2003, 249–67.

————. "Fannie Lou Hamer: New Ideas for the Civil Rights Movement and American Democracy." In *The Role of Ideas in the Civil Rights South: Essays,* edited by Ted Ownby. Jackson, MS: University Press of Mississippi, 2002.

Riggs, Martha Y., ed. *Can I Get a Witness: Prophetic Religious Voices of African American Women: An Anthology.* Maryknoll, NY: Orbis, 1997.

Robertson, Craig. "Civil Rights Activist: Fannie Lou Hamer Remembered." *Delta Democrat Times,* March 16, 1977, 1.

Robnett, Belinda. *How Long? How Long? African American Women in the Struggle for Civil Rights.* New York: Oxford University Press, 1997.

Ross, Rosetta E. *Witnessing and Testifying: Black Women, Religion, and Civil Rights.* Minneapolis: Fortress, 2003.

Rubel, David. *Fannie Lou Hamer: From Sharecropping to Politics.* Englewood Cliffs, NJ: Silver Burdett, 1990.

Sewell, George. "Fannie Lou Hamer." *Black Collegian* 8 (May/June 1978): 18–20.

Sierichs, Bill. "'Sin-Sickness' Probed at Crime Meet." *Jackson Daily News,* March 24, 1976.

Silver, James. *Mississippi: The Closed Society.* New York: Harcourt, Brace & World, Inc., 1963.

Smith, Jessie Carney, ed. *Epic Lives: One Hundred Black Women Who Made a Difference.* Detroit: Visible Ink Press, 1993.

Sugarman, Tracy. *Stranger at the Gates: A Summer in Mississippi.* New York: Hill and Wang, 1966.

————. *We Had Sneakers, They Had Guns: The Kids Who Fought for Civil Rights in Mississippi.* Syracuse, NY: Syracuse University Press, 2009.

Torres, Sasha. *Black, White and in Color: Television and Black Civil Rights.* Princeton, NJ: Princeton University Press, 2003.

Towns, Stuart W., ed. *We Want Our Freedom: Rhetoric of the Civil Rights Movement.* Westport, CT: Praeger, 2002.

Wolman, Jonathon. "Mississippi Elections: By Hook or Crook." *Daily Cardinal,* November 5, 1971, 1.

————. "Mississippi Elections: Facing an Old Political Reality." *Daily Cardinal,* November 11, 1971, 1.

Yockey, Roger. "King Co. 'Adopts' Sunflower County." *The Progress,* March 7, 1969, 3.

Young, Andrew. *An Easy Burden: The Civil Rights Movement and the Transformation of America.* New York: Harper Collins, 1996.

Young, Billie Jean. *Fear Not the Fall: Fannie Lou Hamer: This Little Light . . .* Montgomery: New South, 2004.

Index